POWERSHELL® FOR SYSADMINS

POWERSHELL® FOR SYSADMINS

Workflow Automation Made Easy

by Adam Bertram

no starch press

San Francisco

Printed in USA

First printing

24 23 22 21 20   1 2 3 4 5 6 7 8 9

ISBN-10: 1-59327-918-3
ISBN-13: 978-1-59327-918-9

Publisher: William Pollock
Production Editor: Janelle Ludowise
Cover Illustration: Josh Ellingson
Interior Design: Octopod Studios
Developmental Editors: Alex Freed and Zach Lebowski
Technical Reviewer: Jeffery Hicks
Copyeditor: Sharon Wilkey
Compositor: Danielle Foster
Proofreader: James M. Fraleigh
Indexer: Beth Nauman-Montana

For information on distribution, translations, or bulk sales, please contact No Starch Press, Inc. directly:
No Starch Press, Inc.
245 8th Street, San Francisco, CA 94103
phone: 1.415.863.9900; info@nostarch.com
www.nostarch.com

Library of Congress Cataloging-in-Publication Data

```
Names: Bertram, Adam Richard author.
Title: PowerShell for sysadmins / Adam Bertram.
Description: San Francisco, CA : No Starch Press, 2020. | Includes
   bibliographical references and index. | Summary: "A practical guide to
   using PowerShell. Begins with an introduction for new users, then moves
   on to explaining how to develop scripts to automate daily tasks, and
   finally teaches how to build a large project to automate server
   deployments from scratch."-- Provided by publisher.
Identifiers: LCCN 2019041874 (print) | LCCN 2019041875 (ebook) | ISBN
   9781593279189 (paperback) | ISBN 9781593279196 (ebook)
Subjects: LCSH: Windows PowerShell (Computer program language) | Computer
   networks--Management. | Computer systems.
Classification: LCC QA76.73.W56 B47 2020  (print) | LCC QA76.73.W56
   (ebook) | DDC 005.4/22--dc23
LC record available at https://lccn.loc.gov/2019041874
LC ebook record available at https://lccn.loc.gov/2019041875
```

To those that question the status quo, fight the "that's the way we've always done it" company culture, and always come up with a better solution to problems, this book is dedicated to you.

About the Author

Adam Bertram is a 20-year veteran of IT and an experienced online business professional. He's an entrepreneur, IT influencer, Microsoft MVP, blogger, trainer, author, and content marketing writer for multiple technology companies. Adam is also the founder of the popular IT career development platform TechSnips (*https://techsnips.io/*).

About the Technical Reviewer

Jeffery Hicks is an IT veteran with almost 30 years of experience, much of it spent as an IT infrastructure consultant specializing in Microsoft server technologies with an emphasis in automation and efficiency. He is a multi-year recipient of the Microsoft MVP Award. Jeff has taught and presented on PowerShell and the benefits of automation to IT professionals worldwide. He works today as an independent author, teacher, and consultant.

BRIEF CONTENTS

CONTENTS IN DETAIL

3 COMBINING COMMANDS 37

4 CONTROL FLOW 47

5 ERROR HANDLING 61

6 WRITING FUNCTIONS 69

7 EXPLORING MODULES 79

8 RUNNING SCRIPTS REMOTELY 91

9 TESTING WITH PESTER 107

PART II: AUTOMATING DAY-TO-DAY TASKS 113

10 PARSING STRUCTURED DATA 117

11 AUTOMATING ACTIVE DIRECTORY 137

12 WORKING WITH AZURE 157

PART III: BUILDING YOUR OWN MODULE 213

ACKNOWLEDGMENTS

I couldn't have written this book and accomplished everything I have without the support of my wife, Miranda. Time is a precious commodity and because of her, one I have more of than many others. Miranda is the CEO of the Bertram household. She has somehow managed our two daughters, kept a tidy house, and kept us all fed for the years I've been out focusing my career and helping our family prosper. There's no way I could have accomplished all that I have with my work if she weren't there supporting me and our kids.

I also want to thank Jeffrey Snover for creating the PowerShell scripting language, which has truly changed my life; Jeff Hicks, Don Jones, and Jason Helmick for inspiring me to get more involved with a community; and Microsoft for supporting crazy overachievers with their Microsoft MVP program and other initiatives.

INTRODUCTION

Throughout my career in IT, I've worked a diverse range of jobs: I've been in the trenches answering calls on the help desk, visited users to tell them to reboot as a technician, kept servers up as a systems administrator, designed and built solutions as a systems engineer, and learned the difference between OSPF and RIP routing as a network engineer.

It wasn't until I discovered PowerShell that I realized how passionate I could be for a particular technology. PowerShell has changed my life in more ways than one, and it's the technology that's changed the trajectory of my career most dramatically. This language helped me be a critical asset at my job by knowing how to save countless hours of my team's work, and it got me my first six-figure salary. PowerShell is just so cool that I decided I had to share it with the world, and since then, I've been awarded the prestigious Microsoft MVP award for five years straight.

In this book, I'll show you how to use PowerShell to automate thousands of tasks, build custom tools instead of buying off-the-shelf products, and link various tools together. You may not be interested in becoming an active member of the PowerShell community, but I guarantee that learning PowerShell will give you skills that many businesses need and actively seek.

Why PowerShell?

Once called *Monad* (see *https://www.jsnover.com/Docs/MonadManifesto.pdf*) and pitched as a more intuitive way to automate tasks than VBScript in 2003, Microsoft PowerShell is a universal automation, scripting, and development language. PowerShell was created to bridge the gap between scripting, automation, and operations personnel. It was meant to enable users to automate tasks with scripts without having to learn computer programming. This makes it particularly useful for system administrators who lack a background in software development. If you're a system administrator with not enough time to get everything done, PowerShell is a great ally to have.

PowerShell has now become an open source, ubiquitous, cross-platform scripting and development language. You can use PowerShell not only to provision fully configured server farms, but also to create a text file or set a registry key. Thousands of software products and services have PowerShell support now, thanks to its ever-increasing adoption rate among IT professionals, developers, DevOps engineers, database administrators, and systems engineers.

Who This Book Is For

This book is for IT professionals and system administrators who are tired of clicking around in the same GUI and performing the same task for the 500th time this year. It can also be for DevOps engineers who are struggling to automate new server environments, perform automated testing, or automate an entire continuous integration/continuous delivery (CI/CD) build pipeline.

No single demographic benefits the most from PowerShell. The traditional job role of a PowerShell user is the Microsoft system administrator in a "Windows shop," but PowerShell tends to fit well in the tool belt of any IT operations personnel. If you're in IT and don't consider yourself a developer, this book is for you.

About This Book

In this book, I'll teach by doing, using tons of examples and real-world use cases. Instead of *telling* you what a variable is, I'll *show* you. If you're looking for a traditional textbook, this book isn't for you.

I won't break PowerShell into parts and cover each feature independently, since that's not how you'll use PowerShell in the real world. For example, rather than expect you to know the written definition of a *function* or *for loop*, I'll combine features whenever possible to give you a holistic understanding of the problem at hand and how to solve it.

The book is divided into three parts. **Part I: Fundamentals** gives PowerShell newcomers the knowledge they need to hang with the seasoned veterans. If you're at an intermediate or higher skill level in PowerShell, you can skip to Chapter 8.

Chapters 1–7 cover the PowerShell language itself. You'll learn the basics including how to find help and how to discover new commands, as well as some programming concepts common to other programming languages such as variables, objects, functions, modules, and error-handling basics.

Chapter 8 explains how to use PowerShell remoting to connect to and run commands on remote computers.

Chapter 9 introduces the popular PowerShell testing framework Pester, which you'll use throughout the book.

In **Part II: Automating Day-to-Day Tasks**, you'll apply what you learned in Part I to begin automating common tasks.

Chapters 10–13 cover how to parse structured data as well as common domains many IT administrators work with, such as Active Directory, Azure, and Amazon Web Services (AWS).

Chapter 14 shows you how to build a tool you can use in your own environment to inventory your servers.

In **Part III: Building Your Own Module**, you'll focus on building a single PowerShell module called PowerLab to demonstrate what's possible with PowerShell. We'll cover good module design and best practices around functions. Even if you consider yourself an advanced PowerShell scripter, you're sure to learn something from Part III.

Chapters 15–20 explain how to use PowerShell to automate entire lab or test server environments by demonstrating how to provision Hyper-V virtual machines, install operating systems, and deploy and configure IIS and SQL servers.

I hope this book helps you get your feet wet with PowerShell. If you're a beginner, I hope it gives you the courage to start automating; if you're a seasoned scripter, I hope it shows you some tricks you may not be familiar with.

Let's get scripting!

PART I

FUNDAMENTALS

As the old adage goes, you must learn to crawl before you can walk. When it comes to building tools with PowerShell, it's no different. In Parts II and III of this book, you're going to learn how to build some powerful tools. But before you do that, you'll need to learn the language basics. If you're already an intermediate or expert PowerShell user, you're welcome to skip Part I. Although you may find a nugget or two of knowledge you didn't previously know, it's probably not worth the time it takes to digest this entire part.

But if you're new to PowerShell, this part's for you. We'll explore the PowerShell language and learn about some of the constructs you'll use constantly. We'll cover everything from basic coding concepts, like variables and functions, to writing scripts, running them remotely, and testing them with something called Pester. Because we'll go through only the basics, we won't build too many tools just yet—that's what Part II and Part III are for. Here we'll use small examples to get our grip on the language. You're going to get your first glimpse of what PowerShell is capable of. Let's get started!

1

GETTING STARTED

The name *PowerShell* refers to two things. One is a command line shell, installed by default on all recent versions of Windows (starting with Windows 7) and most recently available on Linux and macOS operating systems via PowerShell Core. The other is a scripting language. Together they refer to one framework that can be used to automate everything from rebooting 100 servers at once to building a complete automation system that controls your entire data center.

In the first chapters of this book, you'll use the PowerShell console to become familiar with the basics of PowerShell. Once you've covered the basics, you'll graduate to more advanced topics including writing scripts, functions, and custom modules.

This chapter covers the basics: some fundamental commands, and how to find and read help pages.

Opening the PowerShell Console

The examples in this book use PowerShell v5.1, the version that comes with Windows 10. Newer versions of PowerShell have more features and bug fixes, but the basic syntax and core functionality of PowerShell hasn't changed dramatically since version 2.

To open PowerShell in Windows 10, enter **PowerShell** in the Start menu. You should immediately see a Windows PowerShell option front and center. Clicking that option should bring up a blue console and a flashing cursor, as in Figure 1-1.

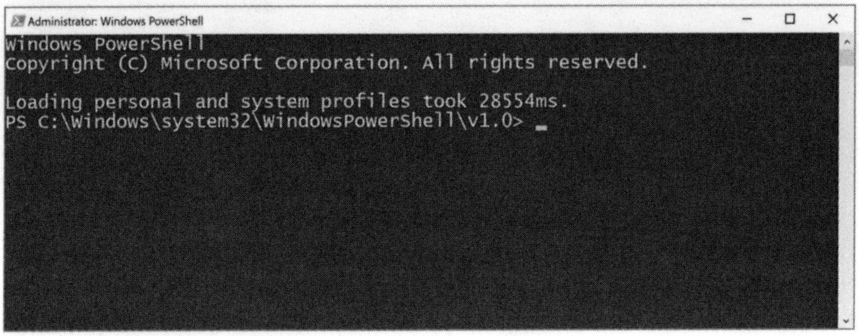

```
Administrator: Windows PowerShell
Windows PowerShell
Copyright (C) Microsoft Corporation. All rights reserved.

Loading personal and system profiles took 28554ms.
PS C:\Windows\system32\WindowsPowerShell\v1.0> _
```

Figure 1-1: A PowerShell console

The flashing cursor indicates that PowerShell is ready for your input. Note that your *prompt*—the line beginning with `PS>`—will probably look different from mine; the file path in the prompt indicates your current location in the system. As you can see in my console's title, I've right-clicked the PowerShell icon and run it as administrator. This gives me full rights, and starts me in the *C:\Windows\system32\WindowsPowerShell\v1.0* directory.

Using DOS Commands

Once PowerShell is open, you can start exploring. If you've previously used the Windows command line, *cmd.exe*, you'll be glad to know that all the commands you're used to (for example, `cd`, `dir`, and `cls`) also work in PowerShell. Under the covers, these DOS "commands" aren't really commands, but command *aliases*, or pseudonyms, that translate from commands you know to commands PowerShell knows. But for now, you don't need to understand the difference—just consider them your familiar DOS friends!

Let's try some of these commands. If you're sitting at the `PS>` prompt and want to check out a specific directory's contents, first navigate to that directory with `cd`, short for *change directory*. Here you'll go to the *Windows* directory:

```
PS> cd .\Windows\
PS C:\Windows>
```

> **USING TAB COMPLETION**
>
> Notice that I specified the *Windows* directory with a dot and backslashes on either side: `.\Windows\`. In fact, you don't have to type all this out because the PowerShell console has a great tab completion feature that lets you hit TAB repeatedly to cycle through the commands that can be used, given what you've already typed.
>
> For example, if you type `Get-` followed by a TAB, you can begin scrolling through all the commands that start with `Get-`. Keep hitting TAB to move forward through the commands; SHIFT-TAB will move you backward. You can also use tab completion on parameters, which I'll cover in "Exploring PowerShell Commands" on page 6, as you can see by typing `Get-Content -` followed by TAB. This time, instead of cycling through commands, PowerShell begins cycling through the available parameters for the `Get-Content` command. When in doubt, press TAB!

Once in the *C:\Windows* folder, you can use the `dir` command to list the contents of your current directory, as shown in Listing 1-1.

```
PS C:\Windows> dir


    Directory: C:\Windows


Mode                LastWriteTime         Length Name
----                -------------         ------ ----
d-----        3/18/2019   4:03 PM                addins
d-----         8/9/2019  10:28 AM                ADFS
d-----        7/24/2019   5:39 PM                appcompat
d-----        8/19/2019  12:33 AM                AppPatch
d-----        9/16/2019  10:25 AM                AppReadiness
--snip--
```

Listing 1-1: Displaying the content of the current directory with the `dir` command

Entering `cls` will clear your screen and give you a fresh console again. If you're familiar with *cmd.exe*, try some of the other *cmd.exe* commands you know to see if they work. Note that although the majority do, not all will. If you're curious about which *cmd.exe* commands exist in PowerShell, once you have the PowerShell console up, you can enter `Get-Alias` in the PowerShell console to return many of the old-school *cmd.exe* commands you're used to, like so:

```
PS> Get-Alias
```

This will allow you to see all the built-in aliases and which PowerShell commands they map to.

Exploring PowerShell Commands

Like nearly all languages, PowerShell has *commands*, the generic term for named executable expressions. A command can be just about anything—from the legacy *ping.exe* tool to the Get-Alias command I referred to earlier. You can even build your own commands. However, if you try to use a nonexistent command, you'll get the infamous red error text, as shown in Listing 1-2.

```
PS> foo
foo : The term 'foo' is not recognized as the name of a cmdlet, function,
script file, or operable program. Check the spelling of the name, or if a
path was included, verify that the path is correct and try again.
At line:1 char:1
+ foo
+ ~~~
    + CategoryInfo          : ObjectNotFound: (foo:String) [], CommandNotFoundException
    + FullyQualifiedErrorId : CommandNotFoundException
```

Listing 1-2: An error is displayed when an unrecognized command is entered.

You can execute Get-Command to see a list of every command PowerShell is aware of by default. You might notice a common pattern. Most commands' names follow the same scheme: *Verb-Noun*. This is a unique trait of PowerShell. To keep the language as intuitive as possible, Microsoft has set guidelines for command names. Although following this naming convention is optional, it is highly recommended for creating your own commands.

PowerShell commands come in a few flavors: cmdlets, functions, aliases, and sometimes external scripts. Most of the built-in commands from Microsoft are *cmdlets*, which are typically commands written in other languages like C#. By running the Get-Command command, as in Listing 1-3, you'll see a CommandType field.

```
PS> Get-Command -Name Get-Alias

CommandType     Name                Version    Source
-----------     ----                -------    ------
Cmdlet          Get-Alias           3.1.0.0    Microsoft.PowerShell.Utility
```

Listing 1-3: Displaying the Get-Alias command's type

Functions, on the other hand, are commands written in PowerShell. You write functions to get things done; you can leave the cmdlets to the software developers. Cmdlets and functions are the most common command types you'll be working with in PowerShell.

You'll use the Get-Command command to explore the plethora of cmdlets and functions available in PowerShell. But as you may have just seen, entering Get-Command with no parameters will leave you tapping your finger for a few seconds as your console scrolls through all the commands available.

A lot of commands in PowerShell have *parameters*, which are values you give (or *pass*) to a command to customize its behavior. For instance, Get-Command has various parameters that allow you to return only specific commands instead of all of them. Looking through `Get-Command`, you may have noticed common verbs such as `Get`, `Set`, `Update`, and `Remove`. If you guessed that all of the `Get` commands *get* information and the others modify information, you'd be right. In PowerShell, what you see is what you get. Commands are named intuitively and generally do what you'd expect.

Since you're just starting out, you don't want to change anything on your system. You do want to retrieve information from various sources. Using the `Verb` parameter on `Get-Command`, you can limit that huge list of commands to only those that use the `Get` verb, for example. To do this, enter the following command at the prompt:

```
PS> Get-Command -Verb Get
```

You'll probably agree that a few too many commands are still displayed, so you can limit the results even further by adding the `Noun` parameter to specify the `Content` noun, as in Listing 1-4.

```
PS> Get-Command -Verb Get -Noun Content

CommandType     Name                Version    Source
-----------     ----                -------    ------
Cmdlet          Get-Content         3.1.0.0    Microsoft.PowerShell.Management
```

Listing 1-4: Displaying only commands that contain the verb Get *and the noun* Content

If these results are too narrow for you, you also can use `Noun` without the `Verb` parameter, as shown in Listing 1-5.

```
PS> Get-Command -Noun Content

CommandType     Name                Version    Source
-----------     ----                -------    ------
Cmdlet          Add-Content         3.1.0.0    Microsoft.PowerShell.Management
Cmdlet          Clear-Content       3.1.0.0    Microsoft.PowerShell.Management
Cmdlet          Get-Content         3.1.0.0    Microsoft.PowerShell.Management
Cmdlet          Set-Content         3.1.0.0    Microsoft.PowerShell.Management
```

Listing 1-5: Displaying only commands that contain the noun Content

You can see that `Get-Command` allows you to separate out the verb and noun. If you'd rather define the entire command as one unit, you can use the `Name` parameter instead and specify the entire command name, as shown in Listing 1-6.

```
PS> Get-Command -Name Get-Content

CommandType     Name                Version    Source
-----------     ----                -------    ------
Cmdlet          Get-Content         3.1.0.0    Microsoft.PowerShell.Management
```

Listing 1-6: Finding the `Get-Content` *cmdlet by command name*

As I said previously, lots of commands in PowerShell have parameters that customize their behavior. You can learn a command's parameters by using the robust PowerShell help system.

Getting Help

PowerShell's documentation isn't unique by any means, but the way the documentation and help content is integrated into the language is truly a work of art. In this section, you'll learn how to display command help pages in the prompt window, get more general information on the language via About topics, and update your documentation with `Update-Help`.

Displaying the Docs

Similar to the `man` command in Linux, PowerShell has the `help` command and the `Get-Help` cmdlet. If you're interested in seeing what one of those `Content` cmdlets does, you can pass that command name to the `Get-Help` command to retrieve the standard `SYNOPSIS`, `SYNTAX`, `DESCRIPTION`, `RELATED LINKS`, and `REMARKS` help sections. These sections provide a breakdown of what the command does, where you can find more information about the command, and even some related commands. Listing 1-7 displays the documentation for the `Add-Content` command.

```
PS> Get-Help Add-Content

NAME
    Add-Content

SYNOPSIS
    Appends content, such as words or data, to a file.

--snip--
```

Listing 1-7: The `Add-Content` command's help page

Providing just the command name to `Get-Help` is useful, but the most helpful part of this content is the `Examples` parameter. This parameter shows examples of real-world uses of the command in a variety of scenarios. Try `Get-Help` *`CommmandName`* `-Examples` on any command and notice that nearly all built-in commands have examples to help you understand what they do. For example, you can run the command on the `Add-Content` cmdlet, as in Listing 1-8.

```
PS> Get-Help Add-Content -Examples

NAME
    Add-Content
```

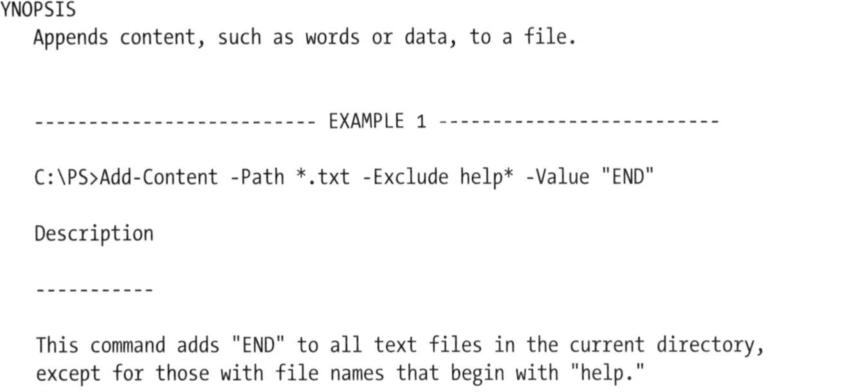

```
SYNOPSIS
    Appends content, such as words or data, to a file.


    -------------------------- EXAMPLE 1 --------------------------

    C:\PS>Add-Content -Path *.txt -Exclude help* -Value "END"

    Description

    -----------

    This command adds "END" to all text files in the current directory,
    except for those with file names that begin with "help."
--snip--
```

Listing 1-8: Getting sample usages of the `Add-Content` *command*

If you want more information, the `Get-Help` cmdlet also has the `Detailed` and `Full` parameters, which give you a complete rundown on what that command does.

Learning About General Topics

In addition to help content for individual commands, the PowerShell help system provides *About topics*, which are help snippets for broader subjects and specific commands. For example, in this chapter you're learning about some of PowerShell's core commands. Microsoft has created an About topic that gives an overall explanation of these commands. To see it, you run **`Get-Help about_Core_Commands`**, as shown in Listing 1-9.

```
PS> Get-Help about_Core_Commands
TOPIC
    about_Core_Commands

SHORT DESCRIPTION
    Lists the cmdlets that are designed for use with Windows PowerShell
    providers.


LONG DESCRIPTION
    Windows PowerShell includes a set of cmdlets that are specifically
    designed to manage the items in the data stores that are exposed by Windows
    PowerShell providers. You can use these cmdlets in the same ways to manage
    all the different types of data that the providers make available to you.
    For more information about providers, type "get-help about_providers".


    For example, you can use the Get-ChildItem cmdlet to list the files in a
    file system directory, the keys under a registry key, or the items that
    are exposed by a provider that you write or download.
```

```
    The following is a list of the Windows PowerShell cmdlets that are designed
    for use with providers:

--snip--
```

Listing 1-9: About topic for PowerShell's core commands

To get a complete list of all the About topics available, use a wildcard for the `Name` parameter. In PowerShell, the *wildcard* character, an asterisk (*), can be used as a placeholder for zero or more characters. You can use a wildcard with the `Get-Help` command's `Name` parameter, as in Listing 1-10.

```
PS> Get-Help -Name About*
```

Listing 1-10: Using a wildcard on the `Get-Help` command's `Name` parameter

By appending the wildcard to `About`, you're asking PowerShell to search for all possible topics that start with *About*. If there are multiple matches, PowerShell will display a list, with brief information about each. To get the full information about one of the matches, you'll have to pass it into `Get-Help` directly, as shown previously in Listing 1-9.

Although the `Get-Help` command has a `Name` parameter, you can pass the parameter argument directly to it by entering `-Name`, as shown in Listing 1-10. This is known as using a *positional parameter*, which determines the value you're passing in based on its (you guessed it) position in the command. Positional parameters are a shortcut that many PowerShell commands have, allowing you to reduce the number of keystrokes.

Updating the Docs

The help system in PowerShell is a great asset for anyone who wants to learn more about the language, but one key feature makes this help system much better: it's dynamic! Documentation tends to get stale after a while. A product ships with documentation, bugs creep in, new features get released, but the documentation on the system stays the same. PowerShell addresses this problem with *updatable help*, which allows the built-in PowerShell cmdlets and any other cmdlets—or functions built by others—to point to an internet URI in order to host up-to-date documentation. Simply enter `Update-Help`, and PowerShell will begin reading the help on your system and checking it against the various online locations.

Note that although updatable help is included with all built-in PowerShell cmdlets, it isn't required for any third-party commands. Also, documentation is only as recent as the developer makes it. PowerShell provides the tools for developers to write better help content, but they still have to keep the repository containing their help files current. Finally, you may occasionally receive an error when running `Update-Help` if the location where the help is stored is not available anymore. In short, don't expect `Update-Help` to *always* show the latest help content for every command in PowerShell.

> **RUNNING POWERSHELL AS ADMINISTRATOR**
>
> At times it's necessary to run the PowerShell console *as Administrator.* This typically happens when you need to modify files, the registry, or anything else that's outside your user profile. For example, the `Update-Help` command mentioned previously needs to modify system-level files and cannot be run properly by a non-Administrator user.
>
> You can run PowerShell as an Administrator by right-clicking in Windows PowerShell and then clicking **Run as Administrator**, as shown in Figure 1-2.

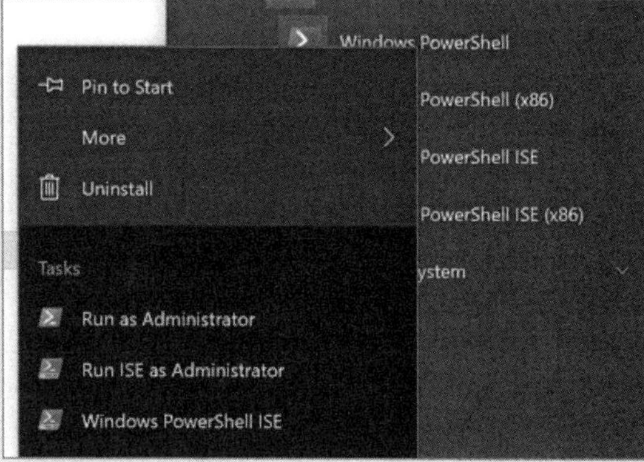

Figure 1-2: Running PowerShell as Administrator

Summary

In this chapter, you learned a few commands that will help you get started. When starting anything new, you're not going to know what you don't know. You just need a seed of knowledge that enables you to explore more by yourself. By understanding the basics of PowerShell commands and how to use `Get-Command` and `Get-Help`, you now have the tools you need to begin learning PowerShell. A big, exciting journey lies ahead of you!

2

BASIC POWERSHELL CONCEPTS

This chapter covers four basic concepts in PowerShell: variables, data types, objects, and data structures. These concepts are fundamental to just about every common programming language, but there's something that makes PowerShell distinctive: everything in PowerShell is an object.

This may not mean much to you now, but keep it in mind as you move through the rest of this chapter. By the end of the chapter, you should have an idea of just how significant this is.

Variables

A *variable* is a place to store *values*. You can think of a variable as a digital box. When you want to use a value multiple times, for example, you can put it in a box. Then, instead of typing the same number over and over in your code, you can put it in a variable and call that variable whenever you need the value. But as you might have guessed from the name, the real power of a variable is that it can change: you can add stuff to a box, swap what's in the box with something else, or take out whatever's in there and show it off for a bit before putting it back.

As you'll see later in the book, this variability lets you build code that can handle a general situation, as opposed to being tailored to one specific scenario. This section covers the basic ways to use a variable.

Displaying and Changing a Variable

All variables in PowerShell start with a dollar sign (`$`), which indicates to PowerShell that you are calling a variable and not a cmdlet, function, script file, or executable file. For example, if you want to display the value of the `MaximumHistoryCount` variable, you have to prepend it with a dollar sign and call it, as in Listing 2-1.

```
PS> $MaximumHistoryCount
4096
```

Listing 2-1: Calling the `$MaximumHistoryCount` variable

The `$MaximumHistoryCount` variable is a built-in variable that determines the maximum number of commands PowerShell saves in its command history; the default is 4096 commands.

You can change a variable's value by entering the variable name—starting with a dollar sign—and then using an equal sign (`=`) and the new value, as in Listing 2-2.

```
PS> $MaximumHistoryCount = 200
PS> $MaximumHistoryCount
200
```

Listing 2-2: Changing the `$MaximumHistoryCount` variable's value

Here you've changed the `$MaximumHistoryCount` variable's value to `200`, meaning PowerShell will save only the previous 200 commands in its command history.

Listings 2-1 and 2-2 use a variable that already exists. Variables in PowerShell come in two broad classes: *user-defined variables*, which are created by the user, and *automatic variables*, which already exist in PowerShell. Let's look at user-defined variables first.

User-Defined Variables

A variable needs to exist before you can use it. Try typing **`$color`** into your PowerShell console, as shown in Listing 2-3.

```
PS> $color
The variable '$color' cannot be retrieved because it has not been set.

At line:1 char:1
+ $color
+ ~~~~
```

```
+ CategoryInfo          : InvalidOperation: (color:String) [], RuntimeException
+ FullyQualifiedErrorId : VariableIsUndefined
```

Listing 2-3: Entering an undefined variable results in an error.

TURNING ON STRICT MODE

If you didn't get the error in Listing 2-3, and your console shows no output, try running the following command to turn on strict mode:

```
PS> Set-StrictMode -Version Latest
```

Turning on strict mode tells PowerShell to throw errors when you violate good coding practices. For example, strict mode forces PowerShell to return an error when you reference an object property that doesn't exist or an undefined variable. It's considered best practice to turn on this mode when writing scripts, as it forces you to write cleaner, more predictable code. When simply running interactive code from the PowerShell console, this setting is typically not used. For more information about strict mode, run `Get Help Set-StrictMode Examples`.

In Listing 2-3, you tried to refer to the `$color` variable before it even existed, which resulted in an error. To create a variable, you need to *declare* it—say that it exists—and then *assign* a value to it (or *initialize* it). You can do these at the same time, as in Listing 2-4, which creates a variable `$color` that contains the value `blue`. You can assign a value to a variable by using the same technique you used to change the value of `$MaximumHistoryCount`—by entering the variable name, followed by the equal sign, and then the value.

```
PS> $color = 'blue'
```

Listing 2-4: Creating a `color` variable with a value of `blue`

Once you've created the variable and assigned it a value, you can reference it by typing the variable name in the console (Listing 2-5).

```
PS> $color
blue
```

Listing 2-5: Checking the value of a variable

The value of a variable won't change unless something, or someone, explicitly changes it. You can call the `$color` variable any number of times, and it will return the value `blue` each time until the variable is redefined.

When you use the equal sign to define a variable (Listing 2-4), you're doing the same thing you'd do with the `Set-Variable` command. Likewise, when you type a variable into the console, and it prints out the value, as in

Listing 2-5, you're doing the same thing you'd do with the `Get-Variable` command. Listing 2-6 recreates Listings 2-4 and 2-5 by using these commands.

```
PS> Set-Variable -Name color -Value blue

PS> Get-Variable -Name color

Name                           Value
----                           -----
color                          blue
```

Listing 2-6: Creating a variable and displaying its value with the `Set-Variable` and `Get-Variable` commands

You can also use `Get-Variable` to return all available variables (as shown in Listing 2-7).

```
PS> Get-Variable

Name                           Value
----                           -----
$                              Get-PSDrive
?                              True
^                              Get-PSDrive
args                           {}
color                          blue
--snip--
```

Listing 2-7: Using `Get-Variable` to return all the variables.

This command will list all the variables currently in memory, but notice that there are some you haven't defined. You'll look at this type of variable in the next section.

Automatic Variables

Earlier I introduced automatic variables, the premade variables that PowerShell itself uses. Although PowerShell allows you to change some of these variables, as you did in Listing 2-2, I typically advise against it because unexpected consequences can arise. In general, you should treat automatic variables as *read-only*. (Now might be a good time to change `$MaximumHistoryCount` back to 4096!)

This section covers a few of the automatic variables that you're likely to use: the `$null` variable, `$LASTEXITCODE`, and the preference variables.

The $null Variable

The `$null` variable is a strange one: it represents nothing. Assigning `$null` to a variable allows you to create that variable but not assign a real value to it, as in Listing 2-8.

```
PS> $foo = $null
PS> $foo
PS> $bar
The variable '$bar' cannot be retrieved because it has not been set.
At line:1 char:1
+ $bar
+ ~~~~
    + CategoryInfo          : InvalidOperation: (bar:String) [], RuntimeException
    + FullyQualifiedErrorId : VariableIsUndefined
```

Listing 2-8: Assigning variables to `$null`

Here, you assign `$null` to the `$foo` variable. Then, when you call `$foo`, nothing is displayed, but no errors occur because PowerShell recognizes the variable.

You can see which variables PowerShell recognizes by passing parameters to the `Get-Variable` command. You can see in Listing 2-9 that PowerShell knows that the `$foo` variable exists but does not recognize the `$bar` variable.

```
PS> Get-Variable -Name foo

Name                           Value
----                           -----
foo


PS> Get-Variable -Name bar
Get-Variable : Cannot find a variable with the name 'bar'.
At line:1 char:1
+ Get-Variable -Name bar
+ ~~~~~~~~~~~~~~~~~~~~~~
    + CategoryInfo          : ObjectNotFound: (bar:String) [Get-Variable], ItemNotFoundException
    + FullyQualifiedErrorId : VariableNotFound,Microsoft.PowerShell.Commands.GetVariableCommand
```

Listing 2-9: Using `Get-Variable` *to find variables*

You may be wondering why we bother defining anything as `$null`. But `$null` is surprisingly useful. For example, as you'll see later in this chapter, you often give a variable a value as a response to something else, like the output of a certain function. If you check that variable, and see that its value is still `$null`, you'll know that something went wrong in the function and can act accordingly.

The LASTEXITCODE Variable

Another commonly used automatic variable is `$LASTEXITCODE`. PowerShell allows you to invoke external executable applications like the old-school *ping.exe*, which pings a website to get a response. When external applications finish running, they finish with an *exit code*, or *return code*, that indicates a message. Typically, a 0 indicates success, and anything else means either a failure or another anomaly. For *ping.exe*, a 0 indicates it was able to successfully ping a node, and a 1 indicates it could not.

When *ping.exe* runs, as in Listing 2-10, you'll see the expected output but not an exit code. That's because the exit code is hidden inside `$LASTEXITCODE`. The value of `$LASTEXITCODE` is always the exit code of the last application that was executed. Listing 2-10 pings *google.com*, returns its exit code, and then pings a nonexistent domain and returns its exit code.

```
PS> ping.exe -n 1 dfdfdfdfd.com

Pinging dfdfdfdfd.com [14.63.216.242] with 32 bytes of data:
Request timed out.

Ping statistics for 14.63.216.242:
    Packets: Sent = 1, Received = 0, Lost = 1 (100% loss),
PS> $LASTEXITCODE
1
PS> ping.exe -n 1 google.com

Pinging google.com [2607:f8b0:4004:80c::200e] with 32 bytes of data:
Reply from 2607:f8b0:4004:80c::200e: time=47ms

Ping statistics for 2607:f8b0:4004:80c::200e:
    Packets: Sent = 1, Received = 1, Lost = 0 (0% loss),
Approximate round trip times in milli-seconds:
    Minimum = 47ms, Maximum = 47ms, Average = 47ms
PS> $LASTEXITCODE
0
```

Listing 2-10: Using ping.exe *to demonstrate the* `$LASTEXITCODE` *variable*

The `$LASTEXITCODE` is 0 when you ping *google.com* but has a value of 1 when you ping the bogus domain name *dfdfdfdfd.com*.

The Preference Variables

PowerShell has a type of automatic variable referred to as *preference variables*. These variables control the default behavior of various output streams: `Error`, `Warning`, `Verbose`, `Debug`, and `Information`.

You can find a list of all of the preference variables by running `Get-Variable` and filtering for all variables ending in *Preference*, as shown here:

```
PS> Get-Variable -Name *Preference

Name                           Value
----                           -----
ConfirmPreference              High
DebugPreference                SilentlyContinue
ErrorActionPreference          Continue
InformationPreference          SilentlyContinue
ProgressPreference             Continue
```

```
VerbosePreference              SilentlyContinue
WarningPreference              Continue
WhatIfPreference               False
```

These variables can be used to configure the various types of output PowerShell can return. For example, if you've ever made a mistake and seen that ugly red text, you've seen the Error output stream. Run the following command to generate an error message:

```
PS> Get-Variable -Name 'doesnotexist'
Get-Variable : Cannot find a variable with the name 'doesnotexist'.
At line:1 char:1
+ Get-Variable -Name 'doesnotexist'
+ ~~~~~~~~~~~~~~~~~~~~~~~~~~~~~~~~~~
    + CategoryInfo          : ObjectNotFound: (doesnotexist:String) [Get-Variable],
                              ItemNotFoundException
    + FullyQualifiedErrorId : VariableNotFound,Microsoft.PowerShell.Commands.GetVariableCommand
```

You should have gotten a similar error message, as this is the default behavior for the Error stream. If for whatever reason you didn't want to be bothered by this error text, and would rather nothing happen, you could redefine the $ErrorActionPreference variable to SilentlyContinue or Ignore, either of which will tell PowerShell not to output any error text:

```
PS> $ErrorActionPreference = 'SilentlyContinue'
PS> Get-Variable -Name 'doesnotexist'
PS>
```

As you can see, no error text is output. Ignoring error output is generally considered bad practice, so change the value of $ErrorActionPreference back to Continue before proceeding. For more information on preference variables, check out the about_help content by running **Get-Help about _Preference_Variables.**

Data Types

PowerShell variables come in a variety of forms, or *types*. All the details of PowerShell's data types are beyond the scope of this chapter. What you need to know is that PowerShell has several data types—including bools, strings, and integers—and you can change a variable's data type without errors. The following code should run with no errors:

```
PS> $foo = 1
PS> $foo = 'one'
PS> $foo = $true
```

This is because PowerShell can figure out data types based on the values you provide it. What's happening under the hood is a little too complicated for this book, but it's important you understand the basic types and how they interact.

Boolean Values

Just about every programming language uses *booleans*, which have a true or false value (1 or 0). Booleans are used to represent binary conditions, like a light switch being on or off. In PowerShell, booleans are called *bools*, and the two boolean values are represented by the automatic variables `$true` and `$false`. These automatic variables are hardcoded into PowerShell and can't be changed. Listing 2-11 shows how to set a variable to be `$true` or `$false`.

```
PS> $isOn = $true
PS> $isOn
True
```

Listing 2-11: Creating a bool variable

You'll see a lot more of bools in Chapter 4.

Integers and Floating Points

You can represent numbers in PowerShell in two main ways: via integer or floating-point data types.

Integer types

Integer data types hold only whole numbers and will round any decimal input to the nearest integer. Integer data types come in *signed* and *unsigned* types. Signed data types can store both positive and negative numbers; unsigned data types store values with no sign.

By default, PowerShell stores integers by using the 32-bit signed `Int32` type. The bit count determines how big (or small) a number the variable can hold; in this case, anything in the range –2,147,483,648 to 2,147,483,647. For numbers outside that range, you can use the 64-bit signed `Int64` type, which has a range of –9,223,372,036,854,775,808 to 9,223,372,036,854,775,807.

Listing 2-12 shows an example of how PowerShell handles `Int32` types.

```
❶ PS> $num = 1
  PS> $num
  1
❷ PS> $num.GetType().name
  Int32
❸ PS> $num = 1.5
  PS> $num.GetType().name
  Double
❹ PS> [Int32]$num
  2
```

Listing 2-12: Using an `Int` type to store different values

Let's walk through each of these steps. Don't worry about all the syntax; for now, focus on the output. First, you create a variable `$num` and give it the value of 1 ❶. Next, you check the type of `$num` ❷ and see that PowerShell interprets 1 as an `Int32`. You then change `$num` to hold a decimal value ❸ and check the type again and see that PowerShell has changed the type to Double. This is because PowerShell will change a variable's type depending on its value. But you can force PowerShell to treat a variable as a certain type by *casting* that variable, as you do at the end by using the [Int32] syntax in front of $num ❹. As you can see, when forced to treat 1.5 as an integer, PowerShell rounds it up to 2.

Now let's look at the Double type.

Floating-Point Types

The Double type belongs to the broader class of variables known as *floating-point* variables. Although they can be used to represent whole numbers, floating-point variables are most often used to represent decimals. The other main type of floating-point variable is Float. I won't go into the internal representation of the Float and Double types. What you need to know is that although Float and Double are capable of representing decimal numbers, these types can be imprecise, as shown in Listing 2-13.

```
PS> $num = 0.1234567910
PS> $num.GetType().name
Double
PS> $num + $num
0.2469135782
PS> [Float]$num + [Float]$num
0.246913582086563
```

Listing 2-13: Precision errors with floating-point types

As you can see, PowerShell uses the Double type by default. But notice what happens when you add $num to itself but cast both as a Float—you get a strange answer. Again, the reasons are beyond the scope of this book, but be aware that errors like this can happen when using Float and Double.

Strings

You've already seen this type of variable. When you defined the $color variable in Listing 2-4, you didn't just type $color = blue. Instead, you enclosed the value in single quotes, which indicates to PowerShell that the value is a series of letters, or a *string*. If you try to assign the blue value to $color without the quotes, PowerShell will return an error:

```
PS> $color = blue
blue : The term 'blue' is not recognized as the name of a cmdlet, function, script file, or
operable program. Check the spelling of the name, or if a path was included, verify that the
path is correct and try again.
At line:1 char:10
+ $color = blue
+          ~~~~
    + CategoryInfo          : ObjectNotFound: (blue:String) [], CommandNotFoundException
    + FullyQualifiedErrorId : CommandNotFoundException
```

Without quotes, PowerShell interprets `blue` as a command and tries to execute it. Because the command `blue` doesn't exist, PowerShell returns an error message that says so. To correctly define a string, you need to use quotes around your value.

Combining Strings and Variables

Strings aren't restricted to words; they can be phrases and sentences as well. For instance, you can assign `$sentence` this string:

```
PS> $sentence = "Today, you learned that PowerShell loves the color blue"
PS> $sentence
Today, you learned that PowerShell loves the color blue
```

But maybe you want to use this same sentence, but with the words *PowerShell* and *blue* as the values of variables. For instance, what if you have a variable called `$name`, another called `$language`, and another called `$color`? Listing 2-14 defines these variables by using other variables.

```
PS> $language = 'PowerShell'
PS> $color = 'blue'

PS> $sentence = "Today, you learned that $language loves the color $color"
PS> $sentence
Today, you learned that PowerShell loves the color blue
```

Listing 2-14: Inserting variables in strings

Notice the use of double quotes. Enclosing your sentence in single quotes doesn't achieve the intended result:

```
PS> 'Today, $name learned that $language loves the color $color'
Today, $name learned that $language loves the color $color
```

This isn't just a weird bug. There's an important difference between single and double quotes in PowerShell.

Using Double vs. Single Quotes

When you're assigning a variable a simple string, you can use single or double quotes, as shown in Listing 2-15.

```
PS> $color = "yellow"
PS> $color
yellow
PS> $color = 'red'
PS> $color
red
PS> $color = ''
PS> $color
```

```
PS> $color = "blue"
PS> $color
blue
```

Listing 2-15: Changing variable values by using single and double quotes

As you can see, it doesn't matter which quotes you use to define a simple string. So why did it matter when you had variables in your string? The answer has to do with *variable interpolation*, or *variable expansion*. Normally, when you enter `$color` by itself into the console and hit ENTER, PowerShell *interpolates*, or *expands*, that variable. These are fancy terms that mean PowerShell is reading the value inside a variable, or opening the box so you can see inside. When you use double quotes to call a variable, the same thing happens: the variable is expanded, as you can see in Listing 2-16.

```
PS> "$color"
blue
PS> '$color'
$color
```

Listing 2-16: Variable behavior inside a string

But notice what happens when you use single quotes: the console outputs the variable itself, not its value. Single quotes tell PowerShell that you mean *exactly* what you're typing, whether that's a word like *blue* or what looks like a variable called `$color`. To PowerShell, it doesn't matter. It won't look past the value in single quotes. So when you use a variable inside single quotes, PowerShell doesn't know to expand that variable's value. This is why you need to use double quotes when inserting variables into your strings.

There's much more to say about bools, integers, and strings. But for now, let's take a step back and look at something more general: objects.

Objects

In PowerShell, *everything* is an object. In technical terms, an *object* is an individual instance of a specific template, called a class. A *class* specifies the kinds of things an object will contain. An object's class determines its *methods*, or actions that can be taken on that object. In other words, the methods are all the things an object can do. For example, a list object might have a `sort()` method that, when called, will sort the list. Likewise, an object's class determines its *properties*, the object's variables. You can think of the properties as all the data about the object. In the case of the list object, you might have a `length` property that stores the number of elements in the list. Sometimes, a class will provide default values for the object's properties, but more often than not, these are values you will provide to the objects you work with.

But that's all very abstract. Let's consider an example: a car. The car starts out as a plan in the design phase. This plan, or template, defines how the car should look, what kind of engine it should have, what kind of chassis it should have, and so on. The plan also lays out what the car will be able to do once it's complete—move forward, move in reverse, and open and close the sunroof. You can think of this plan as the car's class.

Each car is built from this class, and all of that particular car's properties and methods are added to it. One car might be blue, while the same model car might be red, and another car may have a different transmission. These attributes are the properties of a specific car object. Likewise, each of the cars will drive forward, drive in reverse, and have the same method to open and close the sunroof. These actions are the car's methods.

Now with that general understanding of how objects work, let's get our hands dirty and work with PowerShell.

Inspecting Properties

First, let's make a simple object so you can dissect it and uncover the various facets of a PowerShell object. Listing 2-17 creates a simple string object called `$color`.

```
PS> $color = 'red'
PS> $color
red
```

Listing 2-17: Creating a string object

Notice that when you call `$color`, you get only the variable's value. But typically, because they're objects, variables have more information than just their value. They also have properties.

To look at an object's properties, you'll use the `Select-Object` command and the `Property` parameter. You'll pass the `Property` an asterisk argument, as in Listing 2-18, to tell PowerShell to return everything it finds.

```
PS>  Select-Object -InputObject $color -Property *

Length
------
     3
```

Listing 2-18: Investigating object properties

As you can see, the `$color` string has only a single property, called `Length`.

You can directly reference the `Length` property by using *dot notation*: you use the name of the object, followed by a dot and the name of the property you want to access (see Listing 2-19).

```
PS> $color.Length
3
```

Listing 2-19: Using dot notation to check an object's property

Referencing objects like this will become second nature over time.

Using the Get-Member cmdlet

Using `Select-Object`, you discovered that the `$color` string has only a single property. But recall that objects sometimes have methods as well. To take a look at all the methods *and* properties that exist on this string object, you can use the `Get-Member` cmdlet (Listing 2-20); this cmdlet will be your best friend for a long time. It's an easy way to quickly list all of a particular object's properties and methods, collectively referred to as an object's *members*.

```
PS> Get-Member -InputObject $color

   TypeName: System.String

Name                MemberType             Definition
----                ----------             ----------
Clone               Method                 System.Object Clone(), System.Object ICloneable.Clone()
CompareTo           Method                 int CompareTo(System.Object value),
                                           int CompareTo(string strB), int IComparab...
Contains            Method                 bool Contains(string value)
CopyTo              Method                 void CopyTo(int sourceIndex, char[] destination,
                                           int destinationIndex, int co...
EndsWith            Method                 bool EndsWith(string value),
                                           bool EndsWith(string value, System.StringCompari...
Equals              Method                 bool Equals(System.Object obj),
                                           bool Equals(string value), bool Equals(string...
--snip--
Length              Property               int Length {get;}
```

Listing 2-20: Using `Get-Member` to investigate object properties and methods

Now we're talking! It turns out that your simple string object has quite a few methods associated with it. There are lots more to explore, but not all are shown here. The number of methods and properties an object will have depends on its parent class.

Calling Methods

You can reference methods with dot notation. However, unlike a property, a method will always end in a set of opening and closing parentheses and can take one or more parameters.

For example, suppose you want to remove a character in your `$color` variable. You can remove characters from a string by using the `Remove()` method. Let's isolate `$color`'s `Remove()` method with the code in Listing 2-21.

```
PS> Get-Member -InputObject $color -Name Remove
Name   MemberType Definition
----   ---------- ----------
Remove Method     string Remove(int startIndex, int count), string Remove(int startIndex)
```

Listing 2-21: Looking at a string's `Remove()` method

As you can see, there are two definitions. This means you can use the method in two ways: either with `startIndex` and the `count` parameter, or with just `startIndex`.

So to remove the second character in `$color`, you specify the place of the character where you'd like to start removing, which we call the *index*. Indexes start from 0, so the first letter has a starting place of 0, the second an index of 1, and so on. Along with an index, you can provide the number of characters you'd like to remove by using a comma to separate the parameter arguments, as in Listing 2-22.

```
PS> $color.Remove(1,1)
Rd
PS> $color
red
```

Listing 2-22: Calling methods

Using an index of 1, you've told PowerShell that you want to remove characters starting with the string's second character; the second argument tells PowerShell to remove just one character. So you get `Rd`. But notice that the `Remove()` method doesn't permanently change the value of a string variable. If you'd like to keep this change, you'd need to assign the output of the `Remove()` method to a variable, as shown in Listing 2-23.

```
PS> $newColor = $color.Remove(1,1)
PS> $newColor
Rd
```

Listing 2-23: Capturing output of the `Remove()` method on a string

NOTE *If you need to know whether a method returns an object (as `Remove()` does) or modifies an existing object, you can check its description. As you can see in Listing 2-21, `Remove()`'s definition has the word `string` in front of it; this means that the function returns a new string. Functions with the word `void` in front typically modify existing objects. Chapter 6 covers this topic in more depth.*

In these examples, you've used one of the simplest types of object, the string. In the next section, you'll take a look at some more complex objects.

Data Structures

A *data structure* is a way to organize multiple pieces of data. Like the data they organize, data structures in PowerShell are represented by objects stored in variables. They come in three main types: arrays, ArrayLists, and hashtables.

Arrays

So far, I've described a variable as a box. But if a simple variable (such as a `Float` type) is a single box, then an *array* is whole bunch of boxes taped together—a list of items represented by a single variable.

Often you'll need several related variables—say, a standard set of colors. Rather than storing each color as a separate string, and then referencing each of those individual variables, it's much more efficient to store all of those colors in a single data structure. This section will show you how to create, access, modify, and add to an array.

Defining Arrays

First, let's define a variable called `$colorPicker` and assign it an array that holds four colors as strings. To do this, you use the at sign (`@`) followed by the four strings (separated by commas) within parentheses, as in Listing 2-24.

```
PS> $colorPicker = @('blue','white','yellow','black')
PS> $colorPicker
blue
white
yellow
black
```

Listing 2-24: Creating an array

The `@` sign followed by an opening parenthesis and zero or more elements separated by a comma signals to PowerShell that you'd like to create an array.

Notice that after calling `$colorPicker`, PowerShell displays each of the array's elements on a new line. In the next section, you'll learn how to access each element individually.

Reading Array Elements

To access an element in an array, you use the name of the array followed by a pair of square brackets (`[]`) that contain the index of the element you want to access. As with string characters, you start numbering arrays at 0, so the first element is at index 0, the second at index 1, and so on. In PowerShell, using –1 as the index will return the final element.

Listing 2-25 accesses several elements in our `$colorPicker` array.

```
PS> $colorPicker[0]
blue
PS> $colorPicker[2]
yellow
PS> $colorPicker[3]
black
PS> $colorPicker[4]
Index was outside the bounds of the array.
At line:1 char:1
+ $colorPicker[4]
+ ~~~~~~~~~~~~~~~
    + CategoryInfo          : OperationStopped: (:) [], IndexOutOfRangeException
    + FullyQualifiedErrorId : System.IndexOutOfRangeException
```

Listing 2-25: Reading array elements

As you can see, if you try to specify an index number that doesn't exist in the array, PowerShell will return an error message.

To access multiple elements in an array at the same time, you can use the *range operator* (`..`) between two numbers. The range operator will make PowerShell return those two numbers and every number between them, like so:

```
PS> 1..3
1
2
3
```

To use the range operator to access multiple items in an array, you use a range for an index, as shown here:

```
PS> $colorPicker[1..3]
white
yellow
black
```

Now that you've seen how to access elements in an array, let's look at how to change them.

Modifying Elements in an Array

If you want to change an element in an array, you don't have to redefine the entire array. Instead, you can reference an item with its index and use the equal sign to assign a new value, as in Listing 2-26.

```
PS> $colorPicker[3]
black
PS> $colorPicker[3] = 'white'
PS> $colorPicker[3]
white
```

Listing 2-26: Modifying elements in an array

Make sure you double-check that the index number is correct by displaying the element to your console before you modify an element.

Adding Elements to an Array

You can add items to an array with the addition operator (+), as in Listing 2-27.

```
PS> $colorPicker = $colorPicker + 'orange'
PS> $colorPicker
blue
white
yellow
white
orange
```

Listing 2-27: Adding a single item to an array

Notice that you enter `$colorPicker` on both sides of the equal sign. This is because you are asking PowerShell to interpolate the `$colorPicker` variable and then add a new element.

The `+` method works, but there's a quicker, more readable way. You can use the plus and equal signs together to form `+=` (see Listing 2-28).

```
PS> $colorPicker += 'brown'
PS> $colorPicker
blue
white
yellow
white
orange
brown
```

Listing 2-28: Using the += shortcut to add an item to an array

The `+=` operator tells PowerShell to *add this item to the existing array*. This shortcut prevents you from having to type out the array name twice and is much more common than using the full syntax.

You can also add arrays to other arrays. Say you'd like to add the colors pink and cyan to your `$colorPicker` example. Listing 2-29 defines another array with just those two colors and adds them just as you did in Listing 2-28.

```
PS> $colorPicker += @('pink','cyan')
PS> $colorPicker
blue
white
yellow
white
orange
brown
pink
cyan
```

Listing 2-29: Adding multiple elements to an array at once

Adding multiple items at once can save you a lot of time, especially if you're creating an array with a large number of items. Note that PowerShell treats any comma-separated set of values as an array, and you don't explicitly need the `@` or parentheses.

Unfortunately, there is no equivalent of `+=` to remove an element from an array. Removing elements from an array is more complicated than you might think, and we won't cover it here. To understand why, read on!

ArrayLists

Something strange happens when you add to an array. Every time you add an element to an array, you're actually creating a new array from your old (interpolated) array and the new element. The same thing happens when you remove an element from an array: PowerShell destroys your old array and makes a new one. This is because arrays in PowerShell have a fixed size.

When you change them, you can't modify the size, so you have to create a new array. For small arrays like the ones we've been working with, you won't notice this happening. But when you begin to work with *huge* arrays, with tens or hundreds of thousands of elements, you'll see a big performance hit.

If you know you'll have to remove or add many elements to an array, I suggest you use a different data structure called an *ArrayList*. ArrayLists behave nearly identically to the typical PowerShell array, but with one crucial difference: they don't have a fixed size. They can dynamically adjust to added or removed elements, giving a much higher performance when working with large amounts of data.

Defining an ArrayList is exactly like defining an array, except that you need to cast it as an ArrayList. Listing 2-30 re-creates the color picker array but casts it as a `System.Collections.ArrayList` type.

```
PS> $colorPicker = [System.Collections.ArrayList]@('blue','white','yellow','black')
PS> $colorPicker
blue
white
yellow
black
```

Listing 2-30: Creating an ArrayList

As with an array, when you call an ArrayList, each item is displayed on a separate line.

Adding Elements to an ArrayList

To add or remove an element from an ArrayList without destroying it, you can use its methods. You can use the `Add()` and `Remove()` methods to add or remove items from an ArrayList. Listing 2-31 uses the `Add()` method and enters the new element within the method's parentheses.

```
PS> $colorPicker.Add('gray')
4
```

Listing 2-31: Adding a single item to an ArrayList

Notice the output: the number 4, which is the index of the new element you added. Typically, you won't use this number, so you can send the `Add()` method output to the `$null` variable to prevent it from outputting anything, as shown in Listing 2-32.

```
PS> $null = $colorPicker.Add('gray')
```

Listing 2-32: Sending output to `$null`

There are a few ways to negate output from PowerShell commands, but assigning output to `$null` gives the best performance, as the `$null` variable cannot be reassigned.

Removing Elements from an ArrayList

You can remove elements in a similar way, using the `Remove()` method. For example, if you want to remove the value gray from the ArrayList, enter the value within the method's parentheses, as in Listing 2-33.

```
PS> $colorPicker.Remove('gray')
```

Listing 2-33: Removing an item from an ArrayList

Notice that to remove an item, you don't have to know the index number. You can reference the element by its actual value—in this case, `gray`. If the array has multiple elements with the same value, PowerShell will remove the element closest to the start of the ArrayList.

It's hard to see the performance difference with small examples like these. But ArrayLists perform much better on large datasets than arrays. As with most programming choices, you'll need to analyze your specific situation to determine whether it makes more sense to use an array or an ArrayList. The rule of thumb is the larger the collection of items you're working with, the better off you'll be using an ArrayList. If you're working with small arrays of fewer than 100 elements or so, you'll notice little difference between an array and an ArrayList.

Hashtables

Arrays and ArrayLists are great when you need your data associated with only a position in a list. But sometimes you'll want something more direct: a way to correlate two pieces of data. For example, you might have a list of usernames you want to match to real names. In that case, you could use a *hashtable* (or *dictionary*), a PowerShell data structure that contains a list of *key-value pairs*. Instead of using a numeric index, you give PowerShell an input, called a *key*, and it returns the *value* associated with that key. So, in our example, you would index into the hashtable by using the username, and it would return that user's real name.

Listing 2-34 defines a hashtable, called `$users`, that holds information about three users.

```
PS> $users = @{
    abertram = 'Adam Bertram'
    raquelcer = 'Raquel Cerillo'
    zheng21 = 'Justin Zheng'
}
PS> $users
Name                           Value
----                           -----
abertram                       Adam Bertram
raquelcer                      Raquel Cerillo
zheng21                        Justin Zheng
```

Listing 2-34: Creating a hashtable

PowerShell will not let you define a hashtable with duplicate keys. Each key has to uniquely point to a single value, which can be an array or even another hashtable!

Reading Elements from Hashtables

To access a specific value in a hashtable, you use its key. There are two ways to do this. Say you want to find out the real name of the user `abertram`. You could use either of the two approaches shown in Listing 2-35.

```
PS> $users['abertram']
Adam Bertram
PS> $users.abertram
Adam Bertram
```

Listing 2-35: Accessing a hashtable's value

The two options have subtle differences, but for now, you can choose whichever method you prefer.

The second command in Listing 2-35 uses a property: `$users.abertram`. PowerShell will add each key to the object's properties. If you want to see all the keys and values a hashtable has, you can access the `Keys` and `Values` properties, as in Listing 2-36.

```
PS> $users.Keys
abertram
raquelcer
zheng21
PS> $users.Values
Adam Bertram
Raquel Cerillo
Justin Zheng
```

Listing 2-36: Reading hashtable keys and values

If you want to see *all* the properties of a hashtable (or any object), you can run this command:

```
PS> Select-Object -InputObject $yourobject -Property *
```

Adding and Modifying Hashtable Items

To add an element to a hashtable, you can use the `Add()` method or create a new index by using square brackets and an equal sign. Both ways are shown in Listing 2-37.

```
PS> $users.Add('natice', 'Natalie Ice')
PS> $users['phrigo'] = 'Phil Rigo'
```

Listing 2-37: Adding an item to a hashtable

Now your hashtable stores five users. But what happens if you need to change one of the values in your hashtable?

When you're modifying a hashtable, it's always a good idea to check that the key-value pair you want exists. To check whether a key already exists in a hashtable, you can use the `ContainsKey()` method, part of every hashtable created in PowerShell. When the hashtable contains the key, it will return `True`; otherwise, it will return `False`, as shown in Listing 2-38.

```
PS> $users.ContainsKey('johnnyq')
False
```

Listing 2-38: Checking items in a hashtable

Once you've confirmed the key is in the hashtable, you can modify its value by using a simple equal sign, as shown in Listing 2-39.

```
PS> $users['phrigo'] = 'Phoebe Rigo'
PS> $users['phrigo']
Phoebe Rigo
```

Listing 2-39: Modifying a hashtable value

As you've seen, you can add items to a hashtable in a couple of ways. As you'll see in the next section, there's only one way to remove an item from a hashtable.

Removing Items from a Hashtable

Like ArrayLists, hashtables have a `Remove()` method. Simply call it and pass in the key value of the item you want to remove, as in Listing 2-40.

```
PS> $users.Remove('natice')
```

Listing 2-40: Removing an item from a hashtable

One of your users should be gone, but you can call the hashtable to double-check. Remember that you can use the `Keys` property to remind yourself of any key name.

Creating Custom Objects

So far in this chapter, you've been making and using types of objects built into PowerShell. Most of the time, you can stick with these types and save yourself the work of creating your own. But sometimes you'll need to create a custom object with properties and methods that you define.

Listing 2-41 uses the `New-Object` cmdlet to define a new object with a `PSCustomObject` type.

```
PS> $myFirstCustomObject = New-Object -TypeName PSCustomObject
```

Listing 2-41: Creating a custom object by using `New-Object`

This example uses the `New-Object` command, but you could do the same thing by using an equal sign and a cast, as in Listing 2-42. You define a hashtable in which the keys are property names, and the values are property values, and then cast it as `PSCustomObject`.

```
PS> $myFirstCustomObject = [PSCustomObject]@{OSBuild = 'x'; OSVersion = 'y'}
```

Listing 2-42: Creating a custom object by using the `PSCustomObject` *type accelerator*

Notice that Listing 2-42 uses a semicolon (;) to separate the key and value definitions.

Once you have a custom object, you use it as you would any other object. Listing 2-43 passes our custom object to the `Get_Member` cmdlet to check that it is a `PSCustomObject` type.

```
PS> Get-Member  -InputObject $myFirstCustomObject


   TypeName: System.Management.Automation.PSCustomObject

Name        MemberType   Definition
----        ----------   ----------
Equals      Method       bool Equals(System.Object obj)
GetHashCode Method       int GetHashCode()
GetType     Method       type GetType()
ToString    Method       string ToString()
OSBuild     NoteProperty string OSBuild=OSBuild
OSVersion   NoteProperty string OSVersion=Version
```

Listing 2-43: Investigating properties and methods of a custom object

As you can see, your object already has some preexisting methods (for example, one that returns the object's type!), along with the properties you defined when you created the object in Listing 2-42.

Let's access those properties by using dot notation:

```
PS> $myFirstCustomObject.OSBuild
x
PS> $myFirstCustomObject.OSVersion
y
```

Looks good! You'll use `PSCustomObject` objects a lot throughout the rest of the book. They're powerful tools that let you create much more flexible code.

Summary

By now, you should have a general understanding of objects, variables, and data types. If you still don't understand these concepts, please reread this chapter. This is some of the most foundational stuff we'll be covering. A high-level understanding of these concepts will make the rest of this book much easier to understand.

The next chapter covers two ways to combine commands in PowerShell: the pipeline and scripts.

3

COMBINING COMMANDS

So far, you've been using the PowerShell console to call one command at a time. For simple code, this isn't a problem: you run the command you need, and if you need one more, you call that too. But for bigger projects, having to call each command individually is too time-consuming. Luckily, you can combine commands so you can call them as a single unit. In this chapter, you'll learn two ways of combining commands: by using the PowerShell pipeline and by saving your code in external scripts.

Starting a Windows Service

To illustrate why you'd want to combine commands, you'll start by doing a simple example the old way. You'll use two commands: `Get-Service`, which queries Windows services and returns information about them; and `Start-Service`, which starts Windows services. As shown in Listing 3-1, use `Get-Service` to make sure the service exists and then use `Start-Service` to start it.

```
PS> $serviceName = 'wuauserv'
PS> Get-Service -Name $serviceName
Status   Name               DisplayName
------   ----               -----------
Running  wuauserv           Windows Update
PS> Start-Service -Name $serviceName
```

Listing 3-1: Finding a service and starting it by using the `Name` *parameter*

You run `Get-Service` just to make sure PowerShell doesn't throw any errors. Chances are the service is already running. If it is, `Start-Service` will simply return control to the console.

When you're starting just one service, running the commands like this isn't particularly taxing. But you can imagine how monotonous it might get if you were working with hundreds of services. Let's look at how to simplify this problem.

Using the Pipeline

The first way to simplify your code is by chaining together commands by using the PowerShell *pipeline*, a tool that allows you to send the output of one command directly into another command as input. To use the pipeline, use the *pipe operator* (|) between two commands, like so:

```
PS> command1 | command2
```

Here, the output of *command1* is *piped* into *command2*, becoming *command2*'s input. The final command in the pipeline will output to the console.

Many shell scripting languages, including *cmd.exe* and bash, use a pipeline. But what makes the pipeline in PowerShell unique is that it passes objects and not simple strings. Later in this chapter, you'll look at how that happens, but for now, let's rewrite the code in Listing 3-1 by using the pipeline.

Piping Objects Between Commands

To send the output of `Get-Service` into `Start-Service`, use the code in Listing 3-2.

```
PS> Get-Service -Name 'wuauserv' | Start-Service
```

Listing 3-2: Piping existing services to the `Start-Service` *command*

In Listing 3-1, you used the `Name` parameter to tell the `Start-Service` command which service to start. But in this example, you don't have to specify any parameters because PowerShell takes care of that for you. It looks at the output of `Get-Service`, decides what values it should pass to `Start-Service`, and matches the values to the parameters that `Start-Service` takes.

If you wanted to, you could rewrite Listing 3-2 to use no parameters at all:

```
PS> 'wuauserv' | Get-Service | Start-Service
```

PowerShell sends the string wuauserv into Get-Service, and the output of Get-Service into Start-Service—all without you having to specify a thing! You've combined three separate commands into a single line, but you'll still have to reenter that line for every service you want to start. In the next section, you'll see how to use one line to start as many services as you want.

Piping Arrays Between Commands

In a text editor such as Notepad, create a text file called *Services.txt* that contains the strings Wuauserv and W32Time on separate lines, as shown in Figure 3-1.

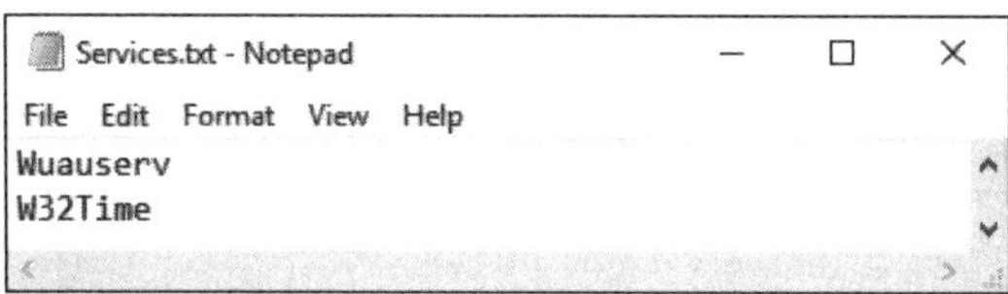

Figure 3-1: A Services.txt *file with* Wuauserv *and* W32Time *listed on separate lines*

This file contains a list of services you want to start. I've used two services here for simplicity's sake, but you could add as many as you like. To display the file to your PowerShell window, use the Get-Content cmdlet's Path parameter:

```
PS> Get-Content -Path C:\Services.txt
Wuauserv
W32Time
```

The Get-Content command reads in a file line by line, adding each line to an array and then returning that array. Listing 3-3 uses the pipeline to pass the array that Get-Content returns into the Get-Service command.

```
PS> Get-Content -Path C:\Services.txt | Get-Service

Status   Name               DisplayName
------   ----               -----------
Stopped  Wuauserv           Windows Update
Stopped  W32Time            Windows Time
```

Listing 3-3: Displaying a list of services to a PowerShell session by piping Services.txt *to* Get-Service

The Get-Content command is reading in the text file and spitting out an array. But instead of sending the array itself through the pipeline, PowerShell *unwraps* it, sending each item in the array individually through the pipeline.

This allows you to execute the same command for every item in the array. By putting every service you want to start in your text file, and tacking on an extra | Start-Service to the command in Listing 3-3, you have a single command that can start as many services as you need.

There's no limit to how many commands you can stitch together using the pipeline. But if you find yourself going over five, you may need to rethink your approach. Note that although the pipeline is powerful, it won't work everywhere: most PowerShell commands accept only certain types of pipeline input, and some don't accept any at all. In the next section, you'll dig a little deeper into how PowerShell handles pipeline input by looking at parameter binding.

Looking at Parameter Binding

When you pass parameters to a command, PowerShell initiates a process known as *parameter binding*, in which it matches each object you pass into the command to the various parameters specified by the command's creator. For a PowerShell command to accept pipeline input, the person who writes the command—whether that's Microsoft or you—has to explicitly build in pipeline support for one or more parameters. You'll notice an error if you attempt to pipe information into a command that doesn't have pipeline support on any parameter, or if PowerShell cannot find a suitable binding. For example, try running the following command:

```
PS> 'string' | Get-Process
Get-Process : The input object cannot be bound to any parameters for the command either...
--snip--
```

You should see that the command won't accept pipeline input. To see if using the pipeline is even possible, you can look at a command's full help content by using the Full parameter on the Get-Help command. Let's use Get-Help to look at the Get-Service command you used in Listing 3-1:

```
PS> Get-Help -Name Get-Service -Full
```

You should get quite a bit of output. Scroll down to the PARAMETERS section. This section lists information about each parameter and gives you more information than you'd get by not using the Detailed or Full parameter at all. Listing 3-4 shows the information for Get-Service's Name parameter.

```
-Name <string[]>
        Required?                    false
        Position?                    0
        Accept pipeline input?       true (ByValue, ByPropertyName)
        Parameter set name           Default
        Aliases                      ServiceName
        Dynamic?                     false
```

Listing 3-4: The Get-Service command's Name parameter information

There's a lot of information here, but we want to focus on the `Accept pipeline input?` field. As you can imagine, this field tells you whether a parameter accepts pipeline input or not; if the parameter didn't accept pipeline input, you'd see `false` next to this field. But notice there's more information here: this parameter accepts pipeline input both via `ByValue` and `ByPropertyName`. Contrast this with the `ComputerName` parameter for the same command, whose information is in Listing 3-5.

```
-ComputerName <string[]>
        Required?                    false
        Position?                    Named
        Accept pipeline input?       true (ByPropertyName)
        Parameter set name           (all)
        Aliases                      Cn
        Dynamic?                     false
```

Listing 3-5: The `Get-Service` command's `ComputerName` parameter information

The `ComputerName` parameter allows you to specify which computer you'd like to run `Get-Service` on. Notice this parameter also accepts a `string` type. So how does PowerShell know that you mean the service name, and not the computer name, when you do something like the following?

```
PS> 'wuauserv' | Get-Service
```

PowerShell matches pipeline input to parameters in two ways. The first is via `ByValue`, which means that PowerShell will look at the *type* of object passed in and interpret it accordingly. Because `Get-Service` specifies that it accepts the `Name` parameter via `ByValue`, it will interpret any string passed to it as `Name` unless otherwise specified. Because parameters passed via `ByValue` depend on the type of input, only one parameter can be passed via `ByValue`.

The second way PowerShell will match a parameter from the pipeline is via `ByPropertyName`. In this case, PowerShell will look at the object passed in, and if it has a property with the appropriate name (`ComputerName`, in this case), then it will look at the value for that property and accept that value as the parameter. So if you wanted to pass in both a service name and a computer name to `Get-Service`, you could create a `PSCustomObject` and pass it in, as in Listing 3-6.

```
PS> $serviceObject = [PSCustomObject]@{Name = 'wuauserv'; ComputerName = 'SERV1'}
PS> $serviceObject | Get-Service
```

Listing 3-6: Passing a custom object into `Get-Service`

By looking at a command's parameter specifications, and using a hashtable to cleanly store the ones you need, you'll be able to use the pipeline to string together all sorts of commands. But as you start to write more complex PowerShell code, you'll need more than the pipeline. In the next section, you'll look at how to externally store your PowerShell code as scripts.

Writing Scripts

Scripts are external files that store a sequence of commands, which you can run by entering a single line in the PowerShell console. As you can see in Listing 3-7, to run a script, you simply enter the path to it in the console.

```
PS> C:\FolderPathToScript\script.ps1
Hello, I am in a script!
```

Listing 3-7: Running a script from the console

Although there's nothing you can do in a script that you can't do in the console, it's much easier to run a single command using a script than it is to type several thousand commands! Not to mention that if you want to change anything in your code, or you make a mistake, you'll need to retype those commands again. As you'll see later in the book, scripting allows you to write complex, robust code. But before you start writing scripts, you have to change some PowerShell settings to make sure you can run them.

Setting the Execution Policy

By default, PowerShell does not allow you to run any scripts. If you try to run an external script in the default PowerShell installation, you'll encounter the error in Listing 3-8.

```
PS> C:\PowerShellScript.ps1
C:\PowerShellScript.ps1: File C:\PowerShellScript.ps1 cannot be loaded because
running scripts is disabled on this system. For more information, see about
_Execution_Policies at http://go.microsoft.com/fwlink/?LinkID=135170.
At line:1 char:1
+ C:\PowerShellScript.ps1
+ ~~~~~~~~~~~~~~~~~~~~~~~
    + CategoryInfo          : SecurityError: (:) [], PSSecurityException
    + FullyQualifiedErrorId : UnauthorizedAccess
```

Listing 3-8: An error that occurs when you try to run scripts

This frustrating error message is the result of PowerShell's *execution policy*, a security measure that decides which scripts can be run. The execution policy has four main configurations:

Restricted This configuration, which is the default, doesn't allow you to run scripts.

AllSigned This configuration allows you to run only scripts that have been cryptographically signed by a trusted party (more on this later).

RemoteSigned This configuration allows you to run any script you write, and any script you download as long as it's been cryptographically signed by a trusted party.

Unrestricted This configuration allows you to run any scripts.

To see which execution policy your machine is currently using, run the command in Listing 3-9.

```
PS> Get-ExecutionPolicy
Restricted
```

Listing 3-9: Displaying the current execution policy with the `Get-ExecutionPolicy` *command*

Chances are you get `Restricted` when you run this command. For the purposes of this book, you'll change the execution policy to `RemoteSigned`. This will allow you to run any script you write, while also ensuring that you use only external scripts that come from trusted sources. To change the execution policy, use the `Set-ExecutionPolicy` command and pass in the policy you want, as in Listing 3-10. Note that you'll need to be running this command as an administrator (see Chapter 1 for a refresher on running commands as an admin). You need to perform this command only once, as the setting is saved in the registry. If you're in a large Active Directory environment, the execution policy can also be set across many computers at once by using Group Policy.

```
PS> Set-ExecutionPolicy -ExecutionPolicy RemoteSigned

Execution Policy Change
The execution policy helps protect you from scripts that you do not trust. Changing the
execution policy might expose you to the security risks described in the about_Execution
_Policies help topic at http://go.microsoft.com/fwlink/?LinkID=135170. Do you want to change
the execution policy?
[Y] Yes  [A] Yes to All  [N] No  [L] No to All  [S] Suspend  [?] Help (default is "N"): A
```

Listing 3-10: Changing your execution policy with the `Set-ExecutionPolicy` *command*

Run the `Get-ExecutionPolicy` command again in order to verify that you successfully changed the policy to `RemoteSigned`. As I said previously, you won't need to set the execution policy every time you open PowerShell. The policy will stay at `RemoteSigned` until you want to change it again.

SCRIPT SIGNING

A *script signature* is an encrypted string appended to the end of the script as a comment; these signatures are generated by a certificate installed on your computer. When you set your policy to `AllSigned` or `RemoteSigned`, you will be able to run only those scripts that are properly signed. Signing a source lets PowerShell know that the script's source is reliable and that the author of the script is who they say they are. A script signature looks something like this:

```
# SIG # Begin signature block
# MIIEMwYJKoZIhvcNAQcCoIIEJDCCBCACAQExCzAJBgUrDgMCGgUAMGkGCisGAQQB
# gjcCAQSgWzBZMDQGCisGAQQBgjcCAR4wJgIDAQAABBAfzDtgWUsITrck0sYpfvNR
# AgEAAgEAAgEAAgEAAgEAMCEwCQYFKw4DAhoFAAQU6vQAn5sf2qIxQqwWUDwTZnJj
--snip--
# m5ugggI9MIICOTCCAaagAwIBAgIQyLeyGZcGA4ZOGqK7VF45GDAJBgUrDgMCHQUA
# Dxoj+2keS9sRR6XPl/ASs68LeF8o9cM=
# SIG # End signature block
```

You should sign any script that you're creating and executing in a professional environment. I won't go into how to do that here, but one of the best resources I've found to explain this concept is the article series "PowerShell Basics—Execution Policy and Code Signing" by Carlos Perez, a popular security guru, which you can find at *https://www.darkoperator.com/blog/2013/3/5/powershell-basics-execution-policy-part-1.html.*

Scripting in PowerShell

Now that your execution policy is set, it's time to write a script and execute it in the console. You can write PowerShell scripts in any text editor you like (Emacs, Vim, Sublime Text, Atom—even Notepad), but the most convenient way to write PowerShell scripts is by using the PowerShell Integrated Scripting Environment (ISE) or Microsoft's Visual Studio Code editor. Technically, the ISE is deprecated, but it comes preinstalled with Windows so it will probably be the first editor you discover.

Using the PowerShell ISE

To start the PowerShell ISE, run the command in Listing 3-11.

```
PS> powershell_ise.exe
```

Listing 3-11: Opening the PowerShell ISE

An interactive console screen that looks like Figure 3-2 should open up.

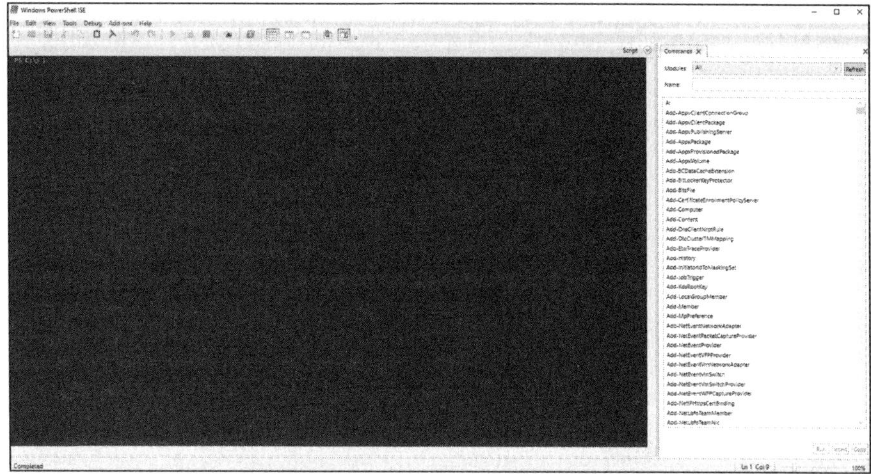

Figure 3-2: The PowerShell ISE

To add a script, click **File ▸ New**. The screen should split, with a white panel opening above the console, as in Figure 3-3.

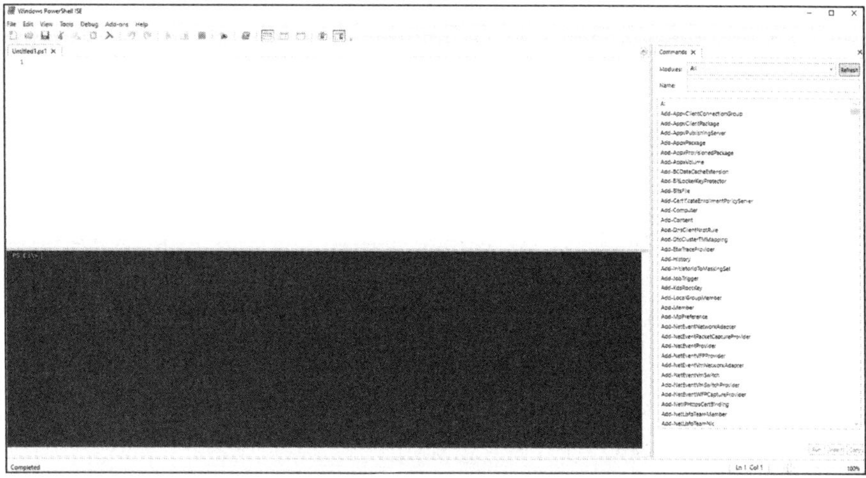

Figure 3-3: The PowerShell ISE with a script opened

Click **File ▸ Save** and save the new file as *WriteHostExample.ps1*. I'll save my script at the root of my C: drive, so it's located at *C:\WriteHostExample.ps1*. Notice that you save your script with the extension *.ps1*; this extension tells your system that the file is a PowerShell script.

You'll be entering all the text for your script in the white panel. The PowerShell ISE allows you to edit and run the script in the same window, which can save you a lot of annoying back and forth as you're editing. The PowerShell ISE has many more features, although I won't cover them here.

PowerShell scripts are simple text files. It doesn't matter which text editor you use, so long as you use the correct PowerShell syntax.

Writing Your First Script

Using whatever editor you like, add the line in Listing 3-12 to your script.

```
Write-Host 'Hello, I am in a script!'
```

Listing 3-12: The first line in your script

Notice there's no `PS>` at the start of the line. From here on out, that's how you'll know whether we're working in the console or writing in a script.

To run this script, head over to your console and type the path to your script, as in Listing 3-13.

```
PS> C:\WriteHostExample.ps1
Hello, I am in a script!
```

Listing 3-13: Executing WriteHostExample.ps1 *in the console*

Here, you use the full path to run *WriteHostExample.ps1*. If you're already in the directory containing the script you want to run, you can use a dot to indicate the current working directory, like so: `.\WriteHostExample.ps1`.

Congratulations, that's it—you've created your first script! It might not look like much, but it's a big step in the right direction. By the end of this book, you'll be defining your own PowerShell modules in scripts with hundreds of lines.

Summary

In this chapter, you learned two valuable methods to combine commands: the pipeline and scripts. You also saw how to change your execution policy, and demystified some of the magic behind the pipeline by looking at parameter binding. We've laid the foundation for creating more-powerful scripts, but we need to cover a few more key concepts before we get there. In Chapter 4, you'll learn how to make your code considerably more robust by using control flow structures such as `if/then` statements and `for` loops.

4

CONTROL FLOW

Let's do a quick recap. In Chapter 3, you learned how to combine commands by using the pipeline and external scripts. In Chapter 2, you learned how to use variables to store values. One of the major benefits of working with variables is they allow you to write code that deals with what a value means: instead of working with the number 3, for example, you'll work with the more general `$serverCount`, so you can write code that runs the same whether you have one, or two, or a thousand servers. Combine this ability to write general solutions with the ability to store your code in a script that you can run on many computers, and you can start solving problems at a much bigger scale.

But in the real world, sometimes it matters whether you're working with one server, or two servers, or a thousand. Right now, you don't have a good way to account for that: your scripts run in one direction—top to bottom—and they don't have any way of changing based on the specific values you're working with. In this chapter, you'll use control flow and conditional logic to write scripts that execute different sequences of instructions based on the values they're working with. By the end of the chapter, you'll know how to use `if/then` statements, `switch` statements, and all manner of loops to give your code some much-needed flexibility.

Understanding Control Flow

You're going to write a script that reads the contents of a file stored in various remote computers. To follow along, download a file called *App_configuration.txt* from the book's resources at *https://github.com/adbertram/PowerShellForSysadmins/* and place it in the root of the *C:* drive of a few remote computers. (If you don't have access to remote servers, just follow along in the text for now.) In this example, I'll be using servers with the names `SRV1`, `SRV2`, `SRV3`, `SRV4`, and `SRV5`.

To access the file's contents, you'll use the `Get-Content` command and provide the path to the file as the argument to the `Path` parameter, as shown here:

```
Get-Content -Path "\\servername\c$\App_configuration.txt"
```

As a first attempt, let's store all our server names in an array, and run this command for every server in the array. Open a new *.ps1* file and enter the code in Listing 4-1.

```
$servers = @('SRV1','SRV2','SRV3','SRV4','SRV5')
Get-Content -Path "\\$($servers[0])\c$\App_configuration.txt"
Get-Content -Path "\\$($servers[1])\c$\App_configuration.txt"
Get-Content -Path "\\$($servers[2])\c$\App_configuration.txt"
Get-Content -Path "\\$($servers[3])\c$\App_configuration.txt"
Get-Content -Path "\\$($servers[4])\c$\App_configuration.txt"
```

Listing 4-1: Getting the contents of a file on multiple servers

In theory, this code will run with no problems. But this example assumes that everything in your environment is pristine. What if `SRV2` is down? What if someone forgot to move *App_configuration.txt* onto `SRV4`? Or used a different file path? You could write a different script for each server, but that solution won't scale—especially as you start to add more and more servers. What you need is code that can execute differently depending on what it encounters.

That's the basic idea behind *control flow,* the ability to have your code execute different sequences of instructions depending on predetermined logic. You can think of your scripts as executing along a certain path. Right now, that path goes straight from the first line of code to the last one, but you can use control flow statements to add forks in the road, circle back to places you've already been, or take you over lines. By introducing different paths for your script to run along, you allow for much greater flexibility, enabling you to write a single script that can handle many situations.

You'll start by looking at the most basic type of control flow: the conditional statement.

Using Conditional Statements

In Chapter 2, you learned about the concept of a boolean: a true or false value. You use booleans to build *conditional statements*, which tell PowerShell to execute a certain code block based on whether an expression (called a *condition*) evaluates to `True` or `False`. A condition is a yes/no question: Do you have more than five servers? Is server 3 up? Does this file path exist? To start using conditional statements, let's see how to translate these kinds of questions into expressions.

Building Expressions by Using Operators

You can write expressions by using *comparison operators*, which compare values. To use a comparison operator, you put it between two values, like this:

```
PS> 1 -eq 1
True
```

You use the `-eq` operator to determine whether two values are equal. Here's a list of the most common comparison operators you'll use:

`-eq` Compares two values and returns `True` if they are equal.

`-ne` Compares two values and returns `True` if they are not equal.

`-gt` Compares two values and returns `True` if the first is greater than the second.

`-ge` Compares two values and returns `True` if the first is greater than or equal to the second.

`-lt` Compares two values and returns `True` if the first is less than the second.

`-le` Compares two values and returns `True` if the first is less than or equal to the second.

`-contains` Returns `True` if the second value is "in" the second. You can use this to determine whether a value is inside an array.

PowerShell offers more advanced comparison operators. I won't go into them now, but I encourage you to read about them in the Microsoft documentation at *https://docs.microsoft.com/en-us/powershell/module/microsoft.powershell.core/about/about_comparison_operators/*, or in the PowerShell help (see Chapter 1).

You can use the preceding operators to compare variables and values. But an expression doesn't have to be a comparison. Sometimes PowerShell commands can be used as conditions. In the previous example, you wanted to know whether a server was online. You can test to see whether a server can be pinged by using the `Test-Connection` cmdlet. Normally, the output of `Test-Connection` returns an object full of information, but by using the `Quiet` parameter, you can force the command to return a simple `True` or `False` and limit the test to a single attempt via the `Count` parameter.

```
PS> Test-Connection -ComputerName offlineserver -Quiet -Count 1
False

PS> Test-Connection -ComputerName onlineserver -Quiet -Count 1
True
```

If you wanted to know whether the server was offline, you could use the -not operator to convert the expression to its opposite:

```
PS> -not (Test-Connection -ComputerName offlineserver -Quiet -Count 1)
True
```

Now that you've seen the basics of expressions, let's look at the simplest conditional statement.

The if Statement

The if statement is straightforward: if *X* is true, then do *Y*. That's it!

To write an if statement, you begin with an if keyword followed by parentheses containing a condition. After the expression comes a code block, demarcated in curly brackets. PowerShell will execute that code block only when the expression evaluates to True. If the if expression evaluates to False or returns nothing at all, the code block is skipped. You can see the basic syntax of an if/then statement in Listing 4-2.

```
if (condition) {
    # code to run if the condition evaluates to be True
}
```

Listing 4-2: The syntax of an if statement

This example uses a bit of new syntax: the hash mark (#) signals a *comment*, which is text PowerShell will ignore. You can use comments to leave yourself, or anyone else reading your code, helpful notes and descriptions.

Now let's take a second look at the code in Listing 4-1 and see how to use an if statement to make sure you don't try to access a server that's not up. In the preceding section, you saw how Test-Connection can be used as an expression that returns True or False, so let's wrap a Test-Connection command in an if statement and then use Get-Content in the following code block to avoid accessing a server that's down. For now, you'll change the code for only the first server, as in Listing 4-3.

```
$servers = @('SRV1','SRV2','SRV3','SRV4','SRV5')
if (Test-Connection -ComputerName $servers[0] -Quiet -Count 1) {
    Get-Content -Path "\\$($servers[0])\c$\App_configuration.txt"
}
Get-Content -Path "\\$($servers[1])\c$\App_configuration.txt"
--snip--
```

Listing 4-3: Using an if statement to selectively get server content

Because you have Get-Content in an if statement, you won't run into any errors if you try to access a dead server; if the test fails, your script will know not to attempt to read the file. You'll try to access the server only if you *already* know it's up. But notice that this code handles only the case in which the condition is true. Often enough, you'll want to have one behavior if a condition is true and another behavior if it's false. In the next section, you'll see how to specify behavior for a false condition by using the else statement.

The else Statement

To add an alternate behavior to your if statement, you use the else keyword after the closing parenthesis of your if block, followed by another pair of curly brackets containing a code block. As shown in Listing 4-4, use an else statement to return an error to the console when the first server isn't responding.

```
if (Test-Connection -ComputerName $servers[0] -Quiet -Count 1) {
    Get-Content -Path "\\$($servers[0])\c$\App_configuration.txt"
} else {
    Write-Error -Message "The server $($servers[0]) is not responding!"
}
```

Listing 4-4: Using the else statement to run code if the condition is not true

The if/else statement works perfectly when you have two mutually exclusive situations. Here, the server is either online or it's not; you need only two branches of code. Let's look at how to handle more complex situations.

The elseif Statement

The else statement works like a catchall: if the first if fails, do this no matter what. For a binary condition, such as a server being up or down, this works well. But sometimes you'll need to account for even more variability. For example, let's say you have a server that you know doesn't have the file you want to get, and you've stored the name of that server in the variable $problemServer (add this line of code to the script on your own!). This means you need an extra check to see whether the server you're dealing with is the problem server. You could account for this statement by using a nested if, as in the following code:

```
if (Test-Connection -ComputerName $servers[0] -Quiet -Count 1) {
    if ($servers[0] -eq $problemServer) {
        Write-Error -Message "The server $servers[0] does not have the right file!"
    } else {
        Get-Content -Path "\\$servers[0]\c$\App_configuration.txt"
    }
} else {
    Write-Error -Message "The server $servers[0] is not responding!"
}
--snip--
```

But a cleaner way to write this same logic is to use an elseif statement, which lets you add an extra condition to check before falling back on the code in the else block. The syntax of an elseif block is identical to that of an if block. So, to check for the problem server by using elseif statements, try the code in Listing 4-5.

```
if (-not (Test-Connection -ComputerName $servers[0] -Quiet -Count 1)) { ❶
    Write-Error -Message "The server $servers[0] is not responding!"
} elseif ($servers[0] -eq $problemServer) ❷
    Write-Error -Message "The server $servers[0] does not have the right file!"
} else {
    Get-Content -Path "\\$servers[0]\c$\App_configuration.txt" ❸
}
--snip--
```

Listing 4-5: Using an elseif block

Notice that you haven't just added an elseif; you've also changed the logic. Now you check to see whether the server is offline by first using the -not operator ❶. Then, once you've determined whether the server is online, you check to see whether it's a problem server ❷. If it's not, you use the else statement to run the default behavior—getting the file ❸. As you can see, there are multiple ways to structure code like this. What matters is that the code works and is readable to someone seeing it with fresh eyes, whether that's a coworker reading it for the first time, or you looking back at a script you wrote a while ago.

You can chain together as many elseif statements as you like, which allows you to account for many scenarios. However, elseif statements are mutually exclusive: when one elseif evaluates to True, PowerShell will run only the code in its block and will not test the rest of the cases. In Listing 4-5, this didn't cause any issues, as you needed to test only whether you were working with the problem server after you had checked that it was up, but it's something to keep in mind moving forward.

The if, else, and elseif statements are great for handling simple yes/no questions. In the next section, you'll learn how to handle slightly more complicated logic.

The switch Statement

Let's tweak our example a bit. Say you have five servers, and *each* server has the file in a different path. Based on what you know now, you'd need to write a separate elseif statement for each individual server. This would work, but there's a cleaner method.

Notice that now you're working with a different kind of condition. Whereas before you wanted the answers to yes/no questions, here you want to know the specific value of one thing: Is the server SRV1? Is it SRV2? And so forth. If you were working with only one or two specific values, an if would do, but in this case, using a switch statement would be cleaner.

A switch statement allows you to execute various pieces of code based on a value. It consists of the switch keyword followed by an expression in parentheses. Inside the switch block are a series of statements that have a value, followed by a set of curly brackets containing a code block, and eventually a default block, as in Listing 4-6.

```
switch (expression) {
    expressionvalue {
        # Do something with code here.
    }
    expressionvalue {
    }
    default {
        # Stuff to do if no matches were found
    }
}
```

Listing 4-6: Template for a switch statement

A switch statement can contain an (almost) unlimited number of values. If the expression evaluates to a value, the code inside that value's block is executed. Critically, unlike with elseif, after one code block runs, PowerShell will continue to evaluate the other conditions unless otherwise specified. If none of the values match the evaluated value, PowerShell executes the code embedded under the default keyword. To force PowerShell to stop evaluating conditions in the switch statement, use the break keyword at the end of the code block, as in Listing 4-7.

```
switch (expression) {
    expressionvalue {
        # Do something with code here.
        break
    }
--snip--
```

Listing 4-7: Using the break keyword in a switch statement

The break keyword can be used to make your switch conditions mutually exclusive. Let's go back to our example of five servers with the same file at different paths. You know that the server you're working with can have only one value (it can't be both SRV1 and SRV2), so you have to use break statements. Your script should look something like Listing 4-8.

```
$currentServer = $servers[0]
switch ($currentServer) {
    $servers[0] {
        # Check if server is online and get content at SRV1 path.
        break
    }
    $servers[1] {
        ## Check if server is online and get content at SRV2 path.
        break
    }

    $servers[2] {
```

```
        ## Check if server is online and get content at SRV3 path.
        break
    }
--snip--
```

Listing 4-8: Checking various servers by using a `switch` *statement*

You could rewrite this code by using only `if` and `elseif` statements (and I encourage you to try!). But however you choose to write it, you'll have to repeat the same structure for each server in your list, meaning that your script is going to get pretty long—and just think about if you wanted to test 500 servers instead of 5. In the next section, you'll learn how to spare yourself that trouble by using one of the most fundamental control flow structures: the loop.

Using Loops

A good rule of thumb for computer work: Don't Repeat Yourself (DRY). If you find yourself doing the same thing more than once, chances are there's a way to automate it. The same is true of writing code: if you're using the same lines of code over and over, there's probably a better solution.

One way to avoid repetitive code is to use loops. A *loop* lets you execute code repeatedly until a condition changes. The *stop condition* can be used to run a loop a set number of times, or until a boolean value has changed, or even to have a loop run infinitely. We call each run of the loop an *iteration.*

PowerShell offers five types of loops: `foreach`, `for`, `do/while`, `do/until`, and `while`. This section explains each type of loop, noting what makes it unique, and highlighting the best situations to use it.

The foreach Loop

We'll start with the type of loop you'll probably use the most in PowerShell, the `foreach` loop. A `foreach` loop goes through a list of objects and performs the same action for every object, ending when it's finished with the last one. This list of objects is typically represented by an array. When you run a loop over a list of objects, we say you're *iterating* over the list.

A `foreach` loop is useful when you have to perform the same task on a lot of different, but related, objects. Let's go back to Listing 4-1 (reproduced here):

```
$servers = @('SRV1','SRV2','SRV3','SRV4','SRV5')
Get-Content -Path "\\$($servers[0])\c$\App_configuration.txt"
Get-Content -Path "\\$($servers[1])\c$\App_configuration.txt"
Get-Content -Path "\\$($servers[2])\c$\App_configuration.txt"
Get-Content -Path "\\$($servers[3])\c$\App_configuration.txt"
Get-Content -Path "\\$($servers[4])\c$\App_configuration.txt"
```

You're going to ignore all the fancy logic you added in the preceding section for now and put this into a `foreach` loop. But unlike other loops in PowerShell, the `foreach` loop can be used in three ways: as a `foreach` statement, as a ForEach-Object cmdlet, or as a foreach() method. Although each is similar to use, you should understand the differences. In the following three sections, you'll rewrite Listing 4-1 by using each type of foreach loop.

The foreach Statement

The first type of foreach you'll look at is the foreach statement. Listing 4-9 has the loop version of Listing 4-1.

```
foreach ($server in $servers) {
    Get-Content -Path "\\$server\c$\App_configuration.txt"
}
```

Listing 4-9: Using a foreach statement

As you can see, the foreach statement is followed by parentheses that contain three elements, in order: a variable, the keyword in, and the object or array to iterate over. The variable you provide can have any name, but I recommend keeping the name as descriptive as possible.

As it moves through the list, PowerShell will *copy* the object it's looking at into the variable. Note that because the variable is just a copy, you cannot directly change the item in the original list. To test this, try running the following:

```
$servers = @('SRV1','SRV2','SRV3','SRV4','SRV5')
foreach ($server in $servers) {
    $server = "new $server"
}
$servers
```

You should get something like this:

```
SRV1
SRV2
SRV3
SRV4
SRV5
```

Nothing changed! This is because you're modifying only a copy of the original variable in the array. This is one of the downsides of using a foreach loop (of any kind). To directly modify the original contents of the list you're looping through, you have to use one of the other loop types.

The ForEach-Object cmdlet

Like the foreach statement, the ForEach-Object cmdlet can iterate over a set of objects and perform an action. But because ForEach-Object is a cmdlet, you have to pass that set of objects and the action to complete as parameters.

Check out Listing 4-10 to see how you'd do the same thing as Listing 4-9 with the ForEach-Object cmdlet.

```
$servers = @('SRV1','SRV2','SRV3','SRV4','SRV5')
ForEach-Object -InputObject $servers -Process {
    Get-Content -Path "\\$_\c$\App_configuration.txt"
}
```

Listing 4-10: Using the ForEach-Object cmdlet

A bit is different here, so let's walk through it. Notice that the `ForEach-Object` cmdlet takes an `InputObject` parameter. In this case, you're using the `$servers` array, but you could use any object, such as a string or integer. In those cases, PowerShell will simply perform a single iteration. The cmdlet also accepts a `Process` parameter, which should be a scriptblock containing the code you'd like to run for each element inside the input object. (A *scriptblock* is a collection of statements that you pass into a cmdlet as a single unit.)

You may have noticed something else strange about Listing 4-10. Instead of using a `$server` variable, as you did with the `foreach` statement, you use the syntax `$_`. This special syntax represents the current object in the pipeline. The major difference between the `foreach` statement and the `ForEach-Object` cmdlet is that the cmdlet accepts pipeline input. In practice, `ForEach-Object` is almost always used by passing in the `InputObject` parameter through the pipeline, like so:

```
$servers | ForEach-Object -Process {
    Get-Content -Path "\\$_\c$\App_configuration.txt"
}
```

The `ForEach-Object` cmdlet can be a major time-saver.

The foreach() Method

The final type of `foreach` loop you'll look at is the `foreach()` object method, introduced in PowerShell V4. The `foreach()` method exists on all arrays in PowerShell, and can be used to accomplish the same thing as `foreach` and `ForEach-Object`. The `foreach()` method accepts a scriptblock parameter that should contain the code to execute each iteration. As with `ForEach-Object`, you use `$_` to capture the current iteration's object, as you can see in Listing 4-11.

```
$servers.foreach({Get-Content -Path "\\$_\c$\App_configuration.txt"})
```

Listing 4-11: Using the foreach() method

The `foreach()` method is considerably faster than the other two, and noticeably so when processing large datasets. I recommend that you use this method over the other two wherever possible.

A `foreach` loop is great when you want to perform a task on an object-by-object basis. But say you want to do something simpler. What if you wanted to execute a task a certain number of times?

The for Loop

To execute code a predetermined number of times, you use a `for` loop. Listing 4-12 shows the syntax for a basic `for` loop.

```
for (❶$i = 0; ❷$i -lt 10; ❸$i++) {
 ❹ $i
}
```

Listing 4-12: A simple `for` *loop*

A `for` loop consists of four pieces: the *iteration variable* declaration ❶, the condition to continue running the loop ❷, the action to perform on the iteration variable after each successful loop ❸, and the code you want to execute ❹. In this example, you start the loop by initializing the variable `$i` to 0. Then, you check to see whether `$i` is less than 10; if it is, you execute the code in the curly brackets, which prints `$ix`. After the code has executed, you increment `$i` by 1 ❸ and then check whether it is still smaller than 10 ❷. You repeat this process until `$i` is no longer less than 10, resulting in 10 iterations.

A `for` loop can be used like this to execute a task any number of times—simply replace the condition ❷ to fit your needs. But the `for` loop has many more uses. One of the most powerful is manipulating the elements in an array. Earlier, you saw how you *couldn't* use a `foreach` loop to change the elements in your array. Let's try again, using a `for` loop:

```
$servers = @('SERVER1','SERVER2','SERVER3','SERVER4','SERVER5')
for ($i = 0; $i -lt $servers.Length; $i++) {
    $servers[$i] = "new $server"
}
$servers
```

Try running this script. The server names should change.

A `for` loop is also particularly useful when performing an action that requires multiple elements in the array. For instance, let's say that your `$servers` array is arranged in a particular order, and you want to know which server comes after which. To do this, you could use a `for` loop:

```
for (❶$i = 1; $i -lt $servers.Length; $i++) {
    Write-Host $servers[$i] "comes after" $servers[$i-1]
}
```

Notice that this time you declare the iteration variable to start at 1 ❶. This ensures that you don't try to access the server that comes before the first one, which would give you an error.

As you'll see over the course of this book, the `for` loop is a powerful tool that has many uses outside the simple examples provided here. For now, let's move on to the next type of loop.

The while Loop

The `while` loop is the simplest loop: while a condition is true, do something. To get a sense of the `while` loop syntax, let's rewrite the `for` loop from Listing 4-12 as shown in Listing 4-13.

```
$counter = 0
while ($counter -lt 10) {
    $counter
    $counter++
}
```

Listing 4-13: A simple counter using a `while` loop

As you can see, to use a `while` loop, just place the condition you want to evaluate inside the parentheses, and the code you want to run inside the curly brackets.

The `while` loop is best used when the number of iterations for the loop is *not* predetermined. Say you have a Windows server (again called `$problemServer`) that's frequently going down. But there's a file you need on it, and you don't want to sit there testing the server every few minutes to get it. You can use a `while` loop to automate this process for you, as in Listing 4-14.

```
while (Test-Connection -ComputerName $problemServer -Quiet -Count 1) {
    Get-Content -Path "\\$problemServer\c$\App_configuration.txt"
    break
}
```

Listing 4-14: Using a `while` loop to deal with a problematic server

By using a `while` loop instead of an `if`, you can repeatedly check to see whether the service is up. Then, once you get the content you need, you can `break` out of the loop to make sure you don't continue to check the server. The `break` keyword can be used in any loop to stop the loop from running. This is especially important when using one of the most common `while` loops: the `while($true)` loop. By using `$true` as your condition, your `while` loop will run forever unless you stop it with a `break` or keyboard input.

The do/while and do/until Loops

Similar to the `while` loop are the `do/while` and `do/until` loops. The two are essentially inverses: the `do/while` loop does something *while* a condition is true, and the `do/until` loop does something *until* a condition is true.

An empty `do/while` loop looks like this:

```
do {

    } while ($true)
```

As you can see, the do code comes before the while condition. The major difference between a while loop and a do/while loop is that a do/while loop will execute the code *before* the condition is evaluated.

This can be useful in certain situations, particularly when you are continually receiving input from a source and want to evaluate it. For example, say you want to prompt the user to ask them for the best programming language. To do so, you could use the code in Listing 4-15. Here, you'll use the do/until loop:

```
do {
    $choice = Read-Host -Prompt 'What is the best programming language?'
} until ($choice -eq 'PowerShell')
Write-Host -Object 'Correct!'
```

Listing 4-15: Using a do/until loop

The do/while and do/until loops are *very* similar. Often this means you can accomplish the same thing using each loop simply by inverting the condition, as you've done here.

Summary

We covered a lot in this chapter. You learned about control flow, and how to use conditional logic to introduce alternative paths through your code. You saw various types of control flow statements, including the if statement, switch statement, and foreach, for, and while loops. Finally, you gained some hands-on experience, using PowerShell to check whether servers are up and to access files on them.

You can use conditional logic to handle some errors, but chances are you'll miss something. In Chapter 5, you'll take a closer look at errors and some techniques you can use to handle them.

5

ERROR HANDLING

You've seen how to use variables and control flow structures to write flexible code that can respond to the imperfections of the real world—servers that aren't up when they should be, files that are in the wrong place, and the like. Some of these things you know to expect and can handle accordingly. But you'll never be able to anticipate every error. There's always something that will break your code. The best you can do is write code that breaks responsibly.

That's the basic premise behind *error handling*, the techniques that developers use to ensure that their code expects and takes care of—or *handles*—errors. In this chapter, you'll learn a few of the most basic error-handling techniques. First, you'll drill down into errors themselves, looking at the difference between terminating and nonterminating errors. Then, you'll learn how to use the `try/catch/finally` construct, and last, you'll examine PowerShell's automatic error variables.

Working with Exceptions and Errors

In Chapter 4, you looked at control flow and how to introduce different paths of execution into your code. When your code encounters a problem, it disrupts the normal flow; we call this flow-disrupting event an *exception*. Mistakes such as dividing by zero, trying to access an element outside the bounds of an array, or trying to open a missing file will all cause PowerShell to *throw* an exception.

Once an exception is thrown, if you do nothing to stop it, it will be wrapped with additional information and sent to the user as an *error*. PowerShell has two types of errors. The first is a *terminating error*: any error that stops execution of the code. For example, say you have a script called *Get-Files.ps1* that finds a list of files in a certain folder and then performs the same action for each of those files. If the script can't find the folder—someone has moved it or named it something unexpected—you'll want to return a terminating error, as the code cannot do anything without access to all the files. But what happens if only one of the files is corrupted?

When you try to access the corrupted file, you'll get another exception. But because you're performing the same independent action on each file, there's no reason that one broken file should stop the rest from running. In that case, you'll write code that treats the exception caused by the single broken file as a *nonterminating error*, one not severe enough to halt the rest of the code.

The general error-handling behavior for nonterminating errors is to output a useful error message and proceed with the rest of the program. You can see this in several of PowerShell's built-in commands. For example, say you want to check the status of the Windows services `bits`, `foo`, and `lanmanserver`. You could use a single `Get-Service` command to check them all at the same time, as in Listing 5-1.

```
PS> Get-Service bits,foo,lanmanserver
Get-Service : Cannot find any service with service name 'foo'.
At line:1 char:1
+ Get-Service bits,foo,lanmanserver
+ ~~~~~~~~~~~~~~~~~~~~~~~~~~~~~~~~~
+ CategoryInfo          : ObjectNotFound: (foo:String) [Get-Service], ServiceCommandException
+ FullyQualifiedErrorId : NoServiceFoundForGivenName,
                          Microsoft.PowerShell.Commands.GetServiceCommand

Status   Name               DisplayName
------   ----               -----------
Running  bits               Background Intelligent Transfer Ser...
Running  lanmanserver       Server
```

Listing 5-1: A nonterminating error

Of course, there is no `foo` service, and PowerShell tells you as much. But notice that PowerShell gets the status for the other services; it doesn't stop executing when it runs into that error. This nonterminating error can be converted to a terminating error to prevent execution of the rest of the code.

It's important to understand that the decision to turn an exception into a nonterminating error or a terminating error is made by a developer. Often, as in Listing 5-1, this decision will be made for you by whoever wrote the cmdlet you're using. In many cases, if the cmdlet encounters an exception, it will return a nonterminating error, writing error output to the console and allowing your script to continue executing. In the next section, you'll see a few ways to turn nonterminating errors into terminating errors.

Handling Nonterminating Errors

Let's say you want to write a simple script that will go into a folder that you know contains several text files and prints out the first line of every text file. If the folder doesn't exist, you want the script to end immediately and report the error; otherwise, if you encounter any other errors, you want the script to keep running and report the error.

You'll start by writing a script that should return a terminating error. Listing 5-2 shows a first attempt at this code. (Though I could've condensed the code into something more succinct, for teaching purposes, I've tried to make each step here as clear as possible.)

```
$folderPath = '.\bogusFolder'
$files = Get-ChildItem -Path $folderPath
Write-Host "This shouldn't run."
$files.foreach({
    $fileText = Get-Content $files
    $fileText[0]
})
```

Listing 5-2: A first attempt at our Get-Files.ps1 *script*

Here, you use `Get-ChildItem` to return all the files contained inside the path you pass it—in this case, a bogus folder. If you run this script, you should get output like the following:

```
Get-ChildItem : Cannot find path 'C:\bogusFolder' because it does not exist.
At C:\Get-Files.ps1:2 char:10
+ $files = Get-ChildItem -Path $folderPath
+          ~~~~~~~~~~~~~~~~~~~~~~~~~~~~~~~~
+ CategoryInfo : ObjectNotFound: (C:\bogusFolder:String) [Get-ChildItem], ItemNotFoundException
    + FullyQualifiedErrorId : PathNotFound,Microsoft.PowerShell.Commands.GetChildItemCommand
This shouldn't run.
```

As you can see, two things happen: PowerShell returns an error, which specifies the type of exception encountered (`ItemNotFoundException`), and the call to `Write-Host` runs. This means that the error you get is nonterminating.

To turn this error into a terminating error, you'll use the `ErrorAction` parameter. This is a *common parameter*, meaning that it's built into every PowerShell cmdlet. The `ErrorAction` parameter determines what action to take if the cmdlet in question encounters a nonterminating error. This parameter has five main options:

Continue Outputs the error message and continues to execute the cmdlet. This is the default value.

Ignore Continues to execute the cmdlet without outputting an error or recording it in the `$Error` variable.

Inquire Outputs the error message and prompts the user for input before continuing.

SilentlyContinue Continues to execute the cmdlet without outputting an error, but records it in the `$Error` variable.

Stop Outputs the error message and stops the cmdlet from executing.

You'll look more at the `$Error` variable later in the chapter. For now, you want to pass `Stop` to `Get-ChildItem`. Update your script and run the code again. You should get the same output without `This shouldn't run`.

The `ErrorAction` parameter is useful for controlling error behavior on a case-by-case basis. To change how PowerShell handles all nonterminating errors, you can use the `$ErrorActionPreference` variable, an automatic variable that controls the default nonterminating error behavior. By default, `$ErrorActionPreference` is set to `Continue`. Note that the `ErrorAction` parameter overrides the value of `$ErrorActionPreference`.

In general, I consider the best practice is to always set `$ErrorActionPreference` to `Stop` to remove the concept of nonterminating errors altogether. This allows you to catch all types of exceptions, and spare yourself the work of knowing in advance which errors are terminating and which are nonterminating. You can accomplish the same task by using the `ErrorAction` parameter on each command to get more granular with defining which commands return terminating errors, but I'd rather set the rule once and forget it than have to remember to add the `ErrorAction` parameter to every command I call.

Now let's look at how to handle terminating errors by using the `try/catch/finally` construct.

Handling Terminating Errors

To prevent terminating errors from stopping a program, you need to *catch* them. You do so with the `try/catch/finally` construct. Listing 5-3 shows the syntax.

```
try {
    # initial code
} catch {
    # code that runs if terminating error found
} finally {
    # code that runs at the end
}
```

Listing 5-3: Syntax for the `try/catch/finally` construct

Using try/catch/finally essentially sets up an error-handling safety net. The try block contains the original code you want to run; if a terminating error happens, PowerShell will redirect flow to the code in the catch block. Regardless of whether the code in catch runs, the code in finally will always run—note that the finally block is optional, unlike try or catch.

To get a better sense of what try/catch/finally can and can't do, let's revisit our *Get-Files.ps1* script. You'll use a try/catch statement to provide a cleaner error message, as in Listing 5-4.

```
$folderPath = '.\bogusFolder'
try {
    $files = Get-ChildItem -Path $folderPath -ErrorAction Stop
    $files.foreach({
        $fileText = Get-Content $files
        $fileText[0]
    })
} catch {
    $_.Exception.Message
}
```

Listing 5-4: Using a try/catch statement to handle terminating errors

When a terminating error is caught in the catch block, the error object is stored in the $_ variable. In this example, you use $_.Exception.Message to return just the exception message. In this case, the code should return something like Cannot find path 'C:\ bogusFolder' because it does not exist. Error objects also contain other information, including the type of exception that was thrown, a stack trace that shows the execution history of the code that occurred before the exception was thrown, and more. However, for now, the most useful piece of information for you is the Message property, as this typically contains the basic information you need in order to see what happened in your code.

By now, your code should work as you expect. By passing Stop into ErrorAction, you ensure that a missing folder will return a terminating error and catch the error. But what will happen if you encounter an error when you try to use Get-Content to access the file?

As an experiment, try running the following code:

```
$filePath = '.\bogusFile.txt'
try {
    Get-Content $filePath
} catch {
    Write-Host "We found an error"
}
```

You should get an error message from PowerShell, not the custom one you wrote in the catch block. This is because Get-Content returns a nonterminating error when an item is not found—and try/catch can find only terminating errors. This means that the code in Listing 5-4 will work as intended—any errors accessing the files themselves will not halt execution of the program, and will simply return to the console.

Notice that you have not used a `finally` block in this code. The `finally` block is a great place to put code that performs necessary cleanup tasks such as disconnecting open database connections, cleaning up PowerShell remoting sessions, and so on. Here, nothing of that sort is necessary.

Exploring the $Error Automatic Variable

Throughout this chapter, you've forced PowerShell to return a lot of errors. Terminating or nonterminating, each one has been stored in a PowerShell automatic variable called `$Error`. The `$Error` variable is a built-in variable that stores an array of all the errors returned in the current PowerShell session, ordered by the time they appear.

To demonstrate the `$Error` variable, let's go to the console and run a command that you know will return a nonterminating error (Listing 5-5).

```
PS> Get-Item -Path C:\NotFound.txt
Get-Item : Cannot find path 'C:\NotFound.txt' because it does not exist.
At line:1 char:1
+ Get-Item -Path C:\NotFound.txt
+ ~~~~~~~~~~~~~~~~~~~~~~~~~~~~~~
+ CategoryInfo : ObjectNotFound: (C:\NotFound.txt:String) [Get-Item], ItemNotFoundException
    + FullyQualifiedErrorId : PathNotFound,Microsoft.PowerShell.Commands.GetItemCommand
```

Listing 5-5: Example error

Now, in the same PowerShell session, examine the `$Error` variable (Listing 5-6).

```
PS> $Error
Get-Item : Cannot find path 'C:\NotFound.txt' because it does not exist.
At line:1 char:1
+ Get-Item -Path C:\NotFound.txt
+ ~~~~~~~~~~~~~~~~~~~~~~~~~~~~~~
+ CategoryInfo : ObjectNotFound: (C:\NotFound.txt:String) [Get-Item], ItemNotFoundException
    + FullyQualifiedErrorId : PathNotFound,Microsoft.PowerShell.Commands.GetItemCommand
--snip--
```

Listing 5-6: The `$Error` variable

Unless you're working in a brand-new session, chances are you see a long list of errors. To access a specific one, you can use index notation just as you would with any other array. The errors in `$Error` are added to the front of the array, so `$Error[0]` is the most recent, `$Error[1]` the second most recent, and so forth.

Summary

Error handling in PowerShell is a massive topic, and this chapter covered only the basics. If you'd like to dive deeper, check out the `about_try_catch_finally` help topic by running `Get-Help about_try_catch_finally`. Another great resource is the *Big Book of PowerShell Error Handling* by Dave Wyatt from the DevOps Collective (*https://leanpub.com/thebigbookofpowershellerrorhandling/*).

The main takeaways here are understanding the difference between terminating and nonterminating errors, the uses of the `try/catch` statement, and the various `ErrorAction` options that will help you build the skills you need to handle any errors your code might throw at you.

So far, you've been doing everything in a single block of code. In the next chapter, you'll see how to organize your code into discrete, executable units called *functions*.

6

WRITING FUNCTIONS

So far, the code you've written has been fairly one-dimensional: your scripts had a single task. And while there's nothing wrong with a script that can only access files in a folder, you'll want code that can do more than one thing as you write more-robust PowerShell tools. There's nothing stopping you from packing more and more into a script. You could write a thousand lines of code that do hundreds of tasks, all in a single, uninterrupted block of code. But that script would be a mess to read and a mess to work with. You could break each task into its own script, but that would be a mess to use. You want one tool that can do many things, not a hundred that can each do a single thing.

To do this, you'll break each task into its own *function*, a labeled piece of code that performs a single task. A function is defined once. You write the code to solve a certain problem once, store it in a function, and anytime you run into that problem, you just use—or *call*—the function that solves it. Functions dramatically increase the usability and readability of your code, making it much easier to work with. In this chapter, you'll learn to write functions, add and manage your functions' parameters, and set up functions to accept pipeline input. But first, let's look at a bit of terminology.

Functions vs. Cmdlets

If the idea of a function sounds familiar, it is probably because it sounds a bit like the cmdlets you've been using throughout this book, such as `Start-Service` and `Write-Host`. These are also named pieces of code that solve a single problem. The difference between a function and a cmdlet is *how* each of these constructs is made. A cmdlet isn't written with PowerShell. It's written in another language, typically something like C#, and then it's compiled and made available inside PowerShell. Functions, on the other hand, are written in PowerShell's simple scripting language.

You can see which commands are cmdlets and which are functions by using the `Get-Command` cmdlet and its `CommandType` parameter, as in Listing 6-1.

```
PS> Get-Command -CommandType Function
```

Listing 6-1: Displaying the available functions

This command will display all the functions currently loaded into your PowerShell session, or inside modules that are available to PowerShell (Chapter 7 covers modules). To see other functions, you have to copy and paste them into the console, add them to an available module, or *dot source* them (which we'll also cover later).

With that out of the way, let's start writing functions.

Defining a Function

Before you can use a function, you need to define it. To define a function, you use the `function` keyword, followed by a descriptive, user-defined name, followed by a set of curly brackets. Inside the curly brackets is a scriptblock that you want PowerShell to execute. Listing 6-2 defines a basic function in the console and executes it.

```
PS> function Install-Software { Write-Host 'I installed some software, Yippee!' }
PS> Install-Software
I installed some software, Yippee!
```

Listing 6-2: Writing a message to the console with a simple function

The function you've defined, `Install-Software`, uses `Write-Host` to display a message in the console. Once it's defined, you can use this function's name to execute the code inside its scriptblock.

A function's name is important. You can name your functions whatever you want, but the name should always describe what the function does. Function-naming convention in PowerShell follows the Verb-Noun syntax, and it's considered best practice to always use this syntax unless absolutely necessary. You can use the Get-Verb command to see a list of recommended verbs. The noun is typically the singular name of whatever entity you're working with—in this case, software.

If you want to change the behavior of a function, you can redefine it, as in Listing 6-3.

```
PS> function Install-Software { Write-Host 'You installed some software, Yay!' }
PS> Install-Software
You installed some software, Yay!
```

Listing 6-3: Redefining the Install-Software function to change its behavior

Now that you've redefined Install-Software, it will display a slightly different message.

Functions can be defined in a script or typed directly into the console. In Listing 6-2, you had a small function, so defining it in the console wasn't a problem. Most of the time, you'll have bigger functions, and it'll be easier to define those functions in a script or a module, and then call that script or module in order to load the function into memory. As you might imagine from Listing 6-3, retyping a hundred-line function every time you want to tweak its functionality could get a little frustrating.

For the rest of this chapter, you'll expand our Install-Software function to accept parameters and accept pipeline input. I suggest you open your favorite editor and store the function in a *.ps1* file as you're working through the chapter.

Adding Parameters to Functions

PowerShell functions can have any number of parameters. When you create your own functions, you'll have the option to include parameters and decide how those parameters work. The parameters can be mandatory or optional, and they can either accept anything or be forced to accept one of a limited list of possible arguments.

For example, the fictional software you're installing via the Install-Software function might have many versions, but currently, the Install-Software function offers a user no way to specify which version they want to install. If you were the only one using the function, you could redefine the function each time you wanted a specific version—but that would be a waste of time and would be prone to potential errors, not to mention that you want others to be able to use your code.

Introducing parameters into your function allows it to have variability. Just as variables allowed you to write scripts that could handle many versions of the same situation, parameters allow you to write a single function that does one thing many ways. In this case, you want it to install multiple versions of the same piece of software, and do so on many computers.

Let's first add a parameter to the function that enables you or a user to specify the version to install.

Creating a Simple Parameter

Creating a parameter on a function requires a `param` block, which will hold all the parameters for the function. You can define a `param` block with the `param` keyword followed by parentheses, as in Listing 6-4.

```
function Install-Software {
    [CmdletBinding()]
    param()

    Write-Host 'I installed software version 2. Yippee!'
}
```

Listing 6-4: Defining a param block

At this point, your function's actual functionality hasn't changed. You've just installed the plumbing, preparing the function for a parameter. You'll use a `Write-Host` command to simulate the software installation so you can focus on writing the function.

NOTE *In the demos this for book, you'll build only* advanced *functions. There are also* basic *functions, but nowadays, they're typically used in only small, niche situations. The differences are too nuanced to go into detail, but if you see a* `[CmdletBinding()]` *reference under the function name, or a parameter defined as* `[Parameter()]`*, you know you're working with an advanced function.*

Once you've added the `param` block, you can create the parameter by putting it within the `param` block's parentheses, as in Listing 6-5.

```
function Install-Software {
    [CmdletBinding()]
    param(
   ❶ [Parameter()]
   ❷ [string] $Version
    )

 ❸ Write-Host "I installed software version $Version. Yippee!"
}
```

Listing 6-5: Creating a parameter

Inside the `param` block, you first define the `Parameter` block ❶. An empty `Parameter` block like the one here does nothing but is required (I'll explain how to use it in the next section).

Let's focus instead on the `[string]` type ❷ in front of the parameter name. By putting the parameter's type between square brackets before the parameter variable name, you can cast the parameter so PowerShell will always try to convert any value that's passed to this parameter into a string—if it isn't one already. Here, anything passed in as `$Version` will always be treated as a string. Casting your parameter to a type isn't mandatory, but I highly encourage it, because explicitly defining the type will significantly reduce errors down the road.

You also add `$Version` into your print statement ❸, which means that when you run the `Install-Software` command with the `Version` parameter and pass it a version number, you should get a statement saying so, as in Listing 6-6.

```
PS> Install-Software -Version 2
I installed software version 2. Yippee!
```

Listing 6-6: Passing a parameter to your function

You've now defined a working parameter to your function. Let's see what you can do with that parameter.

The Mandatory Parameter Attribute

You can use the `Parameter` block to control various *parameter attributes*, which will allow you to change the behavior of the parameter. For example, if you want to make sure anyone calling the function has to pass in a given parameter, you could define that parameter as `Mandatory`.

By default, parameters are optional. Let's force the user to pass in a version by using the `Mandatory` keyword inside the `Parameter` block, as in Listing 6-7.

```
function Install-Software {
    [CmdletBinding()]
    param(
        [Parameter(Mandatory)]
        [string]$Version
    )

    Write-Host "I installed software version $Version. Yippee!"
}
Install-Software
```

Listing 6-7: Using a mandatory parameter

If you run this, you should get the following prompt:

```
cmdlet Install-Software at command pipeline position 1
Supply values for the following parameters:
Version:
```

Once you've set the `Mandatory` attribute, executing the function without the parameter will halt execution until the user inputs a value. The function will wait until the user specifies a value for the `Version` parameter, and once they enter it, PowerShell will execute the function and move on. To avoid this prompt, simply pass the value as a parameter when you call the function with the `-ParameterName` syntax—for example, `Install-Software -Version 2`.

Default Parameter Values

You can also assign a parameter a default value when the parameter is defined. This is useful when you expect a certain value for a parameter most of the time. For example, if you want to install version 2 of this software 90 percent of the time, and you'd rather not have to set the value every time you run this function, you could assign a default value of `2` to the `$Version` parameter, as in Listing 6-8.

```
function Install-Software {
    [CmdletBinding()]
    param(
        [Parameter()]
        [string]$Version = 2
    )

    Write-Host "I installed software version $Version. Yippee!"
}
Install-Software
```

Listing 6-8: Using a default parameter value

Having a default parameter doesn't prevent you from passing one in. Your passed-in value will override the default value.

Adding Parameter Validation Attributes

In addition to making parameters mandatory and giving them default values, you can restrict them to certain values by using *parameter validation attributes*. When possible, limiting the information that users (or even you!) can pass to your functions or scripts will eliminate unnecessary code inside your function. For example, say you pass the value 3 to your `Install-Software` function, knowing that version 3 is an existing version. Your function assumes that every user knows which versions exist, so it doesn't account for what happens when you try to specify version 4. In that case, the function will fail to find the appropriate folder because it doesn't exist.

In Listing 6-9, you use the `$Version` string in a file path. If someone passes a value that doesn't complete an existing folder name (for example, SoftwareV3 or SoftwareV4), the code will fail.

```
function Install-Software {
    param(
        [Parameter(Mandatory)]
        [string]$Version
    )
    Get-ChildItem -Path \\SRV1\Installers\SoftwareV$Version
}

Install-Software -Version 3
```

Listing 6-9: Assuming parameter values

This gives the following error:

```
Get-ChildItem : Cannot find path '\\SRV1\Installers\SoftwareV3' because it does not exist.
At line:7 char:5
+     Get-ChildItem -Path \\SRV1\Installers\SoftwareV3
+     ~~~~~~~~~~~~~~~~~~~~~~~~~~~~~~~~~~~~~~~~~~~~~~~~
    + CategoryInfo          : ObjectNotFound: (\\SRV1\Installers\SoftwareV3:String)
                              [Get-ChildItem], ItemNotFoundException
    + FullyQualifiedErrorId : PathNotFound,Microsoft.PowerShell.Commands.GetChildItemCommand
```

You could write error-handling code to account for this problem, or you could nip the problem in the bud by requiring the user pass only an existing version of the software. To limit the user's input, you'll add parameter validation.

Various kinds of parameter validation exist, but with respect to your `Install-Software` function, the `ValidateSet` attribute works best. The `ValidateSet` attribute enables you to specify a list of values allowed for the parameter. If you're accounting for only the string 1 or 2, you'd ensure that the user can specify only these values; otherwise, the function will fail immediately and notify the user why.

Let's add parameter validation attributes inside the `param` block, right under the original `Parameter` block, as in Listing 6-10.

```
function Install-Software {
    param(
        [Parameter(Mandatory)]
        [ValidateSet('1','2')]
        [string]$Version
    )
    Get-ChildItem -Path \\SRV1\Installers\SoftwareV$Version
}

Install-Software -Version 3
```

Listing 6-10: Using the `ValidateSet` parameter validation attribute

You add the set of items 1 and 2 inside the `ValidateSet` attribute's trailing parentheses, which tells PowerShell that the only values valid for `Version` are 1 or 2. If a user tries to pass something besides what's in the set, they will receive an error message (see Listing 6-11) notifying them that they have only a specific number of options available.

```
Install-Software : Cannot validate argument on parameter 'Version'. The argument "3" does not
belong to the set "1,2" specified by the ValidateSet attribute.
Supply an argument that is in the set and then try the command again.
At line:1 char:25
+ Install-Software -Version 3
+                           ~~~~
+ CategoryInfo          : InvalidData: (:) [Install-Software],ParameterBindingValidationException
    + FullyQualifiedErrorId : ParameterArgumentValidationError,Install-Software
```

Listing 6-11: Passing a parameter value that's not in the `ValidateSet` block

The ValidateSet attribute is a common validation attribute, but others are available. For a complete breakdown of all the ways parameter values can be restricted, check out the Functions_Advanced_Parameters help topic by running Get-Help about_Functions_Advanced_Parameters.

Accepting Pipeline Input

So far, you've created a function with a parameter that can be passed only by using the typical *-ParameterName <Value>* syntax. But in Chapter 3, you learned that PowerShell has a pipeline that allows you to seamlessly pass objects from one command to another. Recall that some functions didn't have pipeline capability—when working with your own functions, that's something you control. Let's add pipeline capabilities to our Install-Software function.

Adding Another Parameter

First, you'll add another parameter to your code that specifies the computer on which you want to install the software. You'll also add that parameter to your Write-Host command to simulate the installation. Listing 6-12 adds the new parameter:

```
function Install-Software {
    param(
        [Parameter(Mandatory)]
        [string]$Version
        [ValidateSet('1','2')],

        [Parameter(Mandatory)]
        [string]$ComputerName
    )
    Write-Host "I installed software version $Version on $ComputerName. Yippee!"

}

Install-Software -Version 2 -ComputerName "SRV1"
```

Listing 6-12: Adding the ComputerName parameter

Just as with $Version, you've added the ComputerName parameter to the param block.

Once you've added the ComputerName parameter to the function, you could iterate over a list of computer names and pass the values for the computer name and the version to the Install-Software function, like so:

```
$computers = @("SRV1", "SRV2", "SRV3")
foreach ($pc in $computers) {
    Install-Software -Version 2 -ComputerName $pc
}
```

But as you've seen a few times already, you should forgo foreach loops like this and use the pipeline instead.

Making the Function Pipeline Compatible

Unfortunately, if you try to use the pipeline straightaway, you'll get errors. Before you add pipeline support to the function, you should decide which type of pipeline input you want the function to accept. As you learned in Chapter 3, a PowerShell function uses two kinds of pipeline input: `ByValue` (entire object) and `ByPropertyName` (a single object property). Here, because our `$computers` list contains only strings, you'll pass those strings via `ByValue`.

To add pipeline support, you add a parameter attribute to the parameter you want by using one of two keywords: `ValueFromPipeline` or `ValueFromPipelineByPropertyName`, as in Listing 6-13.

```
function Install-Software {
    param(
        [Parameter(Mandatory)]
        [string]$Version
        [ValidateSet('1','2')],

        [Parameter(Mandatory, ValueFromPipeline)]
        [string]$ComputerName
    )
    Write-Host "I installed software version $Version on $ComputerName. Yippee!"
}

$computers = @("SRV1", "SRV2", "SRV3")
$computers | Install-Software -Version 2
```

Listing 6-13: Adding pipeline support

Run the script again, and you should get something like this:

```
I installed software version 2 on SRV3. Yippee!
```

Notice that `Install-Software` executes for only the last string in the array. You'll see how to fix this in the next section.

Adding a process Block

To tell PowerShell to execute this function for every object coming in, you must include a `process` block. Inside the `process` block, you put the code you want to execute each time the function receives pipeline input. Add a `process` block to your script, as shown in Listing 6-14.

```
function Install-Software {
    param(
        [Parameter(Mandatory)]
        [string]$Version
        [ValidateSet('1','2')],

        [Parameter(Mandatory, ValueFromPipeline)]
        [string]$ComputerName
    )
```

```
    process {
        Write-Host "I installed software version $Version on $ComputerName. Yippee!"
    }
}

$computers = @("SRV1", "SRV2", "SRV3")
$computers | Install-Software -Version 2
```

Listing 6-14: Adding a process block

Notice that the process keyword is followed by a set of curly brackets, which contain the code your function executes.

With the process block, you should see output for all three servers in $computers:

```
I installed software version 2 on SRV1. Yippee!
I installed software version 2 on SRV2. Yippee!
I installed software version 2 on SRV3. Yippee!
```

The process block should contain the main code you want to execute. You can also use begin and end blocks for code that will execute at the beginning and end of the function call. For more information about building advanced functions including the begin, process, and end blocks, check out the about_Functions_Advanced help topic by running Get-Help about_Functions_Advanced.

Summary

Functions allow you to compartmentalize code into discrete building blocks. They not only help you break your work into smaller, more manageable chunks, but also force you to write readable and testable code. When you use descriptive names for your functions, your code becomes self-documenting, and anyone reading it can intuitively understand what it's doing.

In this chapter, you learned the basics of functions: how to define them, how to specify parameters and their attributes, and how to accept pipeline input. In the next chapter, you'll see how to bundle many functions together by using modules.

7

EXPLORING MODULES

In the preceding chapter, you learned about functions. Functions break a script into manageable units, giving you more efficient, more readable code. But there's no reason a good function should exist in only a script or single session. In this chapter, you'll learn about *modules*, groups of similar functions that are packaged together and distributed for others to use across many scripts.

In its purest form, a PowerShell module is just a text file with a *.psm1* file extension and some optional, extra metadata. Other types of modules that don't fit this description are known as *binary modules* and *dynamic modules*, but they are outside the scope of this book.

Any command that hasn't been explicitly placed in your session almost certainly comes from a module. Many of the commands you've been using throughout this book are part of Microsoft's internal modules that come with PowerShell, but there are also third-party modules and the ones you create yourself. To use a module, you first have to install it. Then, when a command inside a module needs to be used, that module has to be imported into your session; as of PowerShell v3, PowerShell auto-imports modules when a command is referenced.

You'll begin this chapter by looking at the models that are already installed in your system. Then, you'll take apart a model to see its different parts before finally looking at how to download and install PowerShell modules from the PowerShell Gallery.

Exploring Default Modules

PowerShell comes with numerous modules installed by default. In this section, you'll see how to discover and import modules from your session.

Finding Modules in Your Session

You can see the modules imported into your current session by using the `Get-Module` cmdlet (which is itself part of a module). The `Get-Module` cmdlet is a command that allows you to see all the modules on your system available to you in your current session.

Start a fresh PowerShell session and run `Get-Module`, as in Listing 7-1.

```
PS> Get-Module

ModuleType Version    Name                              ExportedCommands
---------- -------    ----                              ----------------
Manifest   3.1.0.0    Microsoft.PowerShell.Management   {Add-Computer, Add-Content...
--snip--
```

Listing 7-1: Viewing imported modules with the `Get-Module` command

Each line you see from this `Get-Module` output is a module that has been imported into the current session, which means all the commands inside that module are immediately available to you. The `Microsoft.PowerShell.Management` and `Microsoft.PowerShell.Utility` modules are imported in any PowerShell session by default.

Notice the `ExportedCommands` column in Listing 7-1. These are the commands you can use from the module. You can easily find all of these commands by using `Get-Command` and specifying the module name. Let's check out all the exported commands inside the `Microsoft.PowerShell.Management` module in Listing 7-2.

```
PS> Get-Command -Module Microsoft.PowerShell.Management

CommandType     Name                  Version    Source
-----------     ----                  -------    ------
Cmdlet          Add-Computer          3.1.0.0    Microsoft.PowerShell.Management
Cmdlet          Add-Content           3.1.0.0    Microsoft.PowerShell.Management
--snip--
```

Listing 7-2: Viewing commands inside a PowerShell module

These are all the commands that are exported from that module; these are the ones that can be explicitly called from outside the module. Some module authors choose to include functions inside their modules that a user cannot use. Any function that is not exported to a user, and only does work inside a script or module, is called a *private function*, or what some developers refer to as a *helper function*.

Using Get-Module without any parameters will return all modules that are imported, but what about the modules that have been installed but not imported?

Finding Modules on Your Computer

To get a list of all modules that are installed and can be imported into your session, you can use Get-Module with the ListAvailable parameter, as in Listing 7-3.

```
PS> Get-Module -ListAvailable
   Directory: C:\Program Files\WindowsPowerShell\Modules

ModuleType Version    Name              ExportedCommands
---------- -------    ----              ----------------
Script     1.2        PSReadline        {Get-PSReadlineKeyHandler,Set-PSReadlineKeyHandler...


   Directory:\Modules


ModuleType Version    Name              ExportedCommands
---------- -------    ----              ----------------
Manifest   1.0.0.0    ActiveDirectory   {Add-ADCentralAccessPolicyMember...
Manifest   1.0.0.0    AppBackgroundTask {Disable-AppBackgroundTaskDiagnosticLog...
--snip--
```

Listing 7-3: Using Get-Module to view all available modules

The ListAvailable parameter tells PowerShell to check a few folders for any subfolders with *.psm1* files in them. PowerShell will then read each of those modules from the filesystem and return a list of each module's name, some metadata, and all the functions that can be used from that module.

PowerShell looks for modules on disk in a few default locations, depending on the type of module:

System modules Nearly all modules that come installed by default with PowerShell will be located in *C:\Windows\System32\WindowsPowerShell\1.0\Modules*. This module path is typically dedicated for internal PowerShell modules only. Technically, you could place modules in this folder, but it's not recommended you do so.

All Users modules Modules are also stored in *C:\Program Files\Windows PowerShell\Modules*. This path is loosely called the *All Users* module path, and it's where you put any modules you'd like available to all users who log into the computer.

Current User modules Lastly, you can store modules in *C:\Users \<LoggedInUser>\Documents\WindowsPowerShell\Modules*. Inside this folder, you'll find all modules that you've created or downloaded that are available to only the current user. Placing modules in this path allows for some separation if multiple users with different requirements will be logging into the computer.

When `Get-Module -ListAvailable` is called, PowerShell will read all these folder paths and return all the modules in each. However, these aren't the only possible module paths, just the defaults.

You can tell PowerShell to add a new module path by using the `$PSModulePath` environment variable, which defines each module folder separated by a semicolon, as shown in Listing 7-4.

```
PS> $env:PSModulePath
C:\Users\Adam\Documents\WindowsPowerShell\Modules;
C:\Program Files\WindowsPowerShell\Modules\Modules;
C:\Program Files (x86)\Microsoft SQL Server\140\Tools\PowerShell\Modules\
```

Listing 7-4: The `PSModulePath` environment variable

You can add folders to the `PSModulePath` environment variable by doing a little string parsing, although this technique may be a little advanced. Here's a quick one-liner:

```
PS> $env:PSModulePath + ';C;\MyNewModulePath'.
```

However, be aware that this adds the new folder in only the current session. To make this change persistent, you need to use the `SetEnvironmentVariable()` method on the `Environment` .NET class, like so:

```
PS> $CurrentValue = [Environment]::GetEnvironmentVariable("PSModulePath", "Machine")
PS> [Environment]::SetEnvironmentVariable("PSModulePath", $CurrentValue + ";C:\
MyNewModulePath", "Machine")
```

Let's now see how to use the modules you have by importing them.

Importing Modules

Once a module folder path is in the `PSModulePath` environment variable, you have to import the module into the current session. Nowadays, because of

PowerShell's auto-importing feature, if you have a module installed, you can usually call the function you want first, and PowerShell will auto-import the module it belongs to. Still, it's important to understand how importing works.

Let's use a default PowerShell module called `Microsoft.PowerShell.Management`. In Listing 7-5, you'll run `Get-Module` twice: once in a fresh PowerShell session, and once after using the `cd` command, an alias for `Set-Location`, a command found in the `Microsoft.PowerShell.Management` module. Look what happens:

```
PS> Get-Module

ModuleType Version    Name                                ExportedCommands
---------- -------    ----                                ----------------
Manifest   3.1.0.0    Microsoft.PowerShell.Utility        {Add-Member, Add-Type...
Script     1.2        PSReadline                          {Get-PSReadlineKeyHandler...


PS> cd\
PS> Get-Module

ModuleType Version    Name                                ExportedCommands
---------- -------    ----                                ----------------
Manifest   3.1.0.0    Microsoft.PowerShell.Management     {Add-Computer, Add-Content...
Manifest   3.1.0.0    Microsoft.PowerShell.Utility        {Add-Member, Add-Type...
Script     1.2        PSReadline                          {Get-PSReadlineKeyHandler....
```

Listing 7-5: PowerShell auto-imports `Microsoft.PowerShell.Management` after using `cd`.

As you can see, `Microsoft.PowerShell.Management` is auto-imported after you use `cd`. The auto-import feature usually works. But if you're expecting a command inside a module to be available and it's not, a problem with the module might be preventing the command's import.

To manually import a module, use the `Import-Module` command, as in Listing 7-6.

```
PS> Import-Module -Name Microsoft.PowerShell.Management
PS> Import-Module -Name Microsoft.PowerShell.Management -Force
PS> Remove-Module -Name Microsoft.PowerShell.Management
```

Listing 7-6: Importing a module manually, reimporting it, and removing it

You'll notice this listing also uses the `Force` parameter and the `Remove-Module` command. If the module has been changed (say you've made changes to a custom module), you can use the `Import-Module` command with the `Force` parameter to unload and reimport the module. The `Remove-Module` unloads a module from a session, although this command is not used often.

The Components of a PowerShell Module

Now that you've learned how to use a PowerShell module, let's see what they look like.

The .psm1 File

Any text file with a *.psm1* file extension can be a PowerShell module. For this file to be useful, it must have functions inside it. While not strictly required, all functions inside a module should be built around the same concept. For example, Listing 7-7 shows some functions dealing with software installation.

```
function Get-Software {
    param()
}

function Install-Software {
    param()
}

function Remove-Software {
    param()
}
```

Listing 7-7: Functions dealing with software installation

Notice that the noun in each command's name stays the same, and only the verb changes. This is best practice when building modules. If you find yourself needing to change the noun, then you should start thinking about breaking one module into multiple modules.

The Module Manifest

Besides a *.psm1* file full of functions, you'll also have a module manifest, or a *.psd1* file. A *module manifest* is an optional but recommended text file written in the form of a PowerShell hashtable. This hashtable contains elements that describe metadata about the module.

It's possible to create a module manifest from scratch, but PowerShell has a `New-ModuleManifest` command that can generate a template for you. Let's use `New-ModuleManifest` to build a module manifest for our software package, as in Listing 7-8.

```
PS> New-ModuleManifest -Path 'C:\Program Files\WindowsPowerShell\Modules\Software\Software.psd1'
-Author 'Adam Bertram' -RootModule Software.psm1
-Description 'This module helps in deploying software.'
```

Listing 7-8: Using the `New-ModuleManifest` to build a module manifest

This command creates a *.psd1* file that looks like this:

```
#
# Module manifest for module 'Software'
#
# Generated by: Adam Bertram
#
# Generated on: 11/4/2019
#

@{

# Script module or binary module file associated with this manifest.
RootModule = 'Software.psm1'

# Version number of this module.
ModuleVersion = '1.0'

# Supported PSEditions
# CompatiblePSEditions = @()

# ID used to uniquely identify this module
GUID = 'c9f51fa4-8a20-4d35-a9e8-1a960566483e'

# Author of this module
Author = 'Adam Bertram'

# Company or vendor of this module
CompanyName = 'Unknown'

# Copyright statement for this module
Copyright = '(c) 2019 Adam Bertram. All rights reserved.'

# Description of the functionality provided by this module
Description = 'This modules helps in deploying software.'

# Minimum version of the Windows PowerShell engine required by this module
# PowerShellVersion = ''

# Name of the Windows PowerShell host required by this module
# PowerShellHostName = ''
--snip--
}
```

As you can see when running the command, there are plenty of fields for which I didn't provide parameters. We're not going to go in depth on module manifests. For now, just know that, at a minimum, always define the `RootModule`, `Author`, `Description`, and perhaps the `version`. All of these attributes are optional, but it's always good practice to get in the habit of adding as much information to the module manifest as possible.

Now that you've seen the anatomy of a module, let's see how to download and install one.

Working with Custom Modules

Thus far, you've been working with only the modules installed in PowerShell by default. In this section, you'll see how to find, install, and uninstall custom modules.

Finding Modules

One of the best parts of modules is sharing them: why waste your time solving a problem that's already been solved? Chances are, if you're running into a problem, the PowerShell Gallery has a solution. The *PowerShell Gallery* (*https://www.powershellgallery.com/*) is a repository of thousands of PowerShell modules and scripts that anyone with an account can freely upload to or download from. It has modules written by single individuals, and modules written by gigantic corporations like Microsoft.

Lucky for us, you can also use the Gallery from PowerShell itself. PowerShell has a built-in module called `PowerShellGet` that provides simple-to-use commands to interact with the PowerShell Gallery. Listing 7-9 uses `Get-Command` to pull up the `PowerShellGet` commands.

```
PS> Get-Command -Module PowerShellGet

CommandType     Name                        Version    Source
-----------     ----                        -------    ------
Function        Find-Command                1.1.3.1    powershellget
Function        Find-DscResource            1.1.3.1    powershellget
Function        Find-Module                 1.1.3.1    powershellget
Function        Find-RoleCapability         1.1.3.1    powershellget
Function        Find-Script                 1.1.3.1    powershellget
Function        Get-InstalledModule         1.1.3.1    powershellget
Function        Get-InstalledScript         1.1.3.1    powershellget
Function        Get-PSRepository            1.1.3.1    powershellget
Function        Install-Module              1.1.3.1    powershellget
Function        Install-Script              1.1.3.1    powershellget
Function        New-ScriptFileInfo          1.1.3.1    powershellget
--snip--
```

Listing 7-9: The `PowerShellGet` *commands*

The `PowerShellGet` module includes commands for finding, saving, and installing modules, as well as publishing your own. You're not quite ready to publish modules yet (you haven't even created your own!), so we'll focus on how to find and install modules from the PowerShell Gallery.

To find a module, you use the `Find-Module` command, which allows you to search the PowerShell Gallery for modules matching a specific name. If you're looking for modules to manage a VMware infrastructure, for example, you can use wildcards with the `Name` parameter to find all modules in the PowerShell Gallery that have the word *VMware* in them, as in Listing 7-10.

```
PS> Find-Module -Name *VMware*

Version      Name                           Repository      Description
-------      ----                           ----------      -----------
6.5.2.6...   VMware.VimAutomation.Core      PSGallery       This Windows...
1.0.0.5...   VMware.VimAutomation.Sdk       PSGallery       This Windows...
--snip--
```

Listing 7-10: Using `Find-Module` to locate modules related to VMware

The `Find-Module` command doesn't download anything; it just shows you what's in the PowerShell Gallery. In the next section, you'll see how to install the modules.

Installing Modules

Once you have a module you want to install, you can use the `Install-Module` command to install it. The `Install-Module` command can take a `Name` parameter, but let's use the pipeline and simply send the objects that `Find-Module` returns directly to the `Install-Module` command (Listing 7-11).

Note that you may receive a warning about an untrusted repository. You will receive this untrusted warning because, by default, the `Find-Module` command uses a PowerShell repository that is untrusted, meaning you must explicitly tell PowerShell to trust all packages inside that repository. Otherwise, it will prompt you to run `Set-PSRepository`, as shown in Listing 7-11, to change the installation policy for that repository.

```
PS> Find-Module -Name VMware.PowerCLI | Install-Module

Untrusted repository You are installing the modules from an untrusted repository. If you trust
this repository, change its InstallationPolicy value by running the Set-PSRepository cmdlet.
Are you sure you want to install the modules from 'https://www.powershellgallery.com/api/v2/'?
[Y] Yes [A] Yes to All [N] No [L] No to All [S] Suspend [?] Help (default is "N"): a
Installing package 'VMware.PowerCLI'
Installing dependent package 'VMware.VimAutomation.Cloud' [oooooooooooooooooooooooooooooooooooo
ooooooooooooooooooooooooo] Installing package 'VMware.VimAutomation.Cloud'
Downloaded 1003175.00 MB out of 1003175.00 MB. [ooooooooooooooooooooooooooooooooooooooooooooooo
oooooooooooooooooooooo]
```

Listing 7-11: Installing a module by using the `Install-Module` command

By default, the command in Listing 7-11 will download the module and place it into the All Users module path in *C:\Program Files*. To check that the module is in this path, you can use the following command:

```
PS> Get-Module -Name VMware.PowerCLI -ListAvailable | Select-Object -Property ModuleBase

ModuleBase
----------
C:\Program Files\WindowsPowerShell\Modules\VMware.PowerCLI\6.5.3.6870460
```

Uninstalling Modules

Newcomers to PowerShell often get confused by the difference between removing and uninstalling a module. As you saw in "Importing Modules" on page 82, you can use `Remove-Module` to *remove* a module from the PowerShell session. But this only unloads the module from the session; it doesn't remove the module from your disk.

To take a module off the disk—or *uninstall* it—you have to use the `Uninstall-Module` cmdlet. Listing 7-12 uninstalls the module you just installed.

```
PS> Uninstall-Module -Name VMware.PowerCLI
```

Listing 7-12: Uninstalling a module

Only modules downloaded from the PowerShell Gallery will be uninstalled via `Uninstall-Module`—the default modules are there to stay!

Creating Your Own Module

So far, you've been working with other people's modules. Of course, one of the amazing things about PowerShell modules is you can create your own and share it with the rest of the world. You'll spend Part III of this book building a real-world module, but for now, let's see how to turn your Software module into a real module.

As you saw earlier, a typical PowerShell module consists of a folder (the *module container*), *.psm1* file (the module), and a *.psd1* file (the module manifest). If the module folder is in one of the three locations (System, All Users, or Current User), PowerShell will automatically see this and import it.

Let's first create the module folder. The module folder must be the same name as the module itself. Since I tend to make modules available for all users on a system, you'll add it to the All Users module path, like so:

```
PS> mkdir 'C:\Program Files\WindowsPowerShell\Modules\Software'
```

Once you create the folder, make a blank *.psm1* file that will eventually hold your functions:

```
PS> Add-Content 'C:\Program Files\WindowsPowerShell\Modules\Software\Software.psm1'
```

Next, create the module manifest just as you did in Listing 7-8:

```
PS> New-ModuleManifest -Path 'C:\Program Files\WindowsPowerShell\Modules\Software\Software.psd1'
-Author 'Adam Bertram' -RootModule Software.psm1
-Description 'This module helps in deploying software.'
```

At this point, PowerShell should be able to see your module, but notice it does not see any exported commands yet:

```
PS> Get-Module -Name Software -List


    Directory: C:\Program Files\WindowsPowerShell\Modules


ModuleType Version    Name                                ExportedCommands
---------- -------    ----                                ----------------
Script     1.0        Software
```

Let's add the three functions you used earlier into the *.psm1* file and see if PowerShell recognizes them now:

```
PS> Get-Module -Name Software -List


    Directory: C:\Program Files\WindowsPowerShell\Modules


ModuleType Version    Name                                ExportedCommands
---------- -------    ----                                ----------------
Script     1.0        Software                            {Get-Software...
```

PowerShell has exported all the commands inside your module and made them available for use. If you want to go the extra mile and choose which commands get exported, you can also open your module manifest and find the `FunctionsToExport` key. In there, you can define each command, separated by a comma, which will then dictate which commands get exported. Although not mandatory, it provides a more granular approach to exporting module functions.

Congrats! You've just created your first module! It won't do much unless you fill the functions in with real functionality, a fun challenge for you to do on your own.

Summary

In this chapter, you learned about modules, groups of like-minded code that prevent you from wasting time on problems that have already been solved. You saw the basic anatomy of a module, as well as how to install, import, remove, and uninstall them. You even made your own basic module!

In Chapter 8, you'll learn how to access remote computers by using PowerShell remoting.

8

RUNNING SCRIPTS REMOTELY

If you're the sole IT person in a small organization, chances are you have several servers to manage. If you have a script you need to run, you could log in to each server, open up the PowerShell console, and run your script there. But you can save a lot of time if you run one script that performs a particular task on each server. In this chapter, you'll learn how to run commands remotely using PowerShell remoting.

PowerShell remoting is a feature that allows a user to remotely run commands in a session on one or many computers at once. A *session*, or more specifically, a `PSSession`, is a PowerShell remoting term that refers to the environment running PowerShell on a remote computer from which you can execute commands. Though executed differently, the Microsoft Sysinternals tool `psexec` is the same concept: you write code that works on your local machine, send that code over to a remote computer, and execute the code as if you were sitting in front of it.

We'll spend most of this chapter looking at sessions—what they are, how to use them, and what to do when you're done with them—but first, you'll need to understand a few things about scriptblocks.

NOTE *Microsoft introduced PowerShell remoting in PowerShell v2, which is built on top of the* Windows Remote Management (WinRM) *service. For this reason, you may, on occasion, see the term WinRM used to refer to PowerShell remoting.*

Working with Scriptblocks

PowerShell remoting makes extensive use of *scriptblocks*, which, like functions, are code packaged into a single executable unit. But they're different from functions in a couple of key ways: they're anonymous—or unnamed—and they can be assigned to variables.

To examine this difference, let's consider an example. Let's define a function, called `New-Thing`, which calls `Write-Host` to display some text in the console (see Listing 8-1).

```
function New-Thing {
    param()
    Write-Host "Hi! I am in New-Thing"
}

New-Thing
```

Listing 8-1: Defining the `New-Thing` function, which displays text in the console window

If you run this script, you should see that it returns the text `"Hi! I am in New-Thing!"` to the console. But notice that for this result, you had to call `New-Thing` for the function to run.

You can replicate the result of the `New-Thing` function call with a scriptblock by first assigning the scriptblock to a variable, as in Listing 8-2.

```
PS> $newThing = { Write-Host "Hi! I am in a scriptblock!" }
```

Listing 8-2: Creating a scriptblock and assigning it to a variable called `$newThing`

To build a scriptblock, place the code you want to execute between curly brackets. You stored our scriptblock in the `$newThing` variable, and you might think that to execute that scriptblock, you could simply call the variable, as shown in Listing 8-3.

```
PS> $newThing = { Write-Host "Hi! I am in a scriptblock!" }
PS> $newThing
 Write-Host "Hi! I am in a scriptblock!"
```

Listing 8-3: Creating and executing a scriptblock

But as you can see, PowerShell reads the contents of `$newThing` literally. It doesn't realize that `Write-Host` is a command it should execute and instead displays the value of the scriptblock.

To tell PowerShell to run the code inside, you need to use an ampersand (`&`) followed by the variable name. Listing 8-4 shows this syntax.

```
PS> & $newThing
Hi! I am in a scriptblock!
```

Listing 8-4: Executing a scriptblock

The ampersand tells PowerShell that the stuff between the curly brackets is code that it should run. The ampersand is one way to execute a code block; however, it does not allow you the customization a command would, which you'll need when using PowerShell remoting to work on remote computers. The next section covers another way to execute scriptblocks.

Using Invoke-Command to Execute Code on Remote Systems

You'll use two main commands when working with PowerShell remoting: `Invoke-Command` and `New-PSSession`. In this section, you'll learn about `Invoke-Command`; the next section covers the `New-PSSession` command.

`Invoke-Command` is probably the command you'll use the most with PowerShell remoting. There are two main ways to use it. The first is when you run what I call *ad hoc commands*—small, one-off expressions you want to execute. The second is using interactive sessions. We'll cover both in this chapter.

An example of an ad hoc command is when you run `Start-Service` to start a service on a remote computer When you execute an ad hoc command by using `Invoke-Command`, PowerShell creates a session behind the scenes, tearing it down as soon as the command has completed. This limits what you can do with just `Invoke-Command`, which is why in the next section, you'll see how to create your own sessions.

But for now, let's see how `Invoke-Command` works with an ad hoc command. Open your PowerShell console, type `Invoke-Command`, and press ENTER, as in Listing 8-5.

```
PS> Invoke-Command

cmdlet Invoke-Command at command pipeline position 1
Supply values for the following parameters:
ScriptBlock:
```

Listing 8-5: Running `Invoke-Command` with no parameters

Your console should immediately ask you to provide a scriptblock. You'll provide the `hostname` command, which will return the hostname of the computer the command is run on.

To pass a scriptblock with `hostname` to `Invoke-Command`, you need to use the required parameter, `ComputerName`, which tells `Invoke-Command` which remote computer to run this command on, as you can see in Listing 8-6. (Note that for this to work, my machine and the remote computer `WEBSRV1` have to be part of the same Active Directory (AD) domain, and my machine needs to have admin rights on `WEBSRV1`.)

```
PS> Invoke-Command -ScriptBlock { hostname } -ComputerName WEBSRV1
WEBSRV1
```

Listing 8-6: Running a simple `Invoke-Command` example

Notice that the output of `hostname` is now the name of the remote computer—in my system, the remote computer is called `WEBSRV1`. You've now executed your first remote command!

NOTE *If you try this on a remote machine with an operating system older than Windows Server 2012 R2, it might not work as expected. If this is the case, you'll first have to enable PowerShell remoting. As of Server 2012 R2, PowerShell remoting is enabled, by default, with the WinRM service running with all the necessary firewall ports open and access rights set up. But if you're running an earlier version of Windows, this has to be done manually, so run* **`Enable-PSRemoting`** *on your remote computer in an elevated console session first before attempting to run* `Invoke-Command` *against an older server. You may also use the* **`Test-WSMan`** *command to confirm whether PowerShell remoting is configured and available.*

Running Local Scripts on Remote Computers

In the previous section, you executed scriptblocks on remote computers. You can also use `Invoke-Command` to execute entire scripts. Instead of using the `Scriptblock` parameter, you can use the `FilePath` parameter and a path to a script on your machine. When using the `FilePath` parameter, `Invoke-Command` will read the contents of the script locally and then execute that code on the remote computer. Contrary to popular belief, the script itself isn't executed on the remote computer.

To demonstrate, let's say you have a script on your local computer in the root of *C:* called *GetHostName.ps1*. This script has one line in it: `hostname`. You'd like to run this script on a remote computer to return the computer's hostname. Note that while we're keeping the script extremely simple, `Invoke -Command` doesn't care what's inside the script. It will happily execute whatever is there.

To run the script, you pass the script file to the `FilePath` parameter on `Invoke-Command`, as shown in Listing 8-7.

```
PS> Invoke-Command -ComputerName WEBSRV1 -FilePath C:\GetHostName.ps1
WEBSRV1
```

Listing 8-7: Running a local script on remote computers

`Invoke-Command` runs the code inside *GetHostName.ps1* on the `WEBSRV1` computer and returns the output back to your local session.

Using Local Variables Remotely

Though PowerShell remoting takes care of a lot of things, you have to watch out when using local variables. Let's say you have a file path on a remote computer that's *C:\File.txt*. Because this file path may change at some point, you may decide to assign that path as a variable; for example, `$serverFilePath`:

```
PS> $serverFilePath = 'C:\File.txt'
```

Now, you may need to reference the *C:\File.txt* path inside a remote scriptblock. In Listing 8-8, you can see what happens when you attempt to reference the variable directly.

```
PS> Invoke-Command -ComputerName WEBSRV1 -ScriptBlock { Write-Host "The value
of foo is $serverFilePath" }
The value of foo is
```

Listing 8-8: Local variables do not work in remote sessions.

Notice that the `$serverFilePath` variable doesn't have a value, because while inside the scriptblock being executed on the remote computer, the variable doesn't exist! When you define a variable in a script or at the console, that variable is stored in a particular *runspace*, which is a container that PowerShell uses to store the information for the session. You may have run into runspaces if you've tried to open two PowerShell consoles at the same time and (failed to) use the variables of one in the other.

By default, variables, functions, and other constructs can't spread over multiple runspaces. However, you can use a couple of methods to use variables, functions, and so forth, in various runspaces. There are two main ways to transfer variables to a remote computer.

Passing Variables with the ArgumentList Parameter

To get the value of a variable into a remote scriptblock, you can use the `ArgumentList` parameter on `Invoke-Command`. This parameter allows you to pass an array of local values to the scriptblock, called `$args`, which you can use in your scriptblock's code. To show how this works, in Listing 8-9, you'll pass the `$serverFilePath` variable, which contains the file path *C:\File.txt*, to the remote scriptblock and then reference it through the `$args` array.

```
PS> Invoke-Command -ComputerName WEBSRV1 -ScriptBlock { Write-Host "The value
of foo is $($args[0])" } -ArgumentList $serverFilePath
The value of foo is C:\File.txt
```

Listing 8-9: Using the `$args` array to pass local variables to a remote session

As you should see, the variable's value, *C:\File.txt*, is now inside the scriptblock. This is because you passed `$serverFilePath` into `ArgumentList` and replaced the `$serverFilePath` reference inside the scriptblock with `$args[0]`. If you want to pass more than one variable into the scriptblock, you can add another value to the `ArgumentList` parameter value and increment the `$args` reference by one where you want to reference the new variable.

Using the $Using Statement to Pass Variable Values

Another way to pass the values of local variables to a remote scriptblock is with the `$using` statement. You can avoid using the `ArgumentList` parameter by prepending `$using` to any local variable name. Before PowerShell sends the scriptblock to the remote computer, it will look for the `$using` statement and expand all the local variables inside the scriptblock.

In Listing 8-10, you'll rewrite Listing 8-9 to use `$using:serverFilePath` instead of `ArgumentList`.

```
PS> Invoke-Command -ComputerName WEBSRV1 -ScriptBlock { Write-Host "The value
of foo is $using:serverFilePath" }
The value of foo is C:\File.txt
```

Listing 8-10: Using `$using` to reference local variables in a remote session

As you should see, the results of Listings 8-9 and 8-10 are the same.

The `$using` statement requires less work and is more intuitive, but down the road, when you begin to write Pester to test your scripts, you'll see that you may have to revert to using the `ArgumentList` parameter: when using the `$using` option, Pester will have no way to evaluate the value in a `$using` variable. When using the `ArgumentList` parameter, the variables passed to the remote session are defined locally, which Pester can interpret and understand. If this doesn't make sense now, it will when you read Chapter 9. For now, the `$using` statement works excellently!

Now that you have a basic understanding of the `Invoke-Command` cmdlet, let's learn a few more sessions.

Working with Sessions

As mentioned earlier, PowerShell remoting uses a concept called a *session*. When you create a session remotely, PowerShell opens a *local session* on the remote computer, which you can use to execute commands there. You don't need to know too many of the technical details of a session. What you do need to know is that you can create, connect to, and disconnect from a session, and it will maintain the same state that you left it in. The session won't end until you remove it.

In the previous section, when you ran `Invoke-Command`, it brought up a new session, ran the code, and tore it down all in one go. In this section, you'll see how to create what I call *full sessions*, sessions that you can enter commands into directly. Using `Invoke-Command` to execute one-off ad hoc commands works well, but it's not too efficient when you need to run a lot of commands that can't all squeeze into a single scriptblock. For example, if you're working on a large script that performs work locally, has to grab information from another source, use that information in a remoting session, grab information from a remoting session to be used locally, and then return to the local computer, you will have to create a script that runs Invoke-Command repeatedly. On top of that, you'll have more issues if you need to set a variable in the remote session and use it again later. Using Invoke-Command as you have so far, this wouldn't work—you'll need a session that stays there after you leave.

Creating a New Session

To create a semipermanent session on a remote computer with PowerShell remoting, you have to explicitly create a full session by using the New-PSSession command, which will create a session on the remote computer and a reference to that session on your local computer.

To create a new PSSession, use New-PSSession with the ComputerName parameter, as in Listing 8-11. In this example, the computer I'm running this on is in the same Active Directory domain as WEBSRV1, and I'm logged in as a domain user with admin rights on WEBSRV1. To connect by using the ComputerName parameter (as I have in Listing 8-11), the user must be a local administrator or at least in the Remote Management Users group on the remote computer. If you're not in an AD domain, you can use the Credential parameter on New-PSSession to pass a PSCredential object containing an alternate credential to authenticate to the remote computer.

```
PS> New-PSSession -ComputerName WEBSRV1

 Id Name        ComputerName   ComputerType    State    ConfigurationName      Availability
 -- ----        ------------   ------------    -----    -----------------      ------------
  3 WinRM3      WEBSRV1        RemoteMachine   Opened   Microsoft.PowerShell   Available
```

Listing 8-11: Creating a new PSSession

As you can see, New-PSSession returns a session. Once the session is established, you can jump in and out of the session with Invoke-Command; instead of using the ComputerName parameter, as you did with the ad hoc command, you'll have to use the Session parameter.

You need to provide the Session parameter with a session object. You can use the Get-PSSession command to see all your current sessions. In Listing 8-12, you'll store the output of Get-PSSession in a variable.

```
PS> $session = Get-PSSession
PS> $session

 Id     Name     ComputerName   ComputerType    State    ConfigurationName      Availability
 --     ----     ------------   ------------    -----    -----------------      ------------
  6     WinRM6   WEBSRV1        RemoteMachine   Opened   Microsoft.PowerShell   Available
```

Listing 8-12: Finding sessions created on the local computer

Because you ran New-PSSession only once, you have only one PSSession created in Listing 8-12. If you have multiple sessions, you can pick the session you want Invoke-Command to use by using the Get-PSSession command's Id parameter.

Invoking Commands in a Session

Now that you have a session in a variable, you can pass that variable to `Invoke-Command` and run some code inside the session, as in Listing 8-13.

```
PS> Invoke-Command -Session $session -ScriptBlock { hostname }
WEBSRV1
```

Listing 8-13: Using an existing session to invoke commands on a remote computer

You should notice that this command runs much faster than when you passed it a command. This is because `Invoke-Command` doesn't have to create and tear down a new session. When you create a full session, not only is it faster, but you also have access to more functionality. For example, as you can see in Listing 8-14, you can set variables in the remote session and return to the session without losing those variables.

```
PS> Invoke-Command -Session $session -ScriptBlock { $foo = 'Please be here next time' }
PS> Invoke-Command -Session $session -ScriptBlock { $foo }
Please be here next time
```

Listing 8-14: Variable values remain over subsequent session connections.

As long as the session stays open, you can do whatever you need in the remote session, and the state of the session will go unchanged. However, this is valid for only your current local session. If you start another PowerShell process, you can't just pick up where you left off. The remote session will still be active, but the reference to that remote session on the local computer will be gone. In that case, the `PSSession` will go into a disconnected state (which you'll see in an upcoming section).

Opening Interactive Sessions

Listing 8-14 used `Invoke-Command` to send commands to a remote computer and receive a response. Running remote commands like this is like running an unmonitored script. It's not interactive, as when you're punching keystrokes into a PowerShell console. If you want to open an interactive console for the session running on a remote computer—for some troubleshooting, for example—you can use the `Enter-PSSession` command.

The `Enter-PSSession` command allows the user to work with the session interactively. It can either create its own session or rely on an existing one created with `New-PSSession`. If you do not specify a session to enter into, `Enter-PSSession` will create a new one and wait for further input, as in Listing 8-15.

```
PS> Enter-PSSession -ComputerName WEBSRV1
[WEBSRV1]: PS C:\Users\Adam\Documents>
```

Listing 8-15: Entering an interactive session

Notice that your PowerShell prompt changes to `[WEBSRV1]: PS`. This prompt indicates that you're no longer running commands locally but in that remote session. At this point, you can run any command you want, as if you're at the console of the remote computer. Working with sessions interactively like this is a great way to eliminate using the *Remote Desktop Protocol (RDP)* application to bring up an interactive GUI to perform tasks, like troubleshooting on a remote computer.

Disconnecting from and Reconnecting to Sessions

If you close your PowerShell console, open it back up again, and try to use `Invoke-Command` in the session you were previously working in, you will receive an error message, as in Listing 8-16.

```
PS> $session = Get-PSSession -ComputerName websrv1
PS> Invoke-Command -Session $session -ScriptBlock { $foo }
Invoke-Command : Because the session state for session WinRM6, a617c702-ed92
-4de6-8800-40bbd4e1b20c, websrv1 is not equal to Open, you cannot run a
command in the session. The session state is Disconnected.
At line:1 char:1
+ Invoke-Command -Session $session -ScriptBlock { $foo }
--snip--
```

Listing 8-16: Attempting to run commands in a disconnected session

PowerShell can find the `PSSession` on the remote computer but can't find the reference on the local machine, which tells you the session is disconnected. This is what happens if you don't correctly disconnect the local session reference to the remote `PSSession`.

You can disconnect existing sessions by using the `Disconnect-PSSession` command. You can clean up any sessions previously created by retrieving them with `Get-PSSession` and then piping those sessions to the `Disconnect-PSSession` command (see Listing 8-17). Or, alternatively, you can use the `Session` parameter on `Disconnect-PSSession` to disconnect one session at a time.

```
PS> Get-PSSession | Disconnect-PSSession

Id Name         ComputerName   ComputerType    State          ConfigurationName     Availability
-- ----         ------------   ------------    -----          -----------------     ------------
 4 WinRM4       WEBSRV1        RemoteMachine   Disconnected   Microsoft.PowerShell None
```

Listing 8-17: Disconnecting a `PSSession`

To properly disconnect from a session, you pass your remote computer's name to the `Session` parameter by either calling it explicitly via `Disconnect-PSSession -Session` *`session object`* or piping an existing session to the command via `Get-PSSession` as in Listing 8-17.

If you'd like to connect to your session again later, after you've disconnected with `Disconnect-PSSession`, close your PowerShell console and then use the `Connect-PSSession` command, as in Listing 8-18. Note that you can see and connect only to disconnected sessions that your account has already created. You will not be able to see sessions other users have created.

```
PS> Connect-PSSession -ComputerName websrv1
[WEBSRV1]: PS>
```

Listing 8-18: Reconnecting to a PSSession

You should now be able to run code on the remote computer as if you never closed your console.

If you still receive an error message, you may have mismatched PowerShell versions. Disconnected sessions work only if the local machine and remote server have the same PowerShell version. For example, if you have PowerShell 5.1 on your local computer, but the remote server you're connecting to is running a version of PowerShell that doesn't support disconnected sessions (such as PowerShell v2 or older), disconnected sessions won't work. Always be sure that both the local machine and remote server have the same PowerShell version.

To check whether your local computer's PowerShell version matches the version on your remote computer, check the value of the `$PSVersionTable` variable, which contains versioning information (see Listing 8-19).

```
PS> $PSVersionTable

Name                           Value
----                           -----
PSVersion                      5.1.15063.674
PSEdition                      Desktop
PSCompatibleVersions           {1.0, 2.0, 3.0, 4.0...}
BuildVersion                   10.0.15063.674
CLRVersion                     4.0.30319.42000
WSManStackVersion              3.0
PSRemotingProtocolVersion      2.3
SerializationVersion           1.1.0.1
```

Listing 8-19: Checking the PowerShell version on a local computer

To check for the version on your remote computer, run `Invoke-Command` on that computer, passing it the `$PSVersionTable` variable, as in Listing 8-20.

```
PS> Invoke-Command -ComputerName WEBSRV1 -ScriptBlock { $PSVersionTable }

Name                           Value
----                           -----
PSRemotingProtocolVersion      2.2
BuildVersion                   6.3.9600.16394
PSCompatibleVersions           {1.0, 2.0, 3.0, 4.0}
PSVersion                      4.0
CLRVersion                     4.0.30319.34014
WSManStackVersion              3.0
SerializationVersion           1.1.0.1
```

Listing 8-20: Checking the PowerShell version on a remote computer

I suggest that, before you disconnect from a session, you check that your versions match; that way, you can avoid losing valuable work on a remote system.

Removing Sessions with Remove-PSSession

Whenever the `New-PSSession` command creates a new session, that session exists both on the remote server and on the local computer. You can open a lot of sessions across many servers at the same time as well, and if some of those sessions are no longer in use, you may eventually need to clean them up. You can do so with the `Remove-PSSession` command, which goes out to the remote computer, tears down that session, and if it exists, removes the local `PSSession` reference. Listing 8-21 is an example of this:

```
PS> Get-PSSession | Remove-PSSession
PS> Get-PSSession
```

Listing 8-21: Removing a `PSSession`

Here, you see that you're running `Get-PSSession` again, and nothing is returned. This means there are no sessions on your local computer.

Understanding PowerShell Remoting Authentication

So far, I've been ignoring the question of authentication. By default, if your local and remote computers are both in the same domain and both have PowerShell remoting enabled, you don't need to explicitly authenticate. But if they're not, you'll need to authenticate somehow.

Two of the most common ways you can authenticate to remote computers with PowerShell remoting are by using Kerberos or CredSSP. If you're in an Active Directory domain, you're probably already using a Kerberos ticket system, whether you know it or not. Active Directory and some Linux systems use Kerberos *realms*, entities that issue tickets to clients. These tickets are then presented to resources and compared (in Active Directory) on domain controllers.

CredSSP, on the other hand, doesn't need Active Directory. CredSSP was introduced way back with Windows Vista and uses a client-side credential service provider (CSP) to enable applications to delegate user credentials to remote computers. CredSSP doesn't require an outside system, such as a domain controller, in order to authenticate two systems.

In an Active Directory environment, PowerShell remoting uses the Kerberos network authentication protocol to make calls out to Active Directory that perform all the authentication under the hood. PowerShell uses the account you're logged onto locally as the user in order to authenticate to the remote computer—just like many other services. This is the beauty of single sign-on.

But sometimes you're forced to change up that authentication type a bit if you're not in an Active Directory environment; for example, when you need to connect to remote computers over the internet or on the local network, but via local credentials on the remote computer. PowerShell supports numerous methods for PowerShell remoting authentication, but the most common—other than just using Kerberos—is CredSSP, which allows a local computer to delegate the user's credentials to the remote computer. This concept is similar to Kerberos, but Active Directory is not needed.

You don't usually need to use a different authentication type when working in an Active Directory environment, but it does come up sometimes, so it's best you're prepared. In this section, you'll learn about a common authentication issue and how to work around it.

The Double Hop Problem

The *double hop problem* has been an issue ever since Microsoft added the PowerShell remoting feature. This problem arises when you're running code inside a remote session, and then attempt to access remote resources from that remote session. For example, if you have a domain controller called DC on your network and you want to check out the files on the root of *C:* by using the `C$` administrative share, you can browse the share remotely from your local machine without an issue (see Listing 8-22).

```
PS> Get-ChildItem -Path '\\dc\c$'


    Directory: \\dc\c$


Mode                LastWriteTime         Length Name
----                -------------         ------ ----
d-----        10/1/2019  12:05 PM                FileShare
d-----       11/24/2019   2:28 PM                inetpub
d-----       11/22/2019   6:37 PM                InstallWindowsFeature
d-----        4/16/2019   1:10 PM                Iperf
```

Listing 8-22: Enumerating files over a UNC share

The issue arises when you create a `PSSession` and attempt to rerun the same command, as in Listing 8-23.

```
PS> Enter-PSSession -ComputerName WEBSRV1
[WEBSRV1]: PS> Get-ChildItem -Path '\\dc\c$'
ls : Access is denied
--snip--
[WEBSRV1]: PS>
```

Listing 8-23: Attempting to access network resources in a session

In this case, PowerShell tells you that access is denied—even when you know your user account has access. This happens because, when you use the default Kerberos authentication, PowerShell remoting doesn't then pass that credential to the other network resource. In other words, it doesn't make both hops. For security reasons, PowerShell adheres to Windows restrictions and refuses to delegate those credentials, and as a result, returns an Access Denied message.

Double Hopping with CredSSP

In this section, you'll learn how to work around the double hop problem. I say *work around* instead of *fix* for a reason. Microsoft has warned that using CredSSP is a security problem, as the credential passed to the first computer is automatically used for all connections from that computer. This means if the original computer is compromised, that credential can be used from that computer to connect to other computers across the network. Nevertheless, other than using some fancy workarounds, like resource-based Kerberos constrained delegation, many users choose to use the CredSSP approach because it's easy to use.

Before you implement CredSSP, you have to enable it on both the client and the server by using the `Enable-WsManCredSSP` command in an elevated PowerShell session. This command has a `Role` parameter, which allows you to define whether CredSSP is being enabled on the client or the server side. First, enable CredSSP on the client side, as in Listing 8-24.

```
PS> Enable-WSManCredSSP ❶-Role ❷Client ❸-DelegateComputer WEBSRV1

CredSSP Authentication Configuration for WS-Management
CredSSP authentication allows the user credentials on this computer to be sent
to a remote computer. If you use CredSSP authentication for a connection to
a malicious or compromised computer, that machine will have access to your
username and password. For more information, see the Enable-WSManCredSSP Help
topic.
Do you want to enable CredSSP authentication?
[Y] Yes  [N] No  [S] Suspend  [?] Help (default is "Y"): y


cfg         : http://schemas.microsoft.com/wbem/wsman/1/config/client/auth
lang        : en-US
Basic       : true
Digest      : true
Kerberos    : true
Negotiate   : true
Certificate : true
CredSSP     : true
```

Listing 8-24: Enabling CredSSP support on the client computer

You enable CredSSP on the client by passing the value `Client` ❷ to the `Role` parameter ❶. You also use the required `DelegateComputer` parameter ❸ here because PowerShell needs to know which computers are allowed to use the credential you'll be delegating it to. You could pass an asterisk (*) to `DelegateComputer` in order to allow delegation to all computers, but for security purposes, it's better to just allow the computers you're working with, in this case, `WEBSRV1`.

Once CredSSP is enabled on the client, you need to do the same on the server (Listing 8-25). Luckily, you can just open up a new remote session without using CredSSP, and then enable CredSSP within the session—rather than having to use Microsoft Remote Desktop to access the server or visit it physically.

```
PS> Invoke-Command -ComputerName WEBSRV1 -ScriptBlock { Enable-WSManCredSSP -Role Server }

CredSSP Authentication Configuration for WS-Management CredSSP authentication allows the server
to accept user credentials from a remote computer. If you enable CredSSP authentication on the
server, the server will have access to the username and password of the client computer if the
client computer sends them. For more information, see the Enable-WSManCredSSP Help topic.
Do you want to enable CredSSP authentication?
[Y] Yes  [N] No  [?] Help (default is "Y"): y

#text
-----
False
True
True
False
True
Relaxed
```

Listing 8-25: Enabling CredSSP support on the server computer

With that, you've enabled CredSSP on both the client and the server: the client is allowing its user credentials to be delegated to the remote server, and the remote server has CredSSP enabled itself. Now you can try to access remote network resources from that remote session again (see Listing 8-26). Note that if you ever need to undo enabling CredSSP, the command `Disable-WsmanCredSSP` will revert your changes.

```
PS> Invoke-Command -ComputerName WEBSRV1 -ScriptBlock { Get-ChildItem -Path '\\dc\c$'  }
❶-Authentication Credssp ❷-Credential (Get-Credential)

cmdlet Get-Credential at command pipeline position 1
Supply values for the following parameters:
Credential


    Directory: \\dc\c$


Mode                LastWriteTime         Length Name                                PSComputerName
----                -------------         ------ ----                                --------------
d-----        10/1/2019  12:05 PM                FileShare                           WEBSRV1
d-----       11/24/2019   2:28 PM                inetpub                             WEBSRV1
d-----       11/22/2019   6:37 PM                InstallWindowsFeature               WEBSRV1
d-----        4/16/2019   1:10 PM                Iperf                               WEBSRV1
```

Listing 8-26: Accessing network resources over a CredSSP-authenticated session

Notice that you have to explicitly tell `Invoke-Command` (or `Enter-PSSession`) that you'd like to use CredSSP authentication ❶, and both commands—whichever you use—require a credential. You get that credential by using the `Get-Credential` command rather than the default Kerberos ❷.

After you execute `Invoke-Command` and provide `Get-Credential` with a username and password with access to the `c$` share on DC, you can see the `Get-ChildItem` command works as expected!

Summary

PowerShell remoting is, by far, the easiest way to remotely execute code on remote systems. As you learned in this chapter, the PowerShell remoting feature is easy to use and intuitive. Once you've grasped the concept of a scriptblock and where that code inside of it is being executed, remote scriptblocks will be second nature to you.

In Part III of this book—where you will build your own robust PowerShell module—you'll use PowerShell remoting in nearly every command. If you had trouble following along in this chapter, please go over it again or begin to experiment. Try different scenarios, break things, fix them, do whatever you can to understand PowerShell remoting. It's one of the most important skills you can learn from this book.

Chapter 9 covers another major skill: testing with Pester.

9

TESTING WITH PESTER

There's no way around it: you need to test your code. It's easy to assume your code has no flaws; it's even easier to be proven wrong. When you test with Pester, you can stop assuming and start knowing.

Testing has been a feature of traditional software development for decades. But while concepts like *unit*, *functional*, *integration*, and *acceptance* testing may be familiar to seasoned software developers, they're relatively new to scripters—those of us who want to automate with PowerShell but don't hold a software engineer job title. Since many organizations are depending more on PowerShell code to run critical production systems, we'll take a page from the programming world and apply it to PowerShell.

In this chapter, you'll learn how to create tests for your scripts and modules so you can be sure your code works, and stays working when you've changed it. You'll do this with the testing framework known as Pester.

Introducing Pester

Pester is an open source testing PowerShell module available in the PowerShell Gallery. Because it's effective, and written in PowerShell, it's become the de facto standard for testing in PowerShell. It allows you to write multiple types of tests, including unit, integration, and acceptance tests. If these test names don't ring a bell, don't worry. In this book, we'll use Pester only to test environmental changes such as whether a virtual machine was created with the right name, whether IIS was installed, or whether the proper operating system was installed. We'll refer to these tests as *infrastructure tests*.

We won't cover how to test for things like whether a function was called, whether a variable was set correctly, or whether a script returned a specific object type—that's all in the world of *unit testing*. If you're curious about unit testing with Pester and want to learn how to use Pester in different situations, check out *The Pester Book* (LeanPub, 2019, *https://leanpub.com/pesterbook/*), which explains just about everything you need to know about testing with PowerShell.

Pester Basics

To use Pester, you must first get it installed. If you have Windows 10, Pester is installed by default, but it's also available in the PowerShell Gallery if you're on another Windows operating system. If you're on Windows 10, chances are Pester will be outdated anyway, so you might as well grab the latest copy from the PowerShell Gallery. Since Pester is available via the PowerShell Gallery, you can run `Install-Module -Name Pester` to download and install it. Once installed, it will have all the commands you need.

It's worth repeating that you'll be using Pester to write and run infrastructure tests, which are meant to validate any expected changes a script performs against its environment. For example, you might run an infrastructure test after creating a new file path by using `Test-Path` to ensure that the file path was created. Infrastructure tests are safeguards put in place to confirm that your code did what you expected it to do.

A Pester File

In its most basic form, a Pester test script consists of a PowerShell script ending in *.Tests.ps1*. You can name the main script anything you like; the naming convention and test structure are entirely up to you. Here, you'll name the script *Sample.Tests.ps1*.

The basic structure of a Pester test script is one or more `describe` blocks that each contain (optional) `context` blocks that each contain `it` blocks that each contain assertions. If that was a lot to process, Listing 9-1 provides a visual guide.

```
C:\Sample.Tests.ps1
    describe
        context
          it
            assertions
```

Listing 9-1: A basic Pester test structure

Let's go through each of these parts.

The describe Block

A `describe` block is a way to group like tests together. In Listing 9-2, you create a `describe` block called `IIS`, which you could use to include all the code to test things like Windows features, app pools, and websites.

The basic syntax for a `describe` block is the word `describe` followed by a name, in single quotes, followed by an opening and closing curly bracket.

```
describe 'IIS' {

}
```

Listing 9-2: A Pester `describe` block

Although this structure looks like an `if/then` condition, don't be fooled! This is a scriptblock that is passed to the `describe` function under the covers. Note that if you're the type who prefers curly brackets on a new line, you're out of luck: the opening curly bracket must come on the same line as the `describe` keyword.

The context Block

Once you create the `describe` block, you can add an optional `context` block. The `context` block groups together similar `it` blocks, which helps organize tests when infrastructure testing. In Listing 9-3, you'll add a `context` block that will contain all the tests for Windows features. It's a good idea to classify tests this way in `context` blocks to more easily manage them.

```
describe 'IIS' {
    context 'Windows features' {
    }
}
```

Listing 9-3: A Pester `context` block

Although optional, the `context` block will become invaluable later when you've created tests to test dozens or hundreds of components!

The it Block

Now let's add an it block inside the context block. An it block is a smaller component that labels the actual test. Its syntax, shown in Listing 9-4, has a name followed by a block, just as you saw with the describe block.

```
describe 'IIS' {
    context 'Windows features' {
        it 'installs the Web-Server Windows feature' {

        }
    }
}
```

Listing 9-4: A Pester `describe` block with a `context` and `it` block

Notice that so far, you more or less just added different labels for the test, in varying scopes. In the next section, you'll add the test itself.

Assertions

Inside the it block, you include one or more assertions. An *assertion* can be thought of as the actual test, or the code that compares the expected state to an actual state. The most common assertion in Pester is the should assertion. The should assertion has different operators that can be used with it, such as be, bein, belessthan, and so on. If you'd like a full list of available operators, the Pester wiki (*https://github.com/pester/Pester/wiki/*) has a full list.

In our IIS example, let's check whether the app pool named test was created on our server. To do that, you first have to write the code to find the current state of the Web-Server Windows feature on the server (we'll call it WEBSRV1). After a little investigation by browsing through the available PowerShell commands with Get-Command and sifting through the Get-WindowsFeature command's help text, you find that the code to do so looks like this:

```
PS> (Get-WindowsFeature -ComputerName WEBSRV1 -Name Web-Server).Installed
True
```

You know that if the Web-Server feature is installed, the Installed property will return True; otherwise, it will return False. Knowing this, you can then assert that when you run this Get-WindowsFeature command, you expect the Installed property to be True. You want to test whether this command's output will *be* equal to True. You can represent this scenario inside an it block, as shown in Listing 9-5.

```
describe 'IIS' {
    context 'Windows features' {
        it 'installs the Web-Server Windows feature' {
            $parameters = @{
```

```
                ComputerName = 'WEBSRV1'
                Name         = 'Web-Server'
            }
            (Get-WindowsFeature @parameters).Installed | should be $true
        }
    }
}
```

Listing 9-5: Asserting a test condition with Pester

Here, you created a rudimentary Pester test to test whether a Windows feature is installed. You first enter the test you want to run, and then pass the results of that test through the pipeline to your testing condition, which, in this case, is `should be $true`.

There's much more to writing Pester tests, and I encourage you to learn the details via *The Pester Book* (*https://leanpub.com/pesterbook/*) or perhaps a series of articles on 4sysops (*https://4sysops.com/archives/powershell-pester-testing-getting-started/*). This should be enough for you to be able to read the tests I provide with this book. Once you finish this book, writing your own Pester tests will be a good way to test your PowerShell skills.

You have a Pester script now. And of course, once you have a script, you need to run it!

Executing a Pester Test

The most common way to execute tests with Pester is by using the `Invoke-Pester` command. This command is a part of the Pester module and allows the tester to pass it a path to the test script, which Pester will then interpret and execute, as in Listing 9-6.

```
PS> Invoke-Pester -Path C:\Sample.Tests.ps1
Executing all tests in 'C:\Sample.Tests.ps1'

Executing script C:\Sample.Tests.ps1

  Describing IIS
    [+] installs the Web-Server Windows feature 2.85s
Tests completed in 2.85s
Tests Passed: 1, Failed: 0, Skipped: 0, Pending: 0, Inconclusive: 0
```

Listing 9-6: Running a Pester test

You can see that the `Invoke-Pester` command has executed the *Sample.Tests.ps1* script and has provided basic information such as displaying the name of the `describe` block, the result of the test, as well as a summary of all the tests that ran during that test run. Note that the `Invoke-Pester` command will always show a summary of the status of each test performed. In this case, the `installs the Web-Server Windows feature` test was successful, indicated by the + symbol and a green output.

Summary

This chapter covered the basics of the Pester testing framework. You downloaded, installed, and built a simple Pester test. This should help you understand how a Pester test is structured and how to execute it. In the coming chapters, you'll use this framework over and over again. You'll be adding lots of `describe` blocks, `it` blocks, and various assertions, but the basic structure will remain relatively unchanged.

This wraps up our final chapter of Part I. You've seen the fundamental syntax and concepts you'll use when scripting with PowerShell. Now let's get to the good stuff in Part II, where you'll get hands-on experience and start looking at real-world problems!

PART II

AUTOMATING DAY-TO-DAY TASKS

If Part I felt more like a school exercise than something practical—the kind of thing you can do today, right here, right now—don't worry, you're not alone! I felt the same way. But you can't always dive in headfirst; sometimes it's good to test the water before you jump in. And that's what Part I accomplished—giving an introduction for those who are new to PowerShell and a refresher for those who aren't.

In Part II, you'll finally get to the fun stuff, taking what you've learned in Part I and *applying* those skills to real-world scenarios. You'll walk through how to use PowerShell to automate some common scenarios many tech professionals deal with every day. If you're a seasoned tech professional, you've undoubtedly encountered some of these scenarios before: sleepily clicking your way through an Active Directory, spending way too much time copying and pasting between Excel sheets, freaking out as you try to rig up some remote-controlled software to connect a dozen machines at a time so you can get management that info they wanted two days ago.

In this part of the book, you'll learn the tools you need to automate tasks like these. Of course, I can't cover everything—there's just too much boring stuff to automate! What follows are a few common scenarios I've encountered in my 20 years in the industry. If your particular problem isn't covered, don't fret! By the end of this book, you'll have the foundation you need to figure out how to automate tasks for yourself.

Part II is broken into four main topics covered in five chapters.

Working with Structured Data

Data is everywhere. If you've worked with it before, you know it comes in a million formats: SQL databases, XML files, JSON objects, CSVs, and all the rest. Every type of data has its own specific structure, and each structure has to be handled differently. In Chapter 10, you'll learn how to read, write, and modify various forms of data.

Automating Active Directory Tasks

Active Directory (AD) is a directory service. At a high level, you can think of a *directory service* as a hierarchical way to keep track of which IT resources a user can access. AD is Microsoft's version of a directory service, and as you might imagine, it's used by thousands and thousands of organizations all over the world, making it an area ripe for automation.

Chapter 11 covers the basics of how to manage various AD objects from the PowerShell console. Once you get used to the AD cmdlets, we'll walk through a few small projects that will help you use various AD cmdlets to automate some of the most mundane tasks you're likely to see.

Controlling the Cloud

Like almost every kind of technology these days, the cloud is heavily supported by PowerShell. Understanding how PowerShell works in cloud environments, including Microsoft Azure and Amazon Web Services (AWS), will open up shiny new frontiers to automate. In Chapters 12 and 13, you'll create virtual machines, web services, and more. You'll even see an example of using PowerShell to interact with both cloud providers at once. Since PowerShell is indifferent to which cloud we use (it's *cloud-agnostic*), we have the ability to control any cloud we want!

Creating a Server Inventory Script

Because the content in this book is cumulative, you'll need a solid foundation before attempting the whirlwind of technical wizardry that is Part III. That's what Chapter 14 is all about, combining all the know-how you've gathered over the course of this book and turning it into a single project. Here, you'll learn how to combine disparate sources of information into a single, cohesive report. This will entail querying computers from AD and interrogating them with CIM/WMI to access useful information such as name, RAM, CPU speed, operating system, IP address, and more.

Summary

By the end of this part, you should have a good idea of the kinds of mundane tasks you can use PowerShell to automate. Having automated a couple of them yourself, you'll see that there's really no need to shell out for expensive software or fancy consultants to manage your environment. PowerShell can complement hundreds of products and services—where there's a will (and PowerShell), there's a way.

10

PARSING STRUCTURED DATA

With ingrained support for any .NET object, and just about every shell method you can think of, PowerShell is able to read, update, and remove data from numerous sources. If you're lucky enough to have your data stored in some kind of structured way, working with that data is even easier.

In this chapter, we'll focus on a few common forms of structured data including CSV, Microsoft Excel spreadsheets, and JSON. You'll learn how to manage each kind of data by using both native PowerShell cmdlets and .NET objects. By the end of the chapter, you should be a data-wrangling pro, able to use PowerShell to manage all sorts of structured data.

CSV Files

One of the easiest, most common ways to store data is to use a CSV file. A *CSV file* is a simple text file representing a table. Each item in the table is separated by a shared, predetermined symbol known as a *delimiter* (commas are the most common delimiter). Every CSV file shares the same basic structure: the first row in the CSV is the header row, containing all the headers for the table's columns; the following rows contain all of the table's contents.

In this section, you'll primarily be working with a couple of CSV cmdlets: `Import-Csv` and `Export-Csv`.

Reading CSV Files

Of all the CSV processing tasks PowerShell is equipped to do, the most common is almost certainly reading. Given how simple and effective the CSV structure is, it should be no surprise that CSV files are used by companies and applications throughout the tech world—hence the popularity of the `Import-Csv` PowerShell command.

But what exactly does it mean to *read* a CSV file? Though a CSV has all the information you want, you can't just import it directly into your program; usually, you have to read through the file and convert it into usable data. This process is known as *parsing*. The `Import-Csv` command parses the CSV file: reading it in, and then transforming the data into PowerShell objects. I will go into the uses of `Import-Csv` in a moment, but first, it's worth taking a dive under the hood to see what `Import-Csv` is doing.

Let's start with a simple spreadsheet containing a few employees at a fictional company, shown in Figure 10-1.

	A	B	C	D
1	First Name	Last Name	Department	Manager
2	Adam	Bertram	IT	Miranda Bertram
3	Barack	Obama	Executive Office	Michelle Obama
4	Miranda	Bertram	Executive Office	
5	Michelle	Obama	Executive Office	

Figure 10-1: Employee CSV file

Figure 10-1 is an Excel screenshot, but you can easily see what the data looks like as a plaintext CSV file. For our sample CSV file, you'll be working with *Employees.csv*, which can be found in this chapter's resources; see Listing 10-1.

```
PS> Get-Content -Path ./Employees.csv -Raw

First Name,Last Name,Department,Manager
Adam,Bertram,IT,Miranda Bertram
Barack,Obama,Executive Office,Michelle Obama
Miranda,Bertram,Executive Office
Michelle,Obama,Executive Office
```

Listing 10-1: Reading a CSV file with `Get-Content`

Here, you're using the Get-Content command to query our text file (CSV). Get-Content is the PowerShell command to use for reading plaintext files of any kind.

You can see that this is a typical CSV file with a header row and multiple data rows separated into columns by a comma delimiter. Notice that you can read the file by using the Get-Content cmdlet. Since a CSV file is a text file, Get-Content works just fine for reading it (this is actually the first step that happens with Import-Csv).

But also notice how Get-Content returns the information: as a simple string. This is what happens when you use the Raw parameter. Otherwise, Get-Content returns an array of strings, with each element representing a row in the CSV file:

```
PS> Get-Content ./Employees.csv -Raw | Get-Member

   TypeName: System.String
   --snip--
```

Though the Get-Content command can read in the data, the command doesn't *understand* a CSV file's schema. Get-Content has no idea that the table has a header row or data rows, and it doesn't know what to do with the delimiter. It just takes in the content and spits it back out. That's why we have Import-Csv.

Using Import-Csv to Process Data

To see how Import-Csv works, compare the output in Listing 10-1 with the output from Import-Csv in Listing 10-2.

```
PS> Import-Csv -Path ./Employees.csv

First Name Last Name Department       Manager
---------- --------- ----------       -------
Adam       Bertram   IT               Miranda Bertram
Barack     Obama     Executive Office Michelle Obama
Miranda    Bertram   Executive Office
Michelle   Obama     Executive Office

PS> Import-Csv -Path ./Employees.csv | Get-Member

   TypeName: System.Management.Automation.PSCustomObject

PS> $firstCsvRow = Import-Csv -Path ./Employees.csv | Select-Object -First
1
PS> $firstCsvRow | Select-Object -ExpandProperty 'First Name'
Adam
```

Listing 10-2: Using Import-Csv

The first thing you'll probably notice is that the headers are now separated from the data entries by a line. This means that Import-Csv reads the file, treats the top row as a header row, and knows to separate it from the rest of the file. You also may notice that there are no more commas—when a command reads and *understands* a CSV file, it knows that the delimiter is used to separate items in the table and shouldn't show up in the table itself.

But what happens if the code has a stray delimiter? Try putting a comma in the middle of *Adam* in *Employees.csv* and run the code. What happens? Now everything in the Adam row is shifted over: *am* is the new Last Name, *Bertram* the new Department, and *IT* the new Manager. `Import-Csv` is smart enough to understand a CSV's format, but not smart enough to understand its content—that's where you come in.

Turning Raw Data into Objects

`Import-Csv` doesn't just read in the CSV and print it out with fancy formatting. The content of the file is put into an array of `PSCustomObjects`. Here, each `PSCustomObject` is an object that holds the data for one row. Each object has properties that correspond to the headers in the header row, and if you want the data for that header's column, all you have to do is access that property. Just by knowing which form of data to expect, `Import-Csv` can take a string of data it has never seen before and turn it into easy-to-use objects. Pretty cool!

Having the data as an array of `PSCustomObjects` allows you to use that data much more effectively. Let's say you want to find only the employees with the last name of *Bertram*. Since each data row in the CSV is a `PSCustomObject`, you can do this by using `Where-Object`:

```
PS> Import-Csv -Path ./Employees.csv | Where-Object { $_.'Last Name' -eq 'Bertram' }

First Name Last Name Department         Manager
---------- --------- ----------         -------
Adam       Bertram   IT                 Miranda Bertram
Miranda    Bertram   Executive Office
```

If, instead, you want to return only rows in the CSV that have a department of Executive Office, you can do so easily! You use the same technique and change the property name from Last Name to Department, and the value from Bertram to Executive Office:

```
PS> Import-Csv -Path ./Employees.csv | Where-Object {$_.Department -eq 'Executive Office' }

First Name Last Name Department       Manager
---------- --------- ---------        --------
Barack     Obama     Executive Office Michelle Obama
Miranda    Bertram   Executive Office
Michelle   Obama     Executive Office
```

What happens if you use semicolons for your delimiter instead of commas? Try changing the CSV file and see what happens. Not good, right? You don't have to use a comma as a delimiter, but commas are the delimiter that Import-Csv natively understands. If you want to use a different delimiter, you have to specify the new delimiter in your Import-Csv command.

To demonstrate, replace all the commas in our *Employees.csv* file with tabs:

```
PS> (Get-Content ./Employees.csv -Raw).replace(',',"`t") | Set-Content ./Employees.csv
PS> Get-Content ./Employees.csv -Raw
First Name  Last Name   Department  Manager
Adam    Bertram IT  Miranda Bertram
Barack  Obama   Executive Office    Michelle Obama
Miranda Bertram Executive Office
Michelle    Obama   Executive Office
```

Once you have a tab-separated file, you can then specify the tab character (represented by a backtick and the t character) as the new delimiter by using the Delimiter parameter (Listing 10-3).

```
PS> Import-Csv -Path ./Employees.csv -Delimiter "`t"

First Name Last Name Department       Manager
---------- --------- ----------       -------
Adam       Bertram   IT               Miranda Bertram
Barack     Obama     Executive Office Michelle Obama
Miranda    Bertram   Executive Office
Michelle   Obama     Executive Office
```

Listing 10-3: Using the Delimiter *parameter of* Import-Csv

Notice that the output is the same as it was in Listing 10-2.

Defining Your Own Header

What if you have a table of data, but you want to change the header row to be more user-friendly? Import-Csv can do this too. As with the new delimiter, you want to pass a parameter in to Import-Csv. Listing 10-4 uses the Header parameter to pass in a series of strings separated by commas (the new headers).

```
PS> Import-Csv -Path ./Employees.csv -Delimiter "`t"
-Header 'Employee FName','Employee LName','Dept','Manager'

Employee FName Employee LName Dept             Manager
-------------- -------------- ----             -------
First Name     Last Name      Department       Manager
Adam           Bertram        IT               Miranda Bertram
Barack         Obama          Executive Office Michelle Obama
Miranda        Bertram        Executive Office
Michelle       Obama          Executive Office
```

Listing 10-4: Using the Header *parameter of* Import-Csv

As you can see, after the command runs, each object in the data row will have the new labels as property names.

Creating CSV Files

So much for reading CSV files. What if you want to make your own? You could type one out by hand, but that would take time and energy, especially if you're dealing with thousands of rows. Luckily, PowerShell also has a native cmdlet for creating CSV files: `Export-Csv`. You can use this cmdlet to create CSV files from any existing PowerShell object; you simply have to tell PowerShell which objects to use as rows, and where it should create the file.

Let's deal with the second requirement first. Say you run some PowerShell commands, and then you want to save the output in the console to a file somehow. You could use `Out-File`, but that would send the unstructured text directly to a new file. You want a nice structured file instead, complete with header rows and delimiters. Enter `Export-Csv`.

As an example, let's say you want to pull all the running processes from your computer and record the process name, company, and description of each one. You can use `Get-Process` to do this and `Select-Object` to narrow down the properties you want to see, as shown here:

```
PS> Get-Process | Select-Object -Property Name,Company,Description

Name                  Company                      Description
----                  -------                      -----------
ApplicationFrameHost Microsoft Corporation        Application Frame Host
coherence             Parallels International GmbH Parallels Coherence service
coherence             Parallels International GmbH Parallels Coherence service
coherence             Parallels International GmbH Parallels Coherence service
com.docker.proxy
com.docker.service    Docker Inc.
Docker.Service
--snip--
```

In Listing 10-5, you can see what happens when you commit this output to the filesystem in a structured manner by using `Export-Csv`.

```
PS> Get-Process | Select-Object -Property Name,Company,Description |
Export-Csv -Path C:\Processes.csv -NoTypeInformation
PS> Get-Content -Path C:\Processes.csv
"Name","Company","Description"
"ApplicationFrameHost","Microsoft Corporation","Application Frame Host"
"coherence","Parallels International GmbH","Parallels Coherence service"
"coherence","Parallels International GmbH","Parallels Coherence service"
"coherence","Parallels International GmbH","Parallels Coherence service"
"com.docker.proxy",,
"com.docker.service","Docker Inc.","Docker.Service"
```

Listing 10-5: Using `Export-Csv`

By piping the output directly to `Export-Csv`, specifying the path to the CSV you'd like to create (using the `Path` parameter), and using the `NoTypeInformation` parameter, you've created a CSV file with the expected header row and data rows.

NOTE *The* `NoTypeInformation` *parameter is not required, but if you don't use it, you will get a line at the top of your CSV file specifying the type of object it came from. Unless you're reimporting the CSV file directly back into PowerShell, this usually isn't desired. An example line looks like* `#TYPE Selected.System.Diagnostics.Process`.

Project 1: Building a Computer Inventory Report

To bring together everything you've learned so far, let's work on a mini-project, something you may run into in your daily life.

Imagine for a moment that your company has acquired another company that has no idea what servers and PCs it has on its network. All it has is a CSV file of IP addresses and the department where each device is located. You've been brought in to figure out what these devices are and to provide a new CSV file to management with the results.

What do you have to do? At a high level, this is a two-step process: read in their CSV and write your own. Your CSV file will need the following information: each IP address you process, the department it's supposed to be in, whether or not the IP address responds to a ping, and the DNS name of that device.

You'll start with a CSV file that looks just like that looks like the following snippet. The IP addresses are part of a full 255.255.255.0 network, so they go all the way up to 192.168.0.254:

```
PS> Get-Content -Path ./IPAddresses.csv
"192.168.0.1","IT"
"192.168.0.2","Accounting"
"192.168.0.3","HR"
"192.168.0.4","IT"
"192.168.0.5","Accounting"
--snip--
```

I've created a script called *Discover-Computer.ps1* that's available in this chapter's resources. As you move through this experiment, start adding code to it.

First, you need to read each row in the CSV file. You do this with `Import-Csv`, which will capture each row of the CSV into a variable for further processing:

```
$rows = Import-Csv -Path C:\IPAddresses.csv
```

Now that you have the data, you need to use it. You'll perform two actions on each IP address: pinging it and finding its hostname. Let's go ahead and test these actions on a row of our CSV to ensure that you have the syntax right.

In the following listing, you use the `Test-Connection` command, which sends a single ICMP packet to the IP address you specify (here the IP address in the first row of our CSV file). The `Quiet` parameter tells the command to return either a `True` or `False` value.

```
PS> Test-Connection -ComputerName $row[0].IPAddress -Count 1 -Quiet
PS> (Resolve-DnsName -Name $row[0].IPAddress -ErrorAction Stop).Name
```

In the second line of this code, you're obtaining the hostname by using the `Resolve-DnsName` command on the same IP address. The `Resolve-DnsName` command returns multiple properties. Here, because you're concerned with only the name, you enclose the entire command in parentheses and use dot notation to return the `Name` property.

Once you're comfortable with the syntax for each action, you need to do this for every row in the CSV. The easiest way to do this is with a `foreach` loop:

```
foreach ($row in $rows) {
    Test-Connection -ComputerName $row.IPAddress -Count 1 -Quiet
    (Resolve-DnsName -Name $row.IPAddress -ErrorAction Stop).Name
}
```

Run the code yourself. What happens? You get a bunch of `True`/`False` lines with hostnames, but no way to know which IP address the output is associated with. You'll have to create a *hashtable* for each row and assign your own elements to it. You also need to account for if or when `Test-Connection` or `Resolve-DnsName` returns an error. Listing 10-6 shows an example of how to do all this.

```
$rows = Import-Csv -Path C:\IPAddresses.csv
foreach ($row in $rows) {
    try { ❶
        $output = @{ ❷
            IPAddress  = $row.IPAddress
            Department = $row.Department
            IsOnline   = $false
            HostName   = $null
            Error      = $null
        }
        if (Test-Connection -ComputerName $row.IPAddress -Count 1 -Quiet) { ❸
            $output.IsOnline = $true
        }
        if ($hostname = (Resolve-DnsName -Name $row.IPAddress -ErrorAction Stop).Name) { ❹
            $output.HostName = $hostName
        }
    } catch {
        $output.Error = $_.Exception.Message ❺
    } finally {
        [pscustomobject]$output ❻
    }
}
```

Listing 10-6: Mini-project—CSV file discovery

Let's walk through what's happening. First, you create a hashtable with values corresponding to the row's columns and the extra information you want ❷. Next, test whether the computer is connected by pinging the IP address ❸. If the computer is connected, set `IsOnline` to `True`. Then do the same with the `HostName`, testing whether it's found ❹ and updating the hashtable's value if it is. If any errors occur, record that in the hashtable's `Error` value ❺. Lastly, turn your hashtable into a `PSCustomObject` and return it (regardless of whether an error is thrown) ❻. Note that you've wrapped this whole function in a `try/catch` block ❶, which will execute the code in the `catch` block if the code in the `try` block throws an error. Because you're using the `ErrorAction` parameter, `Resolve-DnsName` will throw an exception (an error) if something unexpected happens.

Run this, and you should see output that looks like the following:

```
HostName   :
Error      : 1.0.168.192.in-addr.arpa : DNS name does not exist
IsOnline   : True
IPAddress  : 192.168.0.1
Department : HR

HostName   :
Error      : 2.0.168.192.in-addr.arpa : DNS name does not exist
IsOnline   : True
IPAddress  : 192.168.0.2
Department : Accounting
--snip--
```

Congrats! You've done most of the hard work, and now you can tell which IP address is associated with which output. All that's left is to record the output to a CSV. As you learned earlier, you can do this with `Export-Csv`. You'll simply pipe the `PSCustomObject` you created into `Export-Csv`, and the output will go directly into a CSV file rather than being output to the console.

Notice that next, you'll use the `Append` parameter. By default, `Export-Csv` overwrites the CSV file. Using the `Append` parameter adds a row to the end of an existing CSV file rather than overwriting it:

```
PS> [pscustomobject]$output |
Export-Csv -Path C:\DeviceDiscovery.csv -Append
-NoTypeInformation
```

Once the script runs, you'll see that the CSV file will be the exact same as the output you saw in your PowerShell console:

```
PS> Import-Csv -Path C:\DeviceDiscovery.csv

HostName   :
Error      : 1.0.168.192.in-addr.arpa : DNS name does not exist
IsOnline   : True
IPAddress  : 192.168.0.1
Department : HR

HostName   :
Error      :
IsOnline   : True
IPAddress  : 192.168.0.2
Department : Accounting
```

You should now have a CSV file called *DeviceDiscovery.csv* (or whatever you named it) that has rows for each IP address in the original CSV, along with values for all of the original CSV file values and the values that you discovered with `Test-Connection` and `Resolve-DnsName`.

Excel Spreadsheets

It's hard to imagine a business that doesn't use Excel spreadsheets. Chances are, if you get a scripting project, it will involve an Excel spreadsheet. But before we dive deep into the world of Excel, it's worth stating something clearly: if possible, don't use it at all!

A CSV file can store data as effectively as a simple Excel spreadsheet, and CSV files are much easier to manage with PowerShell. Excel spreadsheets come in a proprietary format, and you can't even read them by using PowerShell unless you're using an external library. If you have an Excel workbook with a single worksheet, do yourself a favor and save it as a CSV file. Of course, this isn't always possible, but if it is, you'll thank yourself later. Trust me.

But what if it isn't possible to save it as a CSV? In that case, you need to use a community module. Once upon a time, reading *.xls* or *.xlsx* Excel spreadsheets with PowerShell required a software developer's delicate touch. You had to have Excel installed, and you had to access *COM objects,* complex programming components that take all the fun out of working in PowerShell. Luckily, other people have done the hard work for you, so rather than focus on learning how to use COM, in this section, you'll rely on Doug Finke's wonderful `ImportExcel` module. This freely available community module does not require Excel to be installed, and it's much simpler than COM objects.

First, you need to install the module. The `ImportExcel` module is available via the PowerShell Gallery and can be installed by running `Install-Module ImportExcel`. Once you've installed the `ImportExcel` module, it's time to see what it can do.

Creating Excel Spreadsheets

To start, you need to create an Excel spreadsheet. Now, sure, you could create one the usual way by opening Excel and going through all that jazz—but where's the fun in that? Let's use PowerShell to create a simple spreadsheet with a single worksheet (you have to crawl before you can walk). To do this, you'll use the `Export-Excel` command. Just like `Export-Csv`, `Export-Excel` will read the property names of each object it receives, create a header row from them, and then create the data rows right below.

The easiest way to use `Export-Excel` is to pipe one or more objects into it just as you would with `Export-Csv`. As an example, let's create an Excel workbook with a single worksheet that contains all the running processes on my computer.

The input **`Get-Process | Export-Excel .\Processes.xlsx`** gives us a spreadsheet that looks like Figure 10-2.

	A	B	C	D	E	F	G	H
1	Name	SI	Handles	VM	WS	PM	NPM	Path
2	ApplicationFrameHost	1	315	2.19919E+12	26300416	7204864	17672	C:\WINDOWS\system32\ApplicationFrameHost.exe
3	coherence	0	120	62164992	5607424	1769472	7968	C:\Program Files (x86)\Parallels\Parallels Tools\Services\coherence.exe
4	coherence	1	113	82739200	5255168	1818624	7736	C:\Program Files (x86)\Parallels\Parallels Tools\Services\coherence.exe
5	coherence	1	130	78884864	5672960	1802240	8896	C:\Program Files (x86)\Parallels\Parallels Tools\Services\WOW\coherence.exe
6	com.docker.localhost-forwarder	1	343	35518222336	9560064	31272960	7592	C:\Program Files\Docker\Docker\Resources\com.docker.localhost-forwarder.exe
7	com.docker.proxy	1	74	35512229888	9891840	19812352	6632	C:\Program Files\Docker\Docker\Resources\com.docker.proxy.exe
8	com.docker.service	0	517	650498048	40833024	27496448	43120	C:\Program Files\Docker\Docker\com.docker.service
9	conhost	0	105	2.19908E+12	5926912	1486848	7056	C:\WINDOWS\system32\conhost.exe
10	conhost	0	105	2.19909E+12	5943296	1544192	7192	C:\WINDOWS\system32\conhost.exe

Figure 10-2: The Excel spreadsheet

If you haven't converted to CSVs yet, you're probably working with something more complicated than just a single worksheet. Let's add a couple more worksheets to our existing workbook. To do that, use the `WorksheetName` parameter, as shown in Listing 10-7. This will create additional worksheets by using the objects that are sent to `Export-Excel`.

```
PS> Get-Process | Export-Excel .\Processes.xlsx -WorksheetName 'Worksheet2'
PS> Get-Process | Export-Excel .\Processes.xlsx -WorksheetName 'Worksheet3'
```

Listing 10-7: Adding worksheets to an Excel workbook

Creating a spreadsheet by using `Export-Excel` can be a *whole* lot more complicated, but to save us time (and the Earth a couple of trees), we don't go into it here. If you're curious, check out the help documentation on `Export-Excel` and you'll see the dozens of parameters you can use!

Reading Excel Spreadsheets

Now that you have a spreadsheet you can work with, let's focus on reading the rows inside. To read a spreadsheet, you use the `Import-Excel` command. This command reads a worksheet in a workbook and returns one or more `PSCustomObject` objects representing each row. The simplest way to use this command is to specify the workbook path by using the `Path` parameter. You'll see in Listing 10-8 that `Import-Excel` returns an object that uses the column names as properties.

```
PS> Import-Excel -Path .\Processes.xlsx

Name                       : ApplicationFrameHost
SI                         : 1
Handles                    : 315
VM                         : 2199189057536
WS                         : 26300416
PM                         : 7204864
NPM                        : 17672
Path                       : C:\WINDOWS\system32\ApplicationFrameHost.exe
Company                    : Microsoft Corporation
CPU                        : 0.140625
--snip--
```

Listing 10-8: Using `Import-Excel`

By default, Import-Excel will return only the first worksheet. Our example workbook has multiple worksheets, so you need to figure out a way to go through each sheet. But imagine it's been a while since you last created that spreadsheet, and you can't remember the worksheet names. No problem. You'll use Get-ExcelSheetInfo to find all the worksheets in the workbook, as shown in Listing 10-9.

```
PS> Get-ExcelSheetInfo -Path .\Processes.xlsx

Name        Index Hidden  Path
----        ----- ------  ----
Sheet1          1 Visible C:\Users\adam\Processes.xlsx
Worksheet2      2 Visible C:\Users\adam\Processes.xlsx
Worksheet3      3 Visible C:\Users\adam\Processes.xlsx
```

Listing 10-9: Using Get-ExcelSheetInfo

You'll use this output to pull data from all our worksheets. Make a foreach loop and call Import-Excel for every worksheet inside the workbook, just as in Listing 10-10.

```
$excelSheets = Get-ExcelSheetInfo -Path .\Processes.xlsx
Foreach ($sheet in $excelSheets) {
    $workSheetName = $sheet.Name
    $sheetRows = Import-Excel -Path .\Processes.xlsx -WorkSheetName
    $workSheetName
 ❶ $sheetRows | Select-Object -Property *,@{'Name'='Worksheet';'Expression'={ $workSheetName }
}
```

Listing 10-10: Getting all rows from all worksheets

Notice that you use a calculated property with Select-Object ❶. Typically, when using the Property parameter of Select-Object, a simple string is used, specifying the property you want returned. When you use a calculated property, however, you provide Select-Object with a hashtable containing the name of the property to return and an expression that runs when Select-Object receives input. The result of the expression will be the value of the new, calculated property.

By default, Import-Excel doesn't add the worksheet name as a property to each object—meaning you won't know which worksheet the row comes from. To account for this, you need to create a property called Worksheet on each row object so you have something to reference later.

Adding to Excel Spreadsheets

In the previous section, you created a workbook from scratch. There will inevitably come a time when you need to add rows to a worksheet. Luckily, this is easy enough with the ImportExcel module; you just need to use the Append parameter on the Export-Excel command.

As an example, let's say you want to track process execution history on your computer. You'd like to export all the processes running on your computer over a period of time and then compare results in Excel later. To do so, you need to export all the running processes and make sure to include a timestamp on each row to indicate when the process information was gathered.

Let's add another worksheet to our demo workbook and call it **Processes OverTime**. You'll use a calculated property to add a timestamp property to each process row, like so:

```
PS> Get-Process |
Select-Object -Property *,@{Name = 'Timestamp';Expression = { Get-Date -Format
'MM-dd-yy hh:mm:ss' }} |
Export-Excel .\Processes.xlsx -WorksheetName 'ProcessesOverTime'
```

Run this command, and then open the Processes workbook. You should see a worksheet called ProcessesOverTime with a list of all running processes on your computer, and an additional timestamp column indicating when the process information was queried.

At this point, you'll append additional rows to the worksheet by using the same command you just used, but this time with the `Append` parameter. This command can be run as many times as you like. It will just keep appending rows to the worksheet:

```
PS> Get-Process |
Select-Object -Property *,@{Name = 'Timestamp';Expression = { Get-Date -Format
'MM-dd-yy hh:mm:ss' }} |
Export-Excel .\Processes.xlsx -WorksheetName 'ProcessesOverTime' -Append
```

Once you collect your data, you can review your Excel workbook and all the process information you collected.

Project 2: Creating a Windows Service Monitoring Tool

Let's put together the skills you learned in this section and work on another mini-project. This time, you'll build a process to track Windows service states over time and record them to an Excel worksheet. Then, you'll build a report showing when various services have changed state—basically, you're making a lo-fi monitoring tool.

The first thing you want to do is figure out how to pull all Windows services, returning only their name and state. You can do this easily enough by running `Get-Service | Select-Object -Property Name,Status`. Next, you need to get a timestamp on each row in the Excel worksheet. Just as you did in the lesson, you'll use a calculated property to do this; see Listing 10-11.

```
PS> Get-Service |
Select-Object -Property Name,Status,@{Name = 'Timestamp';Expression =
{ Get-Date -Format 'MM-dd-yy hh:mm:ss' }} |
Export-Excel .\ServiceStates.xlsx -WorksheetName 'Services'
```

Listing 10-11: Exporting service states

You should now have an Excel workbook created called *ServiceStates.xlsx* with a single worksheet called Services that'll look something like Figure 10-3.

	A	B	C
1	Name	Status	Timestamp
2	AdtAgent	Stopped	04-22-18 10:06:58
3	AJRouter	Stopped	04-22-18 10:06:58
4	ALG	Stopped	04-22-18 10:06:58
5	AppHostSvc	Running	04-22-18 10:06:58
6	AppIDSvc	Stopped	04-22-18 10:06:58
7	Appinfo	Stopped	04-22-18 10:06:58

Figure 10-3: The Excel workbook

Before running the same command again, let's change the state of various Windows services. This will allow you to track changes over time. Stop and start a few services to change their states. Then run the same command as in Listing 10-11, although this time using the `Append` parameter to `Export-Excel`. This will get you some data to work with. (Don't forget to use the `Append` parameter, or the command will overwrite the existing worksheet!)

Once you have the data, it's time to summarize it. Excel provides multiple ways to do this, but for now, you'll stick with a pivot table. A *pivot table* is a way to summarize data by grouping one or more properties together and then performing an action on those properties' corresponding values (counting, adding, and so on). Using a pivot table, you can easily spot which services changed states and when they did so.

You'll use the `IncludePivotTable`, `PivotRows`, `PivotColumns`, and `PivotData` parameters to create a summary pivot table (Figure 10-4).

A	B	C	D
Count of Timestamp	Column Labels		
Row Labels	Stopped	Running	Grand Total
AdtAgent	4		4
04-22-18 10:06:58	1		1
04-22-18 10:11:28	1		1
04-22-18 10:14:08	1		1
04-22-18 10:14:53	1		1
AJRouter	4		4
04-22-18 10:06:58	1		1
04-22-18 10:11:28	1		1
04-22-18 10:14:08	1		1
04-22-18 10:14:53	1		1
ALG	4		4
04-22-18 10:06:58	1		1
04-22-18 10:11:28	1		1
04-22-18 10:14:08	1		1
04-22-18 10:14:53	1		1
AppHostSvc	2	2	4
04-22-18 10:06:58		1	1
04-22-18 10:11:28		1	1
04-22-18 10:14:08	1		1
04-22-18 10:14:53	1		1
AppIDSvc	4		4

Figure 10-4: Service state pivot table

As you can see in Listing 10-12, you're reading the data in the Services worksheet and using that data to create a pivot table.

```
PS> Import-Excel .\ServiceStates.xlsx -WorksheetName 'Services' |
Export-Excel -Path .\ServiceStates.xlsx -Show -IncludePivotTable -PivotRows Name,Timestamp
-PivotData @{Timestamp = 'count'} -PivotColumns Status
```

Listing 10-12: Creating an Excel pivot table with PowerShell

The `ImportExcel` PowerShell module has a suite of options you can use here. If you want to keep working with this dataset, play around with it and see what you can do. Take a look at the ImportExcel GitHub repository (*https://github.com/dfinke/ImportExcel*), or if you want to use different data, give that a go. As long as you have the data, PowerShell can manipulate and represent it just about any way you like!

JSON Data

If you've been working in tech for the last five years, you've probably read some JSON. Created in the early 2000s, *JavaScript Object Notation (JSON)* is a machine-readable, human-understandable language that represents hierarchical sets of data. As its name might suggest, it's heavily used in JavaScript applications, meaning it has a strong presence in web development.

A recent surge in the number of online services that use a *REST API*—a technology used to send data between client and server—has led to a similar surge in the use of JSON. If you're doing anything with the web, JSON is a good format to know, and it's one you can easily manage in PowerShell.

Reading JSON

Similar to reading the CSVs, you can read JSON a couple of ways in PowerShell: with parsing or no parsing. Since JSON is just plaintext, PowerShell treats it as a string by default. As an example, look at the JSON file *Employees.json* found in this chapter's resources, reproduced here:

```
{
    "Employees": [
        {
            "FirstName": "Adam",
            "LastName": "Bertram",
            "Department": "IT",
            "Title": "Awesome IT Professional"
        },
        {
            "FirstName": "Bob",
            "LastName": "Smith",
            "Department": "HR",
            "Title": "Crotchety HR guy"
        }
    ]
}
```

If you want only the string output, you can use `Get-Content -Path Employees .json -Raw` to read the file and return a string. But there's not much you can do with a string. You need structure. To get that, you need something that understands the JSON schema (the way individual nodes and arrays of nodes are represented in JSON) and can parse the file accordingly. You need the `ConvertFrom-Json` cmdlet.

The `ConvertFrom-Json` cmdlet is a native cmdlet in PowerShell that takes raw JSON as input and converts it into PowerShell objects. You can see in Listing 10-13 that PowerShell knows `Employees` is a property now.

```
PS> Get-Content -Path .\Employees.json -Raw | ConvertFrom-Json

Employees
---------
{@{FirstName=Adam; LastName=Bertram; Department=IT;
Title=Awesome IT Professional}, @{FirstName=Bob;
LastName=Smith; Department=HR; Title=Crotchety H...
```

Listing 10-13: Converting JSON to objects

If you take a look at the `Employees` property, you'll see that all the employee nodes have been parsed out, with each key representing a column header, and each value representing the row value:

```
PS> (Get-Content -Path .\Employees.json -Raw | ConvertFrom-Json).Employees

FirstName LastName Department Title
--------- -------- ---------- -----
Adam      Bertram  IT         Awesome IT Professional
Bob       Smith    HR         Crotchety HR guy
```

The `Employees` property is now an array of objects that you can query and manipulate just as you would any other array.

Creating JSON Strings

Let's say you have a whole bunch of data from a whole bunch of sources and you want to convert it all to JSON. What do you do? This is the magic of the `ConvertTo-Json` cmdlet: it can convert any object in PowerShell to JSON.

As an example, let's convert the CSV file you built earlier in the chapter into *Employees.json*. First, you need to import our CSV:

```
PS> Import-Csv -Path .\Employees.csv -Delimiter "`t"

First Name Last Name Department       Manager
---------- --------- ----------       -------
Adam       Bertram   IT               Miranda Bertram
Barack     Obama     Executive Office Michelle Obama
Miranda    Bertram   Executive Office
Michelle   Obama     Executive Office
```

To do the conversion, you need to pipe the output to ConvertTo-Json, as in Listing 10-14.

```
PS> Import-Csv -Path .\Employees.csv -Delimiter "`t" | ConvertTo-Json
[
    {
        "First Name":  "Adam",
        "Last Name":  "Bertram",
        "Department":  "IT",
        "Manager":  "Miranda Bertram"
    },
    {
        "First Name":  "Barack",
        "Last Name":  "Obama",
        "Department":  "Executive Office",
        "Manager":  "Michelle Obama"
    },
    {
        "First Name":  "Miranda",
        "Last Name":  "Bertram",
        "Department":  "Executive Office",
        "Manager":  null
    },
    {
        "First Name":  "Michelle",
        "Last Name":  "Obama",
        "Department":  "Executive Office",
        "Manager":  null
    }
]
```

Listing 10-14: Converting objects to JSON

As you might expect by now, there are a couple parameters you can pass in to modify the conversion. A nice one is the Compress parameter, which minifies the output by removing all the potentially unwanted line breaks:

```
PS> Import-Csv -Path .\Employees.csv -Delimiter "`t" | ConvertTo-Json -Compress
[{"First Name":"Adam","Last
Name":"Bertram","Department":"IT","Manager":"Miranda
Bertram"},{"First Name":"Barack","Last
Name":"Obama","Department":"Executive
Office","Manager":"Michelle Obama"},{"First
Name":"Miranda","Last Name":"Bertram","Department":"Executive
Office","Manager":null},{"First Name":"Michelle",
"Last Name":"Obama","Department":"Executive
Office","Manager":null}]
```

If it has a property and a property value, ConvertTo-Json can do its job. The property will always be the node key, and the property value will always be the node value.

Project 3: Querying and Parsing a REST API

Now that you know how to parse JSON, let's do something a little fancier: let's use PowerShell to query a REST API and parse the results. You could use just about any REST API, but some require authentication, and it'll be easier to do this without the extra steps. Let's use one that doesn't require authentication. I've found a REST API at *postcodes.io*, a service that allows you to query UK postal codes from various criteria.

The URI you'll use is *http://api.postcodes.io/random/postcodes*. When you access this URI, it will query the *postcodes.io* API service and return a random postcode in JSON form. To query this URI, you'll use PowerShell's `Invoke-WebRequest` cmdlet:

```
PS> $result = Invoke-WebRequest -Uri 'http://api.postcodes.io/random/postcodes'
PS> $result.Content
{"status":200,"result":{"postcode":"IP12
2FE","quality":1,"eastings":641878,"northings":250383,"country
:"England","nhs_ha":"East of England","longitude":
1.53013518866685,"latitude":52.0988661618569,"european_elector
al_region":"Eastern","primary_care_trust":"Suffolk","region":"
East of England","lsoa":"Suffo
lk Coastal 007C","msoa":"Suffolk Coastal
007","incode":"2FE","outcode":"IP12","parliamentary_constituen
cy":"Suffolk Coastal","admin_district":"Suffolk Coa
stal","parish":"Orford","admin_county":"Suffolk","admin_ward":
"Orford & Eyke","ccg":"NHS Ipswich and East
Suffolk","nuts":"Suffolk","codes":{"admin_distri
ct":"E07000205","admin_county":"E10000029","admin_ward":"E0501
449","parish":"E04009440","parliamentary_constituency":"E14000
81","ccg":"E38000086","nuts"
:"UKH14"}}}
```

Now, let's see if you can convert the result into a PowerShell object:

```
PS> $result = Invoke-WebRequest -Uri 'http://api.postcodes.io/random/postcodes'
PS> $result.Content | ConvertFrom-Json

status result
------ ------
   200 @{postcode=DE7 9HY; quality=1; eastings=445564;
       northings=343166; country=England; nhs_ha=East Midlands;
       longitude=-1.32277519314161; latitude=...

PS> $result = Invoke-WebRequest -Uri 'http://api.postcodes.io/random/postcodes'
PS> $contentObject = $result.Content | ConvertFrom-Json
PS> $contentObject.result

postcode                   : HA7 2SR
quality                    : 1
eastings                   : 516924
northings                  : 191681
country                    : England
nhs_ha                     : London
```

```
longitude                  : -0.312779792807334
latitude                   : 51.6118279308721
european_electoral_region  : London
primary_care_trust         : Harrow
region                     : London
lsoa                       : Harrow 003C
msoa                       : Harrow 003
incode                     : 2SR
outcode                    : HA7
parliamentary_constituency : Harrow East
admin_district             : Harrow
parish                     : Harrow, unparished area
admin_county               :
admin_ward                 : Stanmore Park
ccg                        : NHS Harrow
nuts                       : Harrow and Hillingdon
codes                      : @{admin_district=E09000015;
                             admin_county=E99999999; admin_ward=E05000303;
                             parish=E43000205;
```

You can convert the response to JSON without a problem. But you have to use two commands, `Invoke-WebRequest` and `ConvertFrom-Json`. Wouldn't life be great if you could use only one? It turns out that PowerShell has a command that will do everything for you: `Invoke-RestMethod`.

The `Invoke-RestMethod` cmdlet is similar to `Invoke-WebRequest`; it sends various HTTP verbs to web services and returns the response. Because the *postcodes.io* API service does not require any authentication, you can simply use the `Uri` parameter on `Invoke-RestMethod` to get the API response:

```
PS> Invoke-RestMethod -Uri 'http://api.postcodes.io/random/postcodes'

status result
------ ------
   200 @{postcode=NE23 6AA; quality=1; eastings=426492;
       northings=576264; country=England; nhs_ha=North East;
       longitude=-1.5865793029774; latitude=55...
```

You can see that `Invoke-RestMethod` returns an HTTP status code and the response from the API in the `result` property. So where's the JSON? Well, just as you wanted, it's already been converted to an object for you. There's no need to manually convert the JSON to an object, as you can use the `result` property:

```
PS> (Invoke-RestMethod -Uri 'http://api.postcodes.io/random/postcodes').result

postcode                   : SY11 4BL
quality                    : 1
eastings                   : 332201
northings                  : 331090
country                    : England
nhs_ha                     : West Midlands
longitude                  : -3.00873643515338
```

```
latitude                    : 52.8729967314029
european_electoral_region   : West Midlands
primary_care_trust          : Shropshire County
region                      : West Midlands
lsoa                        : Shropshire 011E
msoa                        : Shropshire 011
incode                      : 4BL
outcode                     : SY11
parliamentary_constituency  : North Shropshire
admin_district              : Shropshire
parish                      : Whittington
admin_county                :
admin_ward                  : Whittington
ccg                         : NHS Shropshire
nuts                        : Shropshire CC
codes                       : @{admin_district=E06000051;
                              admin_county=E99999999; admin_ward=E05009287;
                              parish=E04012256;
```

Working with JSON in PowerShell is a straightforward process. With PowerShell's easy-to-use cmdlets, you're usually spared any complicated string parsing—simply pass in JSON, or a soon-to-be-JSONified object, into the pipeline and watch the magic happen!

Summary

This chapter covered a few ways to structure data, as well as how to work with those structures in PowerShell. PowerShell's native cmdlets make this process a breeze, abstracting away a lot of complicated code and leaving the user with easy-to-use commands. But don't let its simplicity fool you: PowerShell can parse and manipulate nearly any kind of data. Even if it doesn't have a native command to handle the data type, because of its .NET foundation, it's able to dig into any .NET classes for any advanced concepts.

In the next chapter, we'll work with Microsoft's Active Directory (AD). Full of repetitive tasks, AD is a common place to start when learning to use PowerShell; we'll spend a lot of time on this great resource throughout the rest of this book.

11

AUTOMATING ACTIVE DIRECTORY

One of the best products to automate with PowerShell is Microsoft's Active Directory (AD). Employees are constantly entering, leaving, and moving around an organization. A dynamic system is needed to keep track of the ever-shifting flux of employees, and that's where AD comes in. IT pros perform repetitive and similar tasks in AD, making it a perfect site for automation.

In this chapter, we'll walk through using PowerShell to automate a few scenarios involving AD. Although numerous AD objects can be manipulated with PowerShell, we'll cover only three of the most common: user accounts, computer accounts, and groups. These types of objects are the ones an AD administrator will most likely encounter on a day-to-day basis.

Prerequisites

As you follow along with the examples in this chapter, I make a few assumptions about your computer environment.

The first is that you're working on a Windows computer that's already a member of an Active Directory domain. There are ways to work with AD from a workgroup computer using alternate credentials, but that's beyond the scope of this chapter.

The second is that you'll be working with the same domain that your computer is a member of. Complicated cross-domain and forest trust issues are also beyond the scope of this chapter.

The last is that you are logged into your computer with an AD account that has appropriate permissions to read, modify, and create common AD objects such as users, computers, groups, and organizational units. I am doing these exercises from a computer with an account that is part of the Domain Admins group—meaning I have control over everything in my domain. Although this is not completely necessary, and generally not recommended in a production environment, this allows me to demonstrate various topics without being concerned with object rights, which are beyond the scope of this book.

Installing the ActiveDirectory PowerShell Module

As you know by now, there's more than one way to accomplish a task with PowerShell. Likewise, there's not much use in reinventing the wheel when you can use the preexisting tools to make bigger and better ones. In this chapter, you'll use only a single module: `ActiveDirectory`. Although it's not without its shortcomings—obscure parameters, odd filtering syntax, strange error behavior—it's by far the most comprehensive module for managing AD.

The `ActiveDirectory` module comes with the *Remote Server Administration Tools* software package. This is a software bundle of many tools and, unfortunately, at the time of this writing, the only way to get a copy of the `ActiveDirectory` module. Before you continue with this chapter, I encourage you to download and install this package. Once you do, you'll have the `ActiveDirectory` module installed.

To confirm you have `ActiveDirectory` installed, you can use the `Get-Module` command:

```
PS> Get-Module -Name ActiveDirectory -List
Directory: C:\WINDOWS\system32\WindowsPowerShell\v1.0\Modules

ModuleType Version  Name            ExportedCommands
---------- -------  ----            ----------------
Manifest   1.0.0.0  ActiveDirectory {Add-ADCentralAccessPolicyMember,...
```

If you see this output, `ActiveDirectory` is installed.

Querying and Filtering AD Objects

Once you've ensured that you've met all of the prerequisites and have the ActiveDirectory module installed, you're ready to get started.

One of the best ways to get acclimated to a new PowerShell module is to look for all its Get verb commands. Commands that begin with *Get* only read information, so the risk that you'll change something by accident is minimal. Let's take this approach with the ActiveDirectory module and look for commands associated with the objects we'll be working with in this chapter. Listing 11-1 shows how to retrieve only the ActiveDirectory commands that begin with *Get* and have the word *computer* somewhere in the verb portion.

```
PS> Get-Command -Module ActiveDirectory -Verb Get -Noun *computer*

CommandType     Name                               Version    Source
-----------     ----                               -------    ------
Cmdlet          Get-ADComputer                     1.0.0.0    ActiveDirectory
Cmdlet          Get-ADComputerServiceAccount       1.0.0.0    ActiveDirectory

PS> Get-Command -Module ActiveDirectory -Verb Get -Noun *user*

CommandType     Name                               Version    Source
-----------     ----                               -------    ------
Cmdlet          Get-ADUser                         1.0.0.0    ActiveDirectory
Cmdlet          Get-ADUserResultantPasswordPolicy  1.0.0.0    ActiveDirectory

PS> Get-Command -Module ActiveDirectory -Verb Get -Noun *group*

CommandType     Name                               Version    Source
-----------     ----                               -------    ------
Cmdlet          Get-ADAccountAuthorizationGroup    1.0.0.0    ActiveDirectory
Cmdlet          Get-ADGroup                        1.0.0.0    ActiveDirectory
Cmdlet          Get-ADGroupMember                  1.0.0.0    ActiveDirectory
Cmdlet          Get-ADPrincipalGroupMembership     1.0.0.0    ActiveDirectory
```

Listing 11-1: ActiveDirectory module Get commands

You can see a few commands that look interesting. In this chapter, you'll be using Get-ADComputer, Get-ADUser, Get-ADGroupm, and Get-ADGroupMember.

Filtering Objects

Many of the Get AD commands you'll be using have a common parameter called Filter. Filter is similar to the PowerShell Where-Object command as it filters what each command returns, but is different in the way it accomplishes this task.

The Filter parameter uses its own syntax and can be difficult to understand, especially when you're using complex filters. For a full breakdown of the Filter parameter's syntax, you can run Get-Help about_ActiveDirectory_Filter.

For this chapter, we'll keep it simple and avoid any advanced filtering. First, let's use the `Filter` parameter and the `Get-ADUser` command to return all users in the domain, as shown in Listing 11-2. Be careful, though: if you have a lot of user accounts in your domain, you could be waiting a while.

```
PS> Get-ADUser -Filter *


DistinguishedName : CN=adam,CN=Users,DC=lab,DC=local
Enabled           : True
GivenName         :
Name              : adam
ObjectClass       : user
ObjectGUID        : 5e53c562-4fd8-4620-950b-aad8fbaa84db
SamAccountName    : adam
SID               : S-1-5-21-930245869-402111599-3553179568-500
Surname           :
UserPrincipalName :
--snip--
```

Listing 11-2: Finding all user accounts in a domain

As you can see, the `Filter` parameter accepts a string value wildcard character, `*`. On its own, this character tells (most) `Get` commands to return everything they find. Although this can be occasionally useful, most of the time you don't want *all* possible objects. However, used correctly, the wildcard character is a powerful tool.

Let's say you want to find all computer accounts in AD that start with the letter *C*. You can do so by running `Get-ADComputer -Filter 'Name -like "C*"'`, where `C*` represents all characters after a *C*. You could also do it in reverse; say you want to find anyone with a last name that ends in *son*. You could run the command `Get-ADComputer -Filter 'Name -like "*son"'`.

If you want to find all users that have a last name of *Jones*, you could run `Get-ADUser -Filter "surName -eq 'Jones'"`; if you want a single user using the first and last name, you could run `Get-ADUser -Filter "surName -eq 'Jones' -and givenName -eq 'Joe'`. The `Filter` parameter allows you to use various PowerShell operators such as `like` and `eq` to build a filter that returns only the results you're looking for. Active Directory attributes are stored in the AD database using lower camel case, so that's what I've used in the filters, although this isn't technically necessary.

Another command useful for filtering AD objects is the `Search-ADAccount` command. This command has built-in support for common filtering scenarios such as finding all users with an expired password, finding locked-out users, and finding computers that are enabled. Check out the help for the `Search-ADAccount` cmdlet to see the full range of parameters.

Most of the time, the `Search-ADAccount` syntax is self-explanatory. Various switch parameters, including `PasswordNeverExpires`, `AccountDisabled`, and `AccountExpired`, do not require other parameters to function.

Besides these fancy parameters, Search-ADAccount also has various parameters that require additional input—for example, to indicate how old a datetime attribute is or if you need to limit the results by a particular object type (for example, Users or Computers).

Let's use the AccountInactive parameter as an example. Say you want to find all users who haven't used their account in 90 days. This is a great query for Search-ADAccount. By using the syntax in Listing 11-3, using -UsersOnly to filter the type of object and -TimeSpan to filter for objects that have not been active in the last 90 days, you can quickly find all the requested users.

```
PS> Search-ADAccount -AccountInactive -TimeSpan 90.00:00:00 -UsersOnly
```

Listing 11-3: Using Search-ADAccount

The Search-ADAccount cmdlet returns an object type of Microsoft.ActiveDirectory.Management.ADUser. This is the same object type that commands such as Get-ADUser and Get-ADComputer return. Search-ADAccount can be a good shortcut when you're using a Get command and feel stuck trying to figure out what syntax to use for the Filter parameter.

Returning Single Objects

Sometimes you know the exact AD object you're looking for, so there's no need to use Filter at all. Here, you can use the Identity parameter.

Identity is a flexible parameter that allows you to specify attributes that make an AD object unique; thus it returns only a single object. Every user account has a unique attribute called samAccountName. You could use the Filter parameter to find all users with a specific samAccountName, which would look like this:

```
Get-ADUser -Filter "samAccountName -eq 'jjones'"
```

But it's much cleaner to use the Identity parameter instead:

```
Get-ADUser -Identity jjones
```

Project 4: Finding User Accounts That Haven't Changed Their Password in 30 Days

Now that you have a basic understanding of how to query AD objects, let's create a small script and put that knowledge to use. Here's the scenario: you work at a company that's about to implement a new password-expiration policy and your job is to find all the accounts that haven't changed their password in the past 30 days.

First, let's think about what command to use. Your first choice might be the Search-ADAccount command you learned earlier in this chapter. Search-ADAccount has many uses for searching and filtering on various objects, but you can't craft custom filters. To get more granular in your searching, you'll have to build your own filters by using the `Get-ADUser` command.

Once you know what command you're going to use, the next step is to figure out what you want to filter for. You know you want to filter for accounts that haven't changed their password in the past 30 days, but if you look only for that, you'll find more accounts than you need. Why? If you don't filter for accounts that are `Enabled`, you'll probably get old accounts that don't matter anymore (maybe someone who left the company or lost computer privileges). So you look for enabled computers that haven't changed their password in the past 30 days.

Let's start with filtering enabled user accounts. You can do this by using `-Filter "Enabled -eq 'True'"`. Simple enough. The next step is to figure out how to access the attribute that is stored when a user's password is set.

By default, `Get-ADUser` doesn't return all of a user's properties. Using the `Properties` parameter, you can specify which properties you'd like to see; here, you'll use `name` and `passwordlastset`. Notice that some users don't have a `passwordlastset` property. This is because they've never set their own password.

```
PS> Get-AdUser -Filter * -Properties passwordlastset  | select name,passwordlastset

name           passwordlastset
----           ---------------
adam           2/22/2019 6:45:40 AM
Guest
DefaultAccount
krbtgt         2/22/2019 3:03:32 PM
Non-Priv User  2/22/2019 3:12:38 PM
abertram
abertram2
fbar
--snip--
```

Now that you have the attribute name, you need to build a filter for it. Remember that you want only accounts whose passwords changed in the past 30 days. To find a date difference, you need two dates: the oldest possible date (30 days ago) and the newest possible date (today). You can get today's date easily by using the `Get-Date` command. And you can use the `AddDays` method to figure out what the date was 30 days ago. You'll store both in variables for easy access later.

```
PS> $today = Get-Date
PS> $30DaysAgo = $today.AddDays(-30)
```

Now that you have the dates, you can use them in the filter:

```
PS> Get-ADUser -Filter "passwordlastset -lt '$30DaysAgo'"
```

All that's left to do is to add your Enabled condition to the filter. Listing 11-4 shows the steps to do this.

```
$today = Get-Date
$30DaysAgo = $today.AddDays(-30)
Get-ADUser -Filter "Enabled -eq 'True' -and passwordlastset -lt
'$30DaysAgo'"
```

Listing 11-4: Finding enabled user accounts that haven't changed their password in 30 days

You now have some code built up to find all enabled Active Directory users that have set their password in the last 30 days.

Creating and Changing AD Objects

Now that you know how to find existing AD objects, let's learn how to change and create them. This section is divided into two parts: one dealing with users and computers, and one dealing with groups.

Users and Computers

To change users and computer accounts, you'll use a Set command: either Set-ADUser or Set-ADComputer. These commands can change any attribute of an object. Usually, you'll want to pipe in an object you get from a Get command (like those covered in the previous lesson).

As an example, say that an employee named Jane Jones got married, and you're asked to change the last name of her user account. If you didn't know an identity attribute for this user account, you could use the Filter parameter on Get-ADUser to find it. But first, you'd need to discover how AD stores each user's first and last name. You can then use the values of those attributes to pass to the Filter parameter.

One way to find all available attributes stored in AD is with a little .NET. Using a schema object, you can find the user class and enumerate all of its attributes:

```
$schema =[DirectoryServices.ActiveDirectory.ActiveDirectorySchema]::GetCurrentSchema()
$userClass = $schema.FindClass('user')
$userClass.GetAllProperties().Name
```

By reviewing the available attribute list, you then find the givenName and surName attribute to use in the Filter parameter with the Get-ADUser command, finding the user account. Next, you can pass that object to Set-ADUser, as shown in Listing 11-5.

```
PS> Get-ADUser -Filter "givenName -eq 'Jane' -and surName -eq
'Jones'" | Set-ADUser -Surname 'Smith'
PS> Get-ADUser -Filter "givenName -eq 'Jane' -and surName -eq
'Smith'"

DistinguishedName : CN=jjones,CN=Users,DC=lab,DC=local
Enabled           : False
GivenName         : Jane
Name              : jjones
ObjectClass       : user
ObjectGUID        : fbddbd77-ac35-4664-899c-0683c6ce8457
SamAccountName    : jjones
SID               : S-1-5-21-930245869-402111599-3553179568-3103
Surname           : Smith
UserPrincipalName :
```

Listing 11-5: Changing AD object attributes with `Set-ADUser`

You can also change multiple attributes at once. It turns out Jane also moved departments and got a promotion, both of which need to be updated. Not a problem. You just need to use the parameters that match up to the AD attributes:

```
PS> Get-ADUser -Filter "givenName -eq 'Jane' -and surname -eq
'Smith'" | Set-ADUser -Department 'HR' -Title Director
PS> Get-ADUser -Filter "givenName -eq 'Jane' -and surname -eq
'Smith'" -Properties GivenName,SurName,Department,Title

Department        : HR
DistinguishedName : CN=jjones,CN=Users,DC=lab,DC=local
Enabled           : False
GivenName         : Jane
Name              : jjones
ObjectClass       : user
ObjectGUID        : fbddbd77-ac35-4664-899c-0683c6ce8457
SamAccountName    : jjones
SID               : S-1-5-21-930245869-402111599-3553179568-3103
Surname           : Smith
Title             : Director
UserPrincipalName :
```

Finally, you can create AD objects by using `New-AD*` commands. Creating new AD objects is similar to changing existing objects, but here you don't have access to an `Identity` parameter. Creating a new AD computer account is as easy as running `New-ADComputer -Name FOO`; likewise, an AD user can be created by using `New-ADUser -Name adam`. You'll see that the `New-AD*` commands also have parameters that correlate to AD attributes, just like the `Set-AD*` commands do.

Groups

Groups are trickier than users and computers. One way to think about groups is as a container for many AD objects. In that sense, a group is a bunch of things. But at the same time, it's still a *single* container, meaning that just like users and computers, a group is a singular AD object. That means you can query, create, and change groups the same way you would users and computers, with a few slight differences.

Maybe your organization created a new department called AdamBertram Lovers, and it's bursting at the seams with new employees. Now you need to create a group with this name. Listing 11-6 shows an example of how to create such a group. You use the `Description` parameter to pass in a string (the group's description), and the `GroupScope` parameter to ensure that the group created has a scope of `DomainLocal`. You could have chosen `Global` or `Universal` here as well if that's what you required.

```
PS> New-ADGroup -Name 'AdamBertramLovers'
-Description 'All Adam Bertram lovers in the company'
-GroupScope DomainLocal
```

Listing 11-6: Creating an AD group

Once the group exists, you can modify it just as you would a user or computer. To change the description, for example, you could do this:

```
PS> Get-ADGroup -Identity AdamBertramLovers |
Set-ADGroup -Description 'More Adam Bertram lovers'
```

Of course, the key difference between groups and users/computers is that a group can contain users and computers. When a computer or user account is contained within a group, we say that is a *member* of that group. But to add and change members of a group, you can't use the commands you've been using. Instead, you need to use `Add-ADGroupMember` and `Remove-ADGroupMember`.

For example, to add Jane to our group, you can do so using `Add-ADGroupMember`. If Jane wants to leave the group, you can remove her by using `Remove-ADGroupMember`. As you try this, you'll find that running the `Remove-ADGroupMember` command will lead to a prompt asking you to confirm your decision to remove the member:

```
PS> Get-ADGroup -Identity AdamBertramLovers | Add-ADGroupMember Members 'jjones'
PS> Get-ADGroup -Identity AdamBertramLovers | Remove-ADGroupMember-Members 'jjones'

    Confirm
Are you sure you want to perform this action?
Performing the operation "Set" on target
"CN=AdamBertramLovers,CN=Users,DC=lab,DC=local".
[Y] Yes  [A] Yes to All  [N] No  [L] No to All  [S] Suspend
[?]
Help (default is "Y"): a
```

Add the Force parameter if you want to skip this check, but be aware that getting that confirmation may end up saving you one day!

Project 5: Creating an Employee Provisioning Script

Let's bring this all together and tackle another real-world scenario. Your company has hired a new employee. You, the system administrator, now have to perform a series of actions: creating an AD user, creating their computer account, and adding them to specific groups. You'll build a script that will automate this whole process.

But before you start this project—and really, any project—it's important to figure out what the script will do and write down an informal definition. For this script, you need to create the AD user, which will:

- Dynamically create a username for user based on the first name and last name
- Create and assign the user a random password
- Force the user to change their password at logon
- Set the department attribute based on the department given
- Assign the user an internal employee number

Next, add the user account to a group with the same name as the department. Finally, add the user account into an organizational unit with the same name as the department the employee is in.

Now, with these requirements laid out, let's build the script. The finished script will be called *New-Employee.ps1* and is available in the book's resources.

You want this to be a reusable script. Ideally, anytime you have a new employee, you can use the script. This means you need to figure out a smart way to handle the inputs to the script. By looking at the requirements, you know you'll need a first name, a last name, a department, and an employee number. Listing 11-7 provides a script outline with all parameters defined and a try/catch block to catch any terminating errors you may encounter. The #requires statement is set at the top to ensure that whenever this script is run, it checks to see that the machine has the ActiveDirectory module installed.

```
#requires -Module ActiveDirectory

[CmdletBinding()]
param (
    [Parameter(Mandatory)]
    [string]$FirstName,

    [Parameter(Mandatory)]
    [string]$LastName,

    [Parameter(Mandatory)]
    [string]$Department,
```

```
    [Parameter(Mandatory)]
    [int]$EmployeeNumber
)

try {

} catch {
    Write-Error -Message $_.Exception.Message
}
```

Listing 11-7: Base New-Employee.ps1 *script*

Now that you created the base, let's fill out the try block.

First, you need to create an AD user according to the requirements laid out in our informal definition. You have to *dynamically create* a username. There are several ways to do this: some organizations prefer the username to be the first initial and the last name, some prefer first name and last name, and some do something else entirely. Let's say your company uses first initial and last name. If that username is taken, the next character in the first name is added until a unique username is found.

Let's handle the base case first. You'll use the built-in `Substring` method on every string object to get the first initial. You'll then concatenate the last name to the first initial. You'll do this by using *string formatting*, which allows you to define placeholders for multiple expressions in a string and replace the placeholders with values at runtime, like so:

```
$userName = '{0}{1}' -f $FirstName.Substring(0, 1), $LastName
```

After you create the initial username, you need to query AD to see whether this username is already taken by using `Get-ADUser`.

```
Get-ADUser -Filter "samAccountName -eq '$userName'"
```

If this command returns anything, the username is taken, and you need to try the next username. This means you need to figure out a way to dynamically generate new names, always being prepared for the possibility that the new username is taken. A good way to check for various usernames is a `while` loop conditioned on your previous call to `Get-ADUser`. But you'll need another condition to account for what happens if you run out of letters in the first name. You don't want the loop to run forever, so you'll put in another condition, `$userName -notlike "$FirstName*"`, to stop the loop.

The `while` condition looks like this:

```
(Get-ADUser -Filter "samAccountName -eq '$userName'") -and
($userName -notlike "$FirstName*")
```

With the while condition created, you can fill out the rest of the loop:

```
$i = 2
while ((Get-ADUser -Filter "samAccountName -eq '$userName'") -and
($userName -notlike "$FirstName*")) {
    Write-Warning -Message "The username [$($userName)] already exists. Trying another..."
    $userName = '{0}{1}' -f $FirstName.Substring(0, $i), $LastName
    Start-Sleep -Seconds 1
    $i++
}
```

For each iteration of the loop, you add an additional character from the first name to the proposed username by taking the substring of the first name from 0 to i, where `$i` is a counter variable that starts at 2 (the next position in the string) and is increased each time the loop runs. By the time this `while` loop finishes, it will have either found a unique username or exhausted all options.

If an existing username *isn't* found, you're clear to create the username you intended to. If a username *is* found, you have a few other things to check. You need to check whether the *organizational unit (OU)* and group you're putting the user account into exists:

```
if (-not ($ou = Get-ADOrganizationalUnit -Filter "Name -eq '$Department'")) {
    throw "The Active Directory OU for department [$($Department)] could not be found."
} elseif (-not (Get-ADGroup -Filter "Name -eq '$Department'")) {
    throw "The group [$($Department)] does not exist."
}
```

Once you complete all the checks, you need to create the user account. Again, you have to consult our informal definition: *create and assign the user a random password.* You want to generate a random password every time this script runs. An easy way to generate a secure password is to use the `GeneratePassword` static method on the `System.Web.Security.Membership` object, as shown here:

```
Add-Type -AssemblyName 'System.Web'
$password = [System.Web.Security.Membership]::GeneratePassword(
    (Get-Random Minimum 20 -Maximum 32), 3)
$secPw = ConvertTo-SecureString -String $password -AsPlainText -Force
```

I chose to generate a password of at least 20 characters, with a maximum of 32, but this is completely configurable. If desired, you could also find AD's minimum required password by running `Get-ADDefaultDomainPasswordPolicy | Select-object -expand minPasswordLength`. This method even allows you to specify the length and complexity of the new password.

Now that you have the password as a secure string, you have all the parameter values needed to create the user according to the requirements I laid out earlier.

```
$newUserParams = @{
    GivenName             = $FirstName
    EmployeeNumber        = $EmployeeNumber
    Surname               = $LastName
    Name                  = $userName
    AccountPassword       = $secPw
    ChangePasswordAtLogon = $true
    Enabled               = $true
    Department            = $Department
    Path                  = $ou.DistinguishedName
    Confirm               = $false
}
New-ADUser @newUserParams
```

After you make the user, all that's left is to add them to the department group, which you can do with a simple `Add-ADGroupMember` command:

```
Add-ADGroupMember -Identity $Department -Members $userName
```

Be sure to check out the *New-Employee.ps1* script in the book's resources to get a copy of the full implementation of this script.

Syncing from Other Data Sources

Active Directory, especially when used in large enterprises, can contain millions of objects being created and modified by dozens of people every day. With all that activity and all those inputs, problems are bound to arise. One of the biggest you'll run into is keeping the AD database synced up with the rest of the organization.

A company's AD should be organized the same way the company is organized. This might mean that every department has its own associated AD group, every physical office its own OU, and so on. Regardless, as system administrators, we have the difficult task of ensuring that AD is always in sync with the rest of the organization. This is a great task for PowerShell.

Using PowerShell, you can "link" AD with just about any other source of information, meaning you can have PowerShell continually reading external data sources and making the appropriate changes to AD as necessary to create a sync process.

This syncing process, when triggered, roughly consists of the following six steps:

1. Query the external data source (SQL database, CSV file, and so forth).
2. Retrieve objects from AD.
3. Find each object in the source that AD has a unique attribute to match on. This is usually referred to as an *ID*. The ID can be an employee ID or even usernames. The only thing that matters is that the attribute is unique. If no match is found, optionally create or remove the object from AD based on the source.

4. Find a single matching object.
5. Map all external data sources to AD object attributes.
6. Modify existing AD objects or create new ones.

You'll put this plan into action in the next section.

Project 6: Creating a Syncing Script

In this section, you'll learn how to build a script that'll sync employees from a CSV file to AD. To do so, you'll have to draw on some of the commands you learned in Chapter 10, as well as those you just learned in the previous lessons of this chapter. Before we get started, I encourage you to glance at *Employees.csv* and *Invoke-AdCsvSync.ps1* in the book's resources and familiarize yourself with the project files.

The key to building a great AD sync tool is sameness. By this, I don't mean the data sources should be the same—since, technically, they never will be—but instead that you need to create a script that can query each datastore the same way and have each datastore return the same kind of object. The tricky part of this occurs when you have two sources that use different schemas. In that case, you may have to start doing some translation by mapping one field name to another (as you'll do later in the chapter).

Consider this: you already know that AD has common attributes associated with each user account—things like first name, last name, and department, which we'll call a *schema* of attributes. However, chances are the source datastore you'd like to sync with will never have the exact same attributes. And even if it has the same attributes, it might know them by different names. To resolve this issue, you have to build a mapping between the two datastores.

Mapping Data Source Attributes

An easy, effective way to create this mapping is to use a hashtable in which the key is the attribute name in the first datastore, and the value is the attribute name in the second datastore. To see this in action, let's say you work at a company called Acme. Acme wants to sync employee records from a CSV file into AD. Specifically, they want to sync *Employees.csv,* which you can find in the book's resources or here:

```
"fname","lname","dept"
"Adam","Bertram","IT"
"Barack","Obama","Executive Office"
"Miranda","Bertram","Executive Office"
"Michelle","Obama","Executive Office"
```

Given that you know the headers of the CSV, and the property names in AD, you can build a mapping hashtable with the value for the CSV field as the key and the AD attribute name as the value:

```
$syncFieldMap = @{
    fname = 'GivenName'
    lname = 'Surname'
    dept = 'Department'
}
```

This will handle the conversion between the two datastore schemas. But you also need a unique ID for each employee. As of right now, there is no unique ID to match to an AD object in each row of the CSV. You could have more than one Adam, more than one person in the IT department, or more than one person with the last name of Bertram, for example. This means you'll have to generate your own unique ID. To make things easier, assume that no two employees have the same first and last name. Otherwise, the ID to create will probably be dependent on your own organizational schema. With that assumption, you can simply concatenate each datastore's respective first- and last-name fields to create a temporary unique ID.

You'll represent this unique ID in another hashtable. You haven't handled the concatenation just yet, but you've set up the infrastructure to do so:

```
$fieldMatchIds = @{
    AD = @('givenName','surName')
    CSV = @('fname','lname')
}
```

Now that you created a way to map different fields together, you can incorporate that code into a couple of functions to "force" two datastores to return the same properties, allowing an apples-to-apples comparison.

Creating Functions to Return Similar Properties

Now that you have the hashtables, you need to translate field names and build unique IDs. You can create a function that'll query our CSV file and output both attributes that AD understands, and a property you can use to match both datastores. To do that, you'll create a function called `Get-AcmeEmployeeFromCsv` that looks like Listing 11-8. I've assigned the `CsvFilePath` parameter's value to *C:\Employees.csv*, assuming that our CSV is located there:

```
function Get-AcmeEmployeeFromCsv
{
[CmdletBinding()]
    param (
        [Parameter()]
        [string]$CsvFilePath = 'C:\Employees.csv',

        [Parameter(Mandatory)]
        [hashtable]$SyncFieldMap,
```

```
        [Parameter(Mandatory)]
        [hashtable]$FieldMatchIds
    )
    try {
        ## Read each key/value pair in $SyncFieldMap to create calculated
        ## fields which we can pass to Select-Object later. This allows us to
        ## return property names that match Active Directory attributes rather
        ## than what's in the CSV file.
      ❶ $properties = $SyncFieldMap.GetEnumerator() | ForEach-Object {
            @{
                Name = $_.Value
                Expression = [scriptblock]::Create("`$_.$($_.Key)")
            }
        }
        ## Create the unique ID based on the unique fields defined in
        ## $FieldMatchIds
      ❷ $uniqueIdProperty = '"{0}{1}" -f '
        $uniqueIdProperty = $uniqueIdProperty +=
        ($FieldMatchIds.CSV | ForEach-Object { '$_.{0}' -f $_ }) - join ','
        $properties += @{
            Name = 'UniqueID'
            Expression = [scriptblock]::Create($uniqueIdProperty)
        }
        ## Read the CSV file and "transform" the CSV fields to AD attributes
        ## so we can compare apples to apples
      ❸ Import-Csv -Path $CsvFilePath | Select-Object - Property $properties
    } catch {
        Write-Error -Message $_.Exception.Message
    }
}
```

Listing 11-8: The `Get-AcmeEmployeeFromCsv` function

This function works in three broad steps: first, map the properties of the CSV to AD properties ❶; next, create a unique ID and make that a property ❷; last, read in the CSV and use `Select-Object` and a calculated property to return the properties you need ❸.

As you can see in the following code, you can pass the `$syncFieldMap` hashtable and the `$fieldMatchIds` hashtable to your new `Get-AcmeEmployeeFromCsv` function, which you can use to return property names that'll sync up with the Active Directory attributes as well as with your new unique ID:

```
PS> Get-AcmeEmployeeFromCsv -SyncFieldMap $syncFieldMap
-FieldMatchIds $fieldMatchIds

GivenName Department        Surname UniqueID
--------- ----------        ------- --------
Adam      IT                Bertram AdamBertram
Barack    Executive Office Obama   BarackObama
Miranda   Executive Office Bertram MirandaBertram
Michelle  Executive Office Obama   MichelleObama
```

Now you have to build a function that will query from AD. Thankfully, this time around you don't have to convert any property names because the AD property names are your common set. All you'll be doing in this function is calling `Get-ADUser`, and making sure you return the properties you need, as shown in Listing 11-9.

```
function Get-AcmeEmployeeFromAD
{
    [CmdletBinding()]
    param (
        [Parameter(Mandatory)]
        [hashtable]$SyncFieldMap,

        [Parameter(Mandatory)]
        [hashtable]$FieldMatchIds
    )

    try {
        $uniqueIdProperty = '"{0}{1}" -f '
        $uniqueIdProperty += ($FieldMatchIds.AD | ForEach Object { '$_.{0}' -f $_ }) -join ','

        $uniqueIdProperty = @{ ❶
            Name = 'UniqueID'
            Expression = [scriptblock]::Create($uniqueIdProperty)
        }

        Get-ADUser -Filter * -Properties @($SyncFieldMap.Values) | Select-Object *,$uniqueIdProperty ❷

    } catch {
        Write-Error -Message $_.Exception.Message
    }
}
```

Listing 11-9: The `Get-AcmeEmployeeFromAD` function

Again, I'll highlight the broad strokes of this code: first, create the unique ID to perform the matches on ❶; then, query the AD users and return only the values in the field map hashtable, also returning the unique ID that you created earlier ❷.

When you run this, you'll see that it returns the AD user accounts with the appropriate properties and your unique ID property.

Finding Matches in Active Directory

You now have two similar functions that pull information from your datastores and return the same property names. The next move is to find all the matches between our CSV and AD. To make this easier, you'll use the code in Listing 11-10 to create another function called `Find-UserMatch` that'll execute both of these functions and gather both sets of data. Once it has the data, it will look for a match on the `UniqueID` field.

```
function Find-UserMatch {
    [OutputType()]
    [CmdletBinding()]
    param
    (
        [Parameter(Mandatory)]
        [hashtable]$SyncFieldMap,

        [Parameter(Mandatory)]
        [hashtable]$FieldMatchIds
    )
    $adusers = Get-AcmeEmployeeFromAD -SyncFieldMap $SyncFieldMap -FieldMatchIds $FieldMatchIds ❶

    $csvUsers = Get-AcmeEmployeeFromCSV -SyncFieldMap $SyncFieldMap -FieldMatchIds $FieldMatchIds ❷

    $adUsers.foreach({
        $adUniqueId = $_.UniqueID
        if ($adUniqueId) { ❸
            $output = @{
                CSVProperties = 'NoMatch'
                ADSamAccountName = $_.samAccountName
            }
            if ($adUniqueId -in $csvUsers.UniqueId) { ❹
                $output.CSVProperties = ($csvUsers.Where({$_.UniqueId -eq $adUniqueId})) ❺
            }
            [pscustomobject]$output
        }
    })
}
```

Listing 11-10: Finding user matches

Let's walk through this code. First, get a list of users from AD ❶; then, get a list of users from our CSV ❷. For each user from AD, check whether the `UniqueID` property was populated ❸. If it was, check whether a match was found between the CSV and AD users ❹, and if so, in our custom object, create a property called `CSVProperties` that contains all the properties associated with the matched user ❺.

If a match is found, the function will return the AD user's `samAccountName` and all of its CSV properties; otherwise, it will return `NoMatch`. Returning the `samAccountName` gives you a unique ID in AD, which allows you to look up this user later.

```
PS> Find-UserMatch -SyncFieldMap $syncFieldMap -FieldMatchIds $fieldMatchIds

ADSamAccountName CSVProperties
---------------- -------------
user             NoMatch
abertram         {@{GivenName=Adam; Department=IT;
                 Surname=Bertram; UniqueID=AdamBertram}}
dbddar           NoMatch
jjones           NoMatch
BSmith           NoMatch
```

At this point, you have a function that allows you to find 1:1 matches between your AD data and your CSV data. You're now ready to begin the gratifying (yet scary) work of making bulk changes to AD!

Changing Active Directory Attributes

Now you have a way to find out which CSV row pertains to which AD user account. You can use the `Find-UserMatch` function to find the AD user by their unique ID, and then update its AD information to match the data in the CSV, as shown in Listing 11-11.

```
## Find all of the CSV <--> AD user account matches
$positiveMatches = (Find-UserMatch).where({ $_.CSVProperties -ne 'NoMatch' })
foreach ($positiveMatch in $positiveMatches) {
    ## Create the splatting parameters for Set-ADUser using
    ## the identity of the AD samAccountName
    $setADUserParams = @{
        Identity = $positiveMatch.ADSamAccountName
    }

    ## Read each property value that was in the CSV file
    $positiveMatch.CSVProperties.foreach({
        ## Add a parameter to Set-ADUser for all of the CSV
        ## properties excluding UniqueId
        ## Find all of the properties on the CSV row that are NOT UniqueId
        $_.PSObject.Properties.where({ $_.Name -ne 'UniqueID' }).foreach({
            $setADUserParams[$_.Name] = $_.Value
        })
    })
    Set-ADUser @setADUserParams
}
```

Listing 11-11: Syncing CSV to AD attributes

Quite a bit of work goes into creating a robust and flexible AD syncing script. Along the way, you'll encounter tons of little details and hiccups, especially when you're building even more complicated scripts.

We've only scratched the surface of syncing with PowerShell. If you want to see just how much you can do with this concept, check out the `PSADSync` module in the PowerShell Gallery (`Find-Module PSADSync`). This module was built specifically for the task we had here, but handles considerably more complex cases. If you felt a little lost during this exercise, I highly encourage you to go over the code again—as many times as it takes. The only true way to learn PowerShell is to experiment! Run the code, see it break, fix it yourself, and try again.

Summary

In this chapter, you familiarized yourself with the `ActiveDirectory` PowerShell module. You learned how to create and update users, computers, and groups in AD. Through a couple of real-world examples, you saw how to use PowerShell to automate tedious Active Directory work.

In the next two chapters, we're going to the cloud! We'll continue our journey of automating all the things and look at automating some common tasks done both in Microsoft Azure and in Amazon Web Services (AWS).

12

WORKING WITH AZURE

With organizations pushing more and more services to the cloud, it's important that automators understand how to work there. Luckily, thanks to PowerShell's modules, and its ability to work with just about any API, working in the cloud is a breeze. In this and the next chapter, I'll show you how to use PowerShell to automate tasks; in this chapter, you'll work with Microsoft Azure, and in the next, with Amazon Web Services.

Prerequisites

If you'll be running the code in this chapter, I make a few assumptions about your environment. The first is that you have a Microsoft Azure subscription set up. You'll be working with real cloud resources in this chapter, so you will receive charges to your account, but the fees should be reasonable. As long as you don't leave any of the virtual machines you're creating up for too long, the fees should be less than $10.

Once you have an Azure subscription set up, you'll need the `Az` PowerShell module bundle. This bundle of modules provided by Microsoft has hundreds of commands to perform tasks on nearly every Azure service available. You can download it by running **`Install-Module Az`** in your console (make sure to run as the administrator). I should note that I am using version 2.4.0 of the `Az` module. If you're using a later version, I can't guarantee that all of these commands will work exactly the same way.

Azure Authentication

Azure gives us a few ways to authenticate to its service. In this chapter, you'll use a service principal. A *service principal* is an Azure application's identity. It is the object that represents an application that can then be assigned various permissions.

Why are you creating a service principal? You want to authenticate to Azure by using an automated script that requires no user interaction. To do this, Azure requires you to use either a service principal or an organizational account. I want everyone to be able to follow along regardless of the type of account they have, so you'll use a service principal to authenticate to Azure.

Creating a Service Principal

Counterintuitively, the first thing you have to do to create a service principal is authenticate the old-fashioned way. To do this, use `Connect-AzAccount`, which produces a window like Figure 12-1.

Figure 12-1: The `Connect-AzAccount` credential prompt

Provide your Azure username and password, and the window should close, giving an output similar to Listing 12-1.

```
PS> Connect-AzAccount

Environment           : AzureCloud
Account               : email
TenantId              : tenant id
SubscriptionId        : subscription id
SubscriptionName      : subscription name
CurrentStorageAccount :
```

Listing 12-1: Output from `Connect-AzAccount`

Be sure to record the subscription ID and tenant ID. You'll need those in your script a little later. If, for some reason, you don't catch them while authenticating with `Connect-AzAccount` here, you can always get them by using the `Get-AzSubscription` command later.

Now that you're (interactively) authenticated, you can start creating a service principal. It's a three-step process: first, you create a new Azure AD application; then, you create the service principal itself; and last, you create a role assignment for that service principal.

You can create the Azure AD application by using whatever name and URI you like (Listing 12-2). What URI you use doesn't matter for our purposes, but a URI is required to create the AD application. To ensure that you have adequate rights to create an AD application, refer to *https://docs.microsoft.com/en-us/azure/active-directory/develop/app-objects-and-service-principals.*

```
PS> ❶$secPassword = ConvertTo-SecureString -AsPlainText -Force -String 'password'
PS> ❷$myApp = New-AzADApplication -DisplayName AppForServicePrincipal -IdentifierUris
'http://Some URL here' -Password $secPassword
```

Listing 12-2: Creating an Azure AD application

You can see that you're first creating a secure string by using a password ❶. After you have the password in the correct format, you create a new Azure AD application ❷. A service principal requires an Azure AD application to be created.

Next, you use the `New-AzADServicePrincipal` command to create the service principal, as in Listing 12-3. You reference the application created in Listing 12-2.

```
PS> $sp = New-AzADServicePrincipal -ApplicationId $myApp.ApplicationId
PS> $sp

ServicePrincipalNames : {application id, http://appforserviceprincipal}
ApplicationId         : application id
DisplayName           : AppForServicePrincipal
Id                    : service principal id
Type                  : ServicePrincipal
```

Listing 12-3: Creating an Azure service principal with PowerShell

Last, you need to assign a role to the service principal. Listing 12-4 assigns a `Contributor` role to ensure that the service principal has the access it needs to perform all of the tasks in this chapter.

```
PS> New-AzRoleAssignment -RoleDefinitionName Contributor -ServicePrincipalName
$sp.ServicePrincipalNames[0]

RoleAssignmentId   : /subscriptions/subscription id/providers/Microsoft.Authorization/
                     roleAssignments/assignment id
Scope              : /subscriptions/subscription id
DisplayName        : AppForServicePrincipal
SignInName         :
RoleDefinitionName : Contributor
RoleDefinitionId   : id
ObjectId           : id
ObjectType         : ServicePrincipal
CanDelegate        : False
```

Listing 12-4: Creating a role assignment for a service principal

With that, the service principal has been created and assigned a role.

The only thing left to do is save the encrypted password represented as a secure string for the application you just created somewhere on the disk. You can do that by using the `ConvertFrom-SecureString` command. The `ConvertFrom-SecureString` command (the complement of `ConvertTo-SecureString`) converts encrypted text represented as a PowerShell secure string to a general string, allowing you to save and reference it later:

```
PS> $secPassword | ConvertFrom-SecureString | Out-File -FilePath C:\AzureAppPassword.txt
```

Once you have the password saved to disk, you're ready to set up noninteractive authentication for Azure.

Noninteractively Authenticating with Connect-AzAccount

The `Connect-AzAccount` command prompts you to manually input a username and password. In your scripts, you want to be as noninteractive as possible, because the last thing you want to do is depend on someone sitting in front of a computer to type in your password! Luckily, you can also pass a `PSCredential` object to `Connect-AzAccount`.

You'll write a small script to handle noninteractive authentication. First, let's create a `PSCredential` object that contains the Azure app ID and password:

```
$azureAppId = 'application id'
$azureAppIdPasswordFilePath = 'C:\AzureAppPassword.txt'
$pwd = (Get-Content -Path $azureAppIdPasswordFilePath | ConvertTo-SecureString)
$azureAppCred = (New-Object System.Management.Automation.PSCredential $azureAppId,$pwd)
```

Remember the subscription ID and tenant ID you wrote down earlier? You need to pass those into Connect-AzAccount as well:

```
$subscriptionId = 'subscription id'
$tenantId = 'tenant id'
Connect-AzAccount -ServicePrincipal -SubscriptionId $subscriptionId -TenantId $tenantId
-Credential $azureAppCred
```

You're all set up for noninteractive authentication! Now that you have this set up, it will be saved so you don't have to authenticate like this again.

If you want the condensed code, download the *AzureAuthentication.ps1* script from the book's resources for this chapter.

Creating an Azure Virtual Machine and All Dependencies

It's time to set up an Azure virtual machine. *Azure virtual machines* are one of the most popular Azure services, and having the skills to build Azure VMs will be a big advantage for anyone working in an Azure environment.

Now, way back in the day, when I first created my Azure subscription and wanted to play around with a virtual machine, I thought there'd be a single command to set it up—like all I'd have to do was run New-AzureVm, and voila! There'd be a brand-new virtual machine for me to play with. Boy, was I wrong.

Little did I realize the number of dependencies that had to be in place before a virtual machine would actually work. Did you notice how short the prerequisite section of this chapter is? I left it that way for a reason: to get more experience working with PowerShell, you'll install all the dependencies you need to create a virtual machine with Azure. You'll install a resource group, a virtual network, a storage account, a public IP address, a network interface, and an operating system image. In other words, you'll build this VM from the ground up. Let's get started!

Creating a Resource Group

In Azure, everything is a *resource*, and everything must live inside a *resource group*. Your first task is to create a resource group. To do that, you'll use the New-AzResourceGroup command. This command requires a resource group name and the geographic region that it will be created in. For this example, you'll create a resource group named PowerShellForSysAdmins-RG, and you'll place it in the East US region (as shown in Listing 12-5). You can find all available regions by running the Get-AzLocation command.

```
PS> New-AzResourceGroup -Name 'PowerShellForSysAdmins-RG' -Location 'East US'
```

Listing 12-5: Creating an Azure resource group

Once the resource group is created, it's time to build out the network stack your VM will use.

Creating the Network Stack

For your VM to connect to the outside world and other Azure resources, it needs a *network stack*: the subnet, virtual network, public IP address (optional), and virtual network adapter (vNIC) that the VM uses.

The Subnet

Your first step is to create a subnet. A *subnet* is a logical network of IP addresses that can communicate with one another without the use of a router. The subnet will be what goes "into" the virtual network. Subnets segment a virtual network into smaller networks.

To create a subnet config, use the `New-AzVirtualNetworkSubnetConfig` command (Listing 12-6). This command requires a name and the IP address prefix or network identity.

```
PS> $newSubnetParams = @{
    'Name' = 'PowerShellForSysAdmins-Subnet'
    'AddressPrefix' = '10.0.1.0/24'
}
PS> $subnet = New-AzVirtualNetworkSubnetConfig @newSubnetParams
```

Listing 12-6: Creating a virtual network subnet config

You assign the subnet a name of `PowerShellForSysAdmins-Subnet` and use the prefix of 10.0.1.0/24.

The Virtual Network

Now that you've created a subnet config, you can use it to create the virtual network. The *virtual network* is an Azure resource that allows you to segment various resources such as virtual machines from all other resources. A virtual network can be thought of in the same context as a logical network that you may implement on premises in a network router.

To create a virtual network, use the `New-AzVirtualNetwork` command, as shown in Listing 12-7.

```
PS> $newVNetParams = @{
  ❶ 'Name' = 'PowerShellForSysAdmins-vNet'
  ❷ 'ResourceGroupName' = 'PowerShellForSysAdmins-RG'
  ❸ 'Location' = 'East US'
  ❹ 'AddressPrefix' = '10.0.0.0/16'
}
PS> $vNet = New-AzVirtualNetwork @newVNetParams -Subnet $subnet
```

Listing 12-7: Creating a virtual network

Notice that to create a virtual network, you have to specify the name of the network ❶, the resource group ❷, the region (location) ❸, and the overarching private network that your subnet will be a part of ❹.

The Public IP Address

Now that you've set up a virtual network, you need a public IP address so you can connect your VM to the internet and have clients connect to your VM. Note that this step isn't technically necessary if you plan to make your virtual machine available only to other Azure resources. But since you have bigger plans for your VM, you'll go ahead and do it.

Again, you can create a public IP address by using a single command: `New-AzPublicIpAddress`. You've seen most of the parameters for this function before, but notice that there's a new one named `AllocationMethod`. This parameter tells Azure whether to create a dynamic or static IP address resource. As shown in Listing 12-8, specify that you want a dynamic IP address. You assign your virtual machines dynamic IP addresses because it's one less task to worry about. Because you don't require an IP address to always be the same, using dynamic IP addresses frees you from another task.

```
PS> $newPublicIpParams = @{
    'Name' = 'PowerShellForSysAdmins-PubIp'
    'ResourceGroupName' = 'PowerShellForSysAdmins-RG'
    'AllocationMethod' = 'Dynamic' ## Dynamic or Static
    'Location' = 'East US'
}
PS> $publicIp = New-AzPublicIpAddress @newPublicIpParams
```

Listing 12-8: Creating a public IP address

Although this public IP address exists, it's useless because it's not associated with anything yet. You need to *bind* it to a vNIC.

The Virtual Network Adapter

To build the vNIC, you need to execute another single-line command, `New-AzNetworkInterface`, and you can use a lot of the same parameters you've been using. You also need the ID of the subnet and the ID of the public IP address you created earlier. Both the subnet and the public IP address were stored as objects with an ID property; you simply need to access that property, as shown in Listing 12-9.

```
PS> $newVNicParams = @{
    'Name' = 'PowerShellForSysAdmins-vNIC'
    'ResourceGroupName' = 'PowerShellForSysAdmins-RG'
    'Location' = 'East US'
    'SubnetId' = $vNet.Subnets[0].Id
    'PublicIpAddressId' = $publicIp.Id
}
PS> $vNic = New-AzNetworkInterface @newVNicParams
```

Listing 12-9: Creating an Azure vNIC

Your network stack is complete! The next step is creating the storage account.

Creating a Storage Account

You need to store the virtual machine somewhere. That somewhere is called a *storage account*. Creating a basic storage account is as easy as using the New-AzStorageAccount command. As with the past few commands you've seen, you need a name, resource group, and location; but here you have the new Type parameter, which specifies the level of redundancy your storage account will contain. Use the least expensive type of storage account (*locally redundant*), specified by the Standard_LRS argument, as you can see in Listing 12-10.

```
PS> $newStorageAcctParams = @{
    'Name' = 'powershellforsysadmins'
    'ResourceGroupName' = 'PowerShellForSysAdmins-RG'
    'Type' = 'Standard_LRS'
    'Location' = 'East US'
}
PS> $storageAccount = New-AzStorageAccount @newStorageAcctParams
```

Listing 12-10: Creating an Azure storage account

Now that you have somewhere for the VM to live, it's time to set up the operating system image.

Creating the Operating System Image

The *operating system image* is the base to the virtual disk your virtual machine will be using. Instead of installing Windows on your virtual machine, you'll use a preexisting operating system image to get you to the point to where you can just turn it on.

You create an operating system image in two steps: defining some OS configuration settings, and then defining the offer or OS image to use. Azure uses the term *offer* to reference the VM image.

To set up all the configuration settings, you build a VM configuration object. This object defines the name and size of the VM you're creating. You do this by using the New-AzVMConfig command. In Listing 12-11, you create a Standard_A3 VM. (You can find a list of all sizes available by running Get-AzVMSize and specifying the region.).

```
PS> $newConfigParams = @{
    'VMName' = 'PowerShellForSysAdmins-VM'
    'VMSize' = 'Standard_A3'
}
PS> $vmConfig = New-AzVMConfig @newConfigParams
```

Listing 12-11: Creating a VM configuration

Once the configuration is created, you can pass the object as the VM parameter for the Set-AzVMOperatingSystem command. This command allows you to both define operating-system-specific attributes, such as the hostname of the VM, and enable Windows Update and other attributes. We'll keep it simple here, but if you'd like to see everything possible, check out Set-AzVMOperatingSystem information by using Get-Help.

Listing 12-12 creates a Windows operating system object that will have the hostname of Automate-VM (note: the hostname must be fewer than 16 characters). You use the username and password returned by the Get-Credential command to create a new administrative user with the provided password, and you use the EnableAutoUpdate parameter to automatically apply any new Windows updates.

```
PS> $newVmOsParams = @{
    'Windows' = $true
    'ComputerName' = 'Automate-VM'
    'Credential' = (Get-Credential -Message 'Type the name and password of the
    local administrator account.')
    'EnableAutoUpdate' = $true
    'VM' = $vmConfig
}
PS> $vm = Set-AzVMOperatingSystem @newVmOsParams
```

Listing 12-12: Creating an operating system image

Now you need to create a VM offer. An offer is how Azure allows you to choose what kind of operating system will be installed on the VM's OS disk. This example uses a Windows Server 2012 R2 Datacenter image. This image is one provided by Microsoft, so no need to create your own.

Once you've created the offer object, you can create a source image by using the Set-AzVMSourceImage command, as shown in Listing 12-13.

```
PS> $offer = Get-AzVMImageOffer -Location 'East US'❶ -PublisherName
'MicrosoftWindowsServer'❷ | Where-Object { $_.Offer -eq 'WindowsServer' }❸
PS> $newSourceImageParams = @{
    'PublisherName' = 'MicrosoftWindowsServer'
    'Version' = 'latest'
    'Skus' = '2012-R2-Datacenter'
    'VM' = $vm
    'Offer' = $offer.Offer
}
PS> $vm = Set-AzVMSourceImage @newSourceImageParams
```

Listing 12-13: Finding and creating a VM source image

Here, you're querying all offers in the East US region ❶ with a publisher name of MicrosoftWindowsServer ❷. You may use Get-AzVMImagePublisher to find a list of publishers. You then limit the offers to a name of WindowsServer ❸. With the source image allocated, you can now assign the image to the VM object. This completes the setup of the VM's virtual disk.

To assign the image to the VM object, you need a URI for the OS disk you just created, and you need to pass that URI along with the VM object to the Set-AzVMOSDisk command (Listing 12-14).

```
PS> $osDiskName = 'PowerShellForSysAdmins-Disk'
PS> $osDiskUri = '{0}vhds/PowerShellForSysAdmins-VM{1}.vhd' -f $storageAccount
              .PrimaryEndpoints.Blob.ToString(), $osDiskName
PS> $vm = Set-AzVMOSDisk -Name OSDisk -CreateOption 'fromImage' -VM $vm -VhdUri $osDiskUri
```

Listing 12-14: Assigning the operating system disk to the VM

At this point, you have an OS disk, and it's assigned to a VM object. Time to finish this up!

Wrapping Up

You're *almost* done. All that's left is to attach the vNIC you created earlier and, well, create the actual VM.

To attach the vNIC to the VM, you use the `Add-AzVmNetworkInterface` command and pass the VM object you created along with the ID of the vNIC you created earlier—all of which you can see in Listing 12-15.

```
PS> $vm = Add-AzVMNetworkInterface -VM $vm -Id $vNic.Id
```

Listing 12-15: Attaching the vNIC to the VM

And now, at last, you can create the VM, as shown in Listing 12-16. By calling the `New-AzVm` command with the VM object, the resource group, and region, you finally have your VM! Note that this will start the VM, and at this point, you'll begin incurring charges.

```
PS> New-AzVM -VM $vm -ResourceGroupName 'PowerShellForSysAdmins-RG' -Location 'East US'

RequestId IsSuccessStatusCode StatusCode ReasonPhrase
--------- ------------------- ---------- ------------
                         True         OK OK
```

Listing 12-16: Creating the Azure virtual machine

You should have a brand-new VM in Azure called `Automate-VM`. To confirm, you can run `Get-AzVm` to ensure that the VM exists. Check out the output in Listing 12-17.

```
PS> Get-AzVm -ResourceGroupName 'PowerShellForSysAdmins-RG' -Name PowerShellForSysAdmins-VM


ResourceGroupName  : PowerShellForSysAdmins-RG
Id                 : /subscriptions/XXXXXXXXXXXXX/resourceGroups/PowerShellForSysAdmins-RG/
                     providers/Microsoft.Compute/virtualMachines/PowerShellForSysAdmins-VM
VmId               : e459fb9e-e3b2-4371-9bdd-42ecc209bc01
Name               : PowerShellForSysAdmins-VM
Type               : Microsoft.Compute/virtualMachines
Location           : eastus
Tags               : {}
DiagnosticsProfile : {BootDiagnostics}
```

```
Extensions         : {BGInfo}
HardwareProfile    : {VmSize}
NetworkProfile     : {NetworkInterfaces}
OSProfile          : {ComputerName, AdminUsername, WindowsConfiguration, Secrets}
ProvisioningState  : Succeeded
StorageProfile     : {ImageReference, OsDisk, DataDisks}
```

Listing 12-17: Discovering your Azure VM

If you see similar output, you've successfully created an Azure virtual machine!

Automating the VM Creation

Whew! That was a lot of work getting a single virtual machine running and building all of the dependencies; I would hate to have to go through it again when I want to build my next VM. Why don't we create a single function that'll handle all this for us? With a function, we can incorporate all the code we just went through into a single, executable chunk of code that we can reuse over and over again.

If you're feeling adventurous, I created a custom PowerShell function called `New-CustomAzVm`, available in this chapter's resources. It provides an excellent example of how to incorporate all the tasks accomplished in this section into a single, cohesive function with a minimal amount of input.

Deploying an Azure Web App

If you're working with Azure, you'll want to know how to deploy an Azure web app. *Azure web apps* allow you to quickly provision websites and various other web services running on servers such as IIS, Apache, and more without worrying about building the web server itself. Once you learn how to deploy an Azure web app with PowerShell, you'll be able to work the process into larger workflows including development build pipelines, test environment provisioning, lab provisioning, and more.

Deploying an Azure web app is a two-step process: you create an app service plan and then create the web app itself. Azure web apps are a part of Azure App Services, and any resource under this umbrella must have an associated app service plan. *App service plans* tell the web app which kind of underlying compute resources to build the program on.

Creating an App Service Plan and Web App

Creating an Azure service plan is simple enough. As before, you need only a single command. This command requires you to provide the name of the app service plan, the region or location where it will exist, the resource group, and an optional tier that defines the kind of performance provided by the server running underneath the web app.

Just as you did in the previous section, you create a resource group to keep all of your resources together; let's use this command: `New-AzResourceGroup -Name 'PowerShellForSysAdmins-App' -Location 'East US'`. Once the resource group is created, you create the app service plan and place it inside that resource group.

Your web app, called `Automate`, will be in the East US region and in the `Free` tier of apps. You can see all the code to accomplish those tasks in Listing 12-18.

```
PS> New-AzAppServicePlan -Name 'Automate' -Location 'East US'
-ResourceGroupName 'PowerShellForSysAdmins-App' -Tier 'Free'
```

Listing 12-18: Creating an Azure app service plan

Once this command is executed, you'll have the app service plan created and can move on to creating the web app itself.

You may not be surprised to hear that creating an Azure web app with PowerShell is also a single-command process. Just run `New-AzWebApp`, and supply it with the now-common parameters of resource group name, name, and location, along with the app service plan this web app will sit on top of.

Listing 12-19 uses the `New-AzWebApp` command to create a web app with the name `MyApp` inside the `PowerShellForSysAdmins-App` resource group using the app service plan `Automate` (the one that you created earlier). Note that this starts the app, which may incur billing.

```
PS> New-AzWebApp -ResourceGroupName 'PowerShellForSysAdmins-App' -Name
'AutomateApp' -Location 'East US' -AppServicePlan 'Automate'
```

Listing 12-19: Creating an Azure web app

When you run this command, you should see a lot of properties in your output; these are the web app's various settings.

Deploying an Azure SQL Database

Another common Azure task is deploying an Azure SQL database. To deploy an Azure SQL database, you need to do three things: create the Azure SQL server that the database will run on, create the database itself, and then create a SQL Server firewall rule to connect to the database.

As in previous sections, you create a resource group to house all your new resources. Run `New-AzResourceGroup -Name 'PowerShellForSysAdmins-SQL' -Location 'East US'` to do so. Then you'll create the SQL server that the database will run on.

Creating an Azure SQL Server

Creating an Azure SQL server takes yet another single-line command: `New-AzSqlServer`. And yet again, you need to provide the name of the resource, the name of the server itself, and the region—but here, you also need the username and password of the SQL administrator user on the server. This requires a little more work. Because you need to create a credential to pass to `New-AzSqlServer`, let's go ahead and do that first. I covered how to create a `PSCredential` object in the "Creating a Service Principal" on page 158, so we won't go over that here.

```
PS> $userName = 'sqladmin'
PS> $plainTextPassword = 's3cretp@SSwOrd!'
PS> $secPassword = ConvertTo-SecureString -String $plainTextPassword -AsPlainText -Force
PS> $credential = New-Object -TypeName System.Management.Automation.PSCredential -ArgumentList
$userName,$secPassword
```

Once you have a credential, the rest is as easy as putting all the parameters into a hashtable, and passing it into the `New-AzSqlServer` function, as shown in Listing 12-20.

```
PS> $parameters = @{
    ResourceGroupName = 'PowerShellForSysAdmins-SQL'
    ServerName = 'PowerShellForSysAdmins-SQLSrv'
    Location =  'East US'
    SqlAdministratorCredentials = $credential
}
PS> New-AzSqlServer @parameters

ResourceGroupName        : PowerShellForSysAdmins-SQL
ServerName               : powershellsysadmins-sqlsrv
Location                 : eastus
SqlAdministratorLogin    : sqladmin
SqlAdministratorPassword :
ServerVersion            : 12.0
Tags                     :
Identity                 :
FullyQualifiedDomainName : powershellsysadmins-sqlsrv.database.windows.net
ResourceId               : /subscriptions/XXXXXXXXXXXXXX/resourceGroups
                           /PowerShellForSysAdmins-SQL/providers/Microsoft.Sql
                           /servers/powershellsysadmins-sqlsrv
```

Listing 12-20: Creating the Azure SQL server

Now that the SQL server has been created, you have the bedrock for your database.

Creating the Azure SQL Database

To create the SQL database, use the `New-AzSqlDatabase` command, as shown in Listing 12-21. Along with the common parameter of `ResourceGroupName`, pass in the name of the server that you just created and the name of the database you want to create (in this example, `AutomateSQLDb`).

```
PS> New-AzSqlDatabase -ResourceGroupName 'PowerShellForSysAdmins-SQL'
-ServerName 'PowerShellSysAdmins-SQLSrv' -DatabaseName 'AutomateSQLDb'

ResourceGroupName             : PowerShellForSysAdmins-SQL
ServerName                    : PowerShellSysAdmins-SQLSrv
DatabaseName                  : AutomateSQLDb
Location                      : eastus
DatabaseId                    : 79f3b331-7200-499f-9fba-b09e8c424354
Edition                       : Standard
CollationName                 : SQL_Latin1_General_CP1_CI_AS
CatalogCollation              :
MaxSizeBytes                  : 268435456000
Status                        : Online
CreationDate                  : 9/15/2019 6:48:32 PM
CurrentServiceObjectiveId     : 00000000-0000-0000-0000-000000000000
CurrentServiceObjectiveName   : S0
RequestedServiceObjectiveName : S0
RequestedServiceObjectiveId   :
ElasticPoolName               :
EarliestRestoreDate           : 9/15/2019 7:18:32 PM
Tags                          :
ResourceId                    : /subscriptions/XXXXXXX/resourceGroups
                                /PowerShellForSysAdmins-SQL/providers
                                /Microsoft.Sql/servers/powershellsysadmin-sqlsrv
                                /databases/AutomateSQLDb
CreateMode                    :
ReadScale                     : Disabled
ZoneRedundant                 : False
Capacity                      : 10
Family                        :
SkuName                       : Standard
LicenseType                   :
```

Listing 12-21: Creating an Azure SQL database

At this point, you have a running SQL database in Azure. But when you try to connect to it, it won't work. By default, when a new Azure SQL database is created, it's locked down from any outside connections. You need to create a firewall rule so you can allow connections to your database.

Creating the SQL Server Firewall Rule

The command to create a firewall rule is `New-AzSqlServerFirewallRule`. The command takes in the resource group name, the name of the server you created earlier, the name for the firewall rule, and start and end IP addresses. The start and end IP addresses allow you to specify a single IP address or a range of IPs to allow into your database. Since you'll be working on only one local computer to manage Azure, let's limit the connections to your SQL server to be from only your current computer. To do that, you first need to figure out your public IP address. You can easily do this via a PowerShell one-liner: **`Invoke-RestMethod http://ipinfo.io/json | Select -ExpandProperty ip`**.

You can then use the public IP address for both the StartIPAddress and EndIPAddress parameters. However, note that if your public IP address changes, you'll need to do all this again.

Also, be aware that the server name in Listing 12-22 must be made up of all lowercase letters, hyphens, and/or numbers. Otherwise, you'll get an error when you attempt to create the firewall rule.

```
PS> $parameters = @{
    ResourceGroupName = 'PowerShellForSysAdmins-SQL'
    FirewallRuleName = 'PowerShellForSysAdmins-FwRule'
    ServerName = 'powershellsysadmin-sqlsrv'
    StartIpAddress = 'Your Public IP Address'
    EndIpAddress = 'Your Public IP Address'
}
PS> New-AzSqlServerFirewallRule @parameters

ResourceGroupName : PowerShellForSysAdmins-SQL
ServerName        : powershellsys-sqlsrv
StartIpAddress    : 0.0.0.0
EndIpAddress      : 0.0.0.0
FirewallRuleName  : PowerShellForSysAdmins-FwRule
```

Listing 12-22: Creating an Azure SQL server firewall rule

That's it! Your database should be up and running.

Testing Your SQL Database

To test your database, let's make a small function that uses the System.Data.SqlClient.SqlConnection object's Open() method to attempt a simple connection; see Listing 12-23.

```
function Test-SqlConnection {
    param(
        [Parameter(Mandatory)]
      ❶ [string]$ServerName,

        [Parameter(Mandatory)]
        [string]$DatabaseName,

        [Parameter(Mandatory)]
      ❷ [pscredential]$Credential
    )

    try {
        $userName = $Credential.UserName
      ❸ $password = $Credential.GetNetworkCredential().Password
      ❹ $connectionString = 'Data Source={0};database={1};User
        ID={2};Password={3}' -f $ServerName,$DatabaseName,$userName,$password
        $sqlConnection = New-Object System.Data.SqlClient.SqlConnection
        $ConnectionString
      ❺ $sqlConnection.Open()
        $true
```

```
    } catch {
        if ($_.Exception.Message -match 'cannot open server') {
            $false
        } else {
            throw $_
        }
    } finally {
      ❻ $sqlConnection.Close()
    }
}
```

Listing 12-23: Testing a SQL connection to the Azure SQL database

You use the SQL server's fully qualified domain name created earlier as the `ServerName` parameter for this function ❶ along with the SQL administrator username and password inside a `PSCredential` object ❷.

Then you break apart the `PSCredential` object into a plaintext username and password ❸, create the connection string to make the database connection ❹, invoke the `Open()` method on the `SqlConnection` object to attempt to connect to the database ❺, and then finally close the database connection ❻.

You can execute this function by running **`Test-SqlConnection -ServerName 'powershellsysadmins-sqlsrv.database.windows.net' -DatabaseName 'AutomateSQLDb' -Credential (Get-Credential)`**. If you can connect to the database, the function will return `True`; otherwise, it will return `False` (and further investigation will be needed).

You can clean everything up by removing the resource group with the command **`Remove-AzResourceGroup -ResourceGroupName 'PowerShellForSysAdmins-SQL'`**.

Summary

In this chapter, you dove headfirst into automating Microsoft Azure with PowerShell. You set up noninteractive authentication, and deployed a virtual machine, web app, and SQL database. And you did it all from PowerShell, sparing you any visits to the Azure portal.

You couldn't have done this without the `Az` PowerShell module and the hard work of the people who created it. Like other PowerShell cloud modules, all these commands rely on various APIs that are being called under the hood. Thanks to the module, you didn't have to worry about learning how to call REST methods or use endpoint URLs.

In the next chapter, you'll take a look at using PowerShell to automate Amazon Web Services.

13

WORKING WITH AWS

In the preceding chapter, you learned about using Microsoft Azure with PowerShell. Now let's see what we can do with Amazon Web Services (AWS). In this chapter, you'll go deep into using PowerShell with AWS. Once you've learned how to authenticate to AWS with PowerShell, you'll learn how to create an EC2 instance from scratch, deploy an Elastic Beanstalk (EBS) application, and create an Amazon Relational Database Service (Amazon RDS) Microsoft SQL Server database.

Like Azure, AWS is a juggernaut in the cloud world. Chances are high that if you're in IT, you'll be working with AWS in some way in your career. And as with Azure, there's a handy PowerShell module for working with AWS: `AWSPowerShell`.

You can install `AWSPowerShell` from the PowerShell Gallery the same way you installed the `AzureRm` module, by calling **`Install-Module AWSPowerShell`**. Once this module is downloaded and installed, you're ready to go.

Prerequisites

I'm assuming you already have an AWS account and that you have access to the root user. You can sign up for an AWS free tier account at *https://aws.amazon.com/free/*. You won't need to do everything as root, but you will need it to create your first *identity and access management (IAM)* user. You'll also need to have the `AWSPowerShell` module downloaded and installed, as noted earlier.

AWS Authentication

In AWS, authentication is done using the IAM service, which handles authentication, authorization, accounting, and auditing in AWS. To authenticate to AWS, you must have an IAM user created under your subscription, and that user has to have access to the appropriate resources. The first step to working with AWS is creating an IAM user.

When an AWS account is created, a root user is automatically created, so you'll use the root user to create your IAM user. *Technically*, you could use the root user to do anything in AWS, but that is highly discouraged.

Authenticating with the Root User

Let's create the IAM user you'll use throughout the rest of the chapter. First, however, you need to somehow authenticate it. Without another IAM user, the only way to do that is with the root user. Sadly, this means you have to abandon PowerShell for a moment. You'll have to use the AWS Management Console's GUI to get the root user's access and secret keys.

Your first move is to log into your AWS account. Navigate to the right-hand corner of the screen and click the account drop-down menu, shown in Figure 13-1.

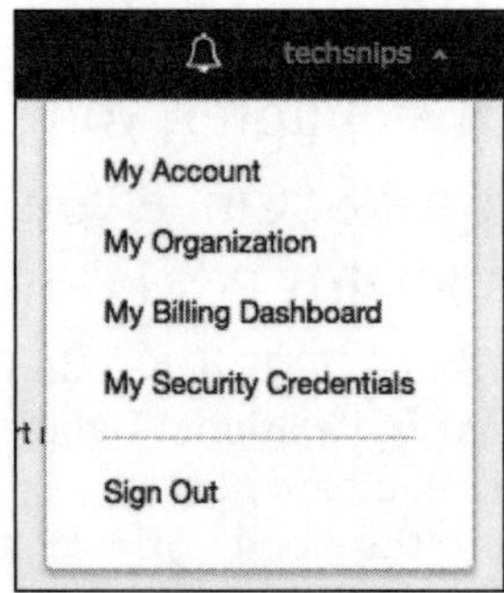

Figure 13-1: My Security Credentials option

Click the **My Security Credentials** option. A screen will pop up, warning that messing with your security credentials isn't a good idea; see Figure 13-2. But you need to do it here to create an IAM user.

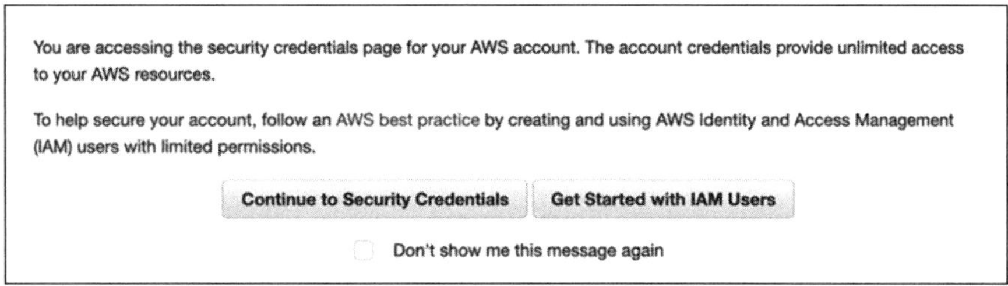

You are accessing the security credentials page for your AWS account. The account credentials provide unlimited access to your AWS resources.
To help secure your account, follow an AWS best practice by creating and using AWS Identity and Access Management (IAM) users with limited permissions.
Continue to Security Credentials
Get Started with IAM Users
Don't show me this message again

Figure 13-2: Authentication warning

Click **Continue to Security Credentials**, then click **Access Keys**. Clicking **Create New Access Key** should present a way to view your account's access key ID and secret key. It should also give you an option to download a key file containing both. If you haven't already, download the file and put it in a safe spot. For now, though, you need to copy the access key and secret key from this page and add them to your default profile in your PowerShell session.

Pass both of these keys to the `Set-AWSCredential` command, which saves them so they can be reused by the commands that'll create an IAM user. Check out Listing 13-1 for the full command.

```
PS> Set-AWSCredential -AccessKey 'access key' -SecretKey 'secret key'
```

Listing 13-1: Setting AWS access keys

With that done, you're ready to create an IAM user.

Creating an IAM User and Role

Now that you're authenticated as the root user, you can create an IAM user. Use the `New-IAMUser` command, specifying the name of the IAM user you'd like to use (in this example, `Automator`). When you create the user, you should see output like that in Listing 13-2.

```
PS> New-IAMUser -UserName Automator

Arn                 : arn:aws:iam::013223035658:user/Automator
CreateDate          : 9/16/2019 5:01:24 PM
PasswordLastUsed    : 1/1/0001 12:00:00 AM
Path                : /
PermissionsBoundary :
UserId              : AIDAJU2WN5KIFOUMPDSR4
UserName            : Automator
```

Listing 13-2: Creating an IAM user

The next step is to give the user the appropriate permission. You do that by assigning this user a role that's assigned a policy. AWS groups certain permissions in units called *roles*, which allow the administrator to more easily delegate permissions (a strategy known as *role-based access control*, or *RBAC*). The *policy* then determines what permissions a role has access to.

You can create a role by using the New-IAMRole command, but first you need to create what AWS calls a *trust relationship policy document*: a string of text in JSON that defines the services that this user can access and the level at which they can access them.

Listing 13-3 is an example of a trust relationship policy document.

```
{
    "Version": "2019-10-17",
    "Statement": [
        {
            "Effect": "Allow",
            "Principal" : { "AWS": "arn:aws:iam::013223035658:user/Automator" },
            "Action": "sts:AssumeRole"
        }
    ]
}
```

Listing 13-3: Example trust policy document

This JSON changes the role itself (modifying its trust policy) to allow your Automator user to use it. It is giving the AssumeRole permission to your user. This is required to create the role. For more information about how to create a trust relationship policy document, refer to *https://docs.aws.amazon.com/IAM/latest/UserGuide/id_roles_manage_modify.html.*

Assign this JSON string to a $json variable and then pass it as the value of the AssumeRolePolicyDocument parameter in New-IamRole, as shown in Listing 13-4.

```
PS> $json = '{
>>     "Version": "2019-10-17",
>>     "Statement": [
>>         {
>>             "Effect": "Allow",
>>             "Principal" : { "AWS": "arn:aws:iam::013223035658:user/Automator" },
>>             "Action": "sts:AssumeRole"
>>         }
>>     ]
>> }'
PS> New-IAMRole -AssumeRolePolicyDocument $json -RoleName 'AllAccess'

Path             RoleName                          RoleId                 CreateDate
----             --------                          ------                 ----------
/                AllAccess                         AROAJ2B7YC3HH6M6F2WOM  9/16/2019 6:05:37 PM
```

Listing 13-4: Creating a new IAM role

Now that the IAM role is created, you need to give it permission to access the various resources you'll be working with. Rather than spend the next 12 dozen pages detailing AWS IAM roles and security, let's do something simple and give the Automator full access to everything (effectively making it a root user).

Note that in practice, you should *not* do this. It's always best to limit access to only those necessary. Check out the AWS IAM Best Practices guide (*https://docs.aws.amazon.com/IAM/latest/UserGuide/best-practices.html*) for more information. But for now, let's assign this user the AdministratorAccess managed policy by using the Register-IAMUserPolicy command. You'll need the Amazon Resource Name (ARN) of the policy. To do that, you can use the Get-IAMPolicies command and filter by policy name, storing that name in a variable, and passing the variable into Register-IAMUserPolicy (all of which you can see in Listing 13-5).

```
PS> $policyArn = (Get-IAMPolicies | where {$_.PolicyName -eq 'AdministratorAccess'}).Arn
PS> Register-IAMUserPolicy -PolicyArn $policyArn -UserName Automator
```

Listing 13-5: Attaching a policy to the user

The last thing you need to do is generate an access key that will let you authenticate your user. Do this with the New-IAMAcessKey command, as shown in Listing 13-6.

```
PS> $key = New-IAMAccessKey -UserName Automator
PS> $key

AccessKeyId     : XXXXXXXX
CreateDate      : 9/16/2019 6:17:40 PM
SecretAccessKey : XXXXXXXXX
Status          : Active
UserName        : Automator
```

Listing 13-6: Creating an IAM access key

Your new IAM user is all set up. Now let's authenticate it.

Authenticating Your IAM User

In an earlier section, you authenticated with the root user—this was a temporary measure. You need to authenticate your IAM user so you can actually get some work done! You need to authenticate your IAM user before you can do just about anything in AWS. You'll again use the Set -AWSCredential command to update your profile with your new access and secret keys. Change the command a bit, though, by using the StoreAs parameter, as shown in Listing 13-7. Because you'll be using this IAM user throughout the rest of the session, you'll store the access and secret key in the AWS default profile so you don't have to run this command again for every session.

```
PS> Set-AWSCredential -AccessKey $key.AccessKeyId -SecretKey
$key.SecretAccessKey -StoreAs 'Default'
```

Listing 13-7: Setting default AWS access keys

The final command to run is **Initialize-AWSDefaultConfiguration -Region '*your region here*'**, which prevents having to specify the region every time you call a command. This is a one-time step. You can find all regions by running Get-AWSRegion to find the closest region to you.

That's it! You now have an authenticated session in AWS and can move on to working with AWS services. To confirm, run Get-AWSCredentials with the ListProfileDetail parameter to look for all saved credentials. If all is well, you will see the default profile show up:

```
PS> Get-AWSCredentials -ListProfileDetail
ProfileName StoreTypeName         ProfileLocation
----------- -------------         ---------------
Default     NetSDKCredentialsFile
```

Creating an AWS EC2 Instance

In Chapter 12, you created an Azure virtual machine. Here, you'll do something similar by creating an *AWS EC2 instance*. An AWS EC2 instance offers the same learning opportunity that an Azure virtual machine does; creating VMs is an extremely common occurrence, whether you're using Azure or AWS. However, to create a VM in AWS, you need to approach provisioning in a different way than with Azure. Here, the underlying APIs are different, meaning the commands you run will be different, but in a nutshell, you'll be performing essentially the same task: creating a virtual machine. It doesn't help that AWS has its own lingo! I've tried to mirror the steps we took to create the VM in the preceding chapter, but of course, because of the architectural and syntactic differences between Azure and AWS, you will see some noticeable differences.

Luckily, just as with Azure, you have a module called AWSPowerShell that makes it easier to write everything from scratch. Just as you did in the preceding chapter, you'll build from the ground up: setting up all the dependencies you need and then creating the EC2 instance.

The Virtual Private Cloud

The first dependency you need is a network. You can use an existing network or build your own. Because this book is hands-on, you'll build your own network from scratch. In Azure, you did this with a vNet, but in AWS, you'll work with *virtual private clouds (VPCs)*, which are a network fabric that allows the virtual machine to connect with the rest of the cloud. To replicate the same settings an Azure vNet might have, you'll simply create a VPC with a single subnet set to its most basic level. Because there is such a wide range of configuration options to choose from, I decided it's best to mirror our Azure network configuration as closely as possible.

Before you get started, you need to know the subnet you'd like to create. Let's use 10.10.0.0/24 as our example network. You'll store that information and a variable, and use the New-EC2Vpc command, as shown in Listing 13-8.

```
PS> $network = '10.0.0.0/16'
PS> $vpc = New-EC2Vpc -CidrBlock $network
PS> $vpc

CidrBlock                   : 10.0.0.0/24
CidrBlockAssociationSet     : {vpc-cidr-assoc-03f1edbc052e8c207}
DhcpOptionsId               : dopt-3c9c3047
InstanceTenancy             : default
Ipv6CidrBlockAssociationSet : {}
IsDefault                   : False
State                       : pending
Tags                        : {}
VpcId                       : vpc-03e8c773094d52eb3
```

Listing 13-8: Creating an AWS VPC

Once you create the VPC, you have to manually enable DNS support (Azure did this for you automatically). Manually enabling DNS support should point the servers attached to this VPC to an internal Amazon DNS server. Likewise, you need to manually give a public hostname (another thing Azure took care of for you). To do this, you need to enable DNS hostnames. Do both of these by using the code in Listing 13-9.

```
PS> Edit-EC2VpcAttribute -VpcId $vpc.VpcId -EnableDnsSupport $true
PS> Edit-EC2VpcAttribute -VpcId $vpc.VpcId -EnableDnsHostnames $true
```

Listing 13-9: Enabling VPC DNS support and hostnames

Notice that you use the `Edit-EC2VpcAttribute` command for both. As its name suggests, this command lets you edit several of your EC2 VPC's attributes.

The Internet Gateway

The next step is creating an internet gateway. This allows your EC2 instance to route traffic to and from the internet. Again, you need to do this manually, here using the `New-EC2InternetGateway` command (Listing 13-10).

```
PS> $gw = New-EC2InternetGateway
PS> $gw

Attachments InternetGatewayId     Tags
----------- -----------------     ----
{}          igw-05ca5aaa3459119b1 {}
```

Listing 13-10: Creating an internet gateway

Once the gateway is created, you have to attach it to your VPC by using the `Add-EC2InternetGateway` command, as shown in Listing 13-11.

```
PS> Add-EC2InternetGateway -InternetGatewayId $gw.InternetGatewayId -VpcId $vpc.VpcId
```

Listing 13-11: Attaching a VPC to an internet gateway

With the VPC out of the way, let's take the next step and add a route to your network.

Routes

With the gateway created, you now need to create a route table and a route so that the EC2 instances on your VPC can access the internet. A *route* is a path that network traffic takes to find the destination. A *route table* is a, well, table of routes. Your route needs to go in a table, so you'll create the route table first. Use the `New-EC2RouteTable` command, passing in your VPC ID (Listing 13-12).

```
PS> $rt = New-EC2RouteTable -VpcId $vpc.VpcId
PS> $rt

Associations     : {}
PropagatingVgws  : {}
Routes           : {}
RouteTableId     : rtb-09786c17af32005d8
Tags             : {}
VpcId            : vpc-03e8c773094d52eb3
```

Listing 13-12: Creating a route table

Inside the route table, you create a route that points to the gateway you just created. You're creating a *default route*, or *default gateway*, meaning a route that outgoing network traffic will take if a more specific route isn't defined. You'll route all traffic (0.0.0.0/0) through your internet gateway. Use the `New-EC2Route` command, which will return `True` if successful, as shown in Listing 13-13.

```
PS> New-EC2Route -RouteTableId $rt.RouteTableId -GatewayId
$gw.InternetGatewayId -DestinationCidrBlock '0.0.0.0/0'

True
```

Listing 13-13: Creating a route

As you can see, your route should be successfully created!

Subnet

Next, you have to create a subnet inside your larger VPC and associate it with your route table. Remember that a subnet defines the logical network that your EC2 instance's network adapter will be a part of. To create one, you use the `New-EC2Subnet` command, and then use the `Register-EC2RouteTable` command to register the subnet to the route table you built earlier. First, though, you need to define an *availability zone* (where AWS datacenters will be hosting your subnet) for the subnet. If you're not sure which availability zone you want to use, you can use the `Get-EC2AvailabilityZone` command to enumerate all of them. Listing 13-14 shows what should happen if you do.

```
PS> Get-EC2AvailabilityZone

Messages RegionName State     ZoneName
-------- ---------- -----     --------
{}       us-east-1  available us-east-1a
{}       us-east-1  available us-east-1b
{}       us-east-1  available us-east-1c
{}       us-east-1  available us-east-1d
{}       us-east-1  available us-east-1e
{}       us-east-1  available us-east-1f
```

Listing 13-14: Enumerating EC2 availability zones

If it's all the same to you, let's use the `us-east-1d` availability zone. Listing 13-15 shows the code to create the subnet, using the `New-EC2Subnet` command, which takes the VPC ID you created earlier, a CIDR block (subnet), and finally that availability zone you found as well as the code to register the table (using the `Register-EC2RouteTable` command).

```
PS> $sn = New-EC2Subnet -VpcId $vpc.VpcId -CidrBlock '10.0.1.0/24' -AvailabilityZone 'us-east-1d'
PS> Register-EC2RouteTable -RouteTableId $rt.RouteTableId -SubnetId $sn.SubnetId
rtbassoc-06a8b5154bc8f2d98
```

Listing 13-15: Creating and registering a subnet

Now that you have the subnet created and registered, you're all done with the network stack!

Assigning an AMI to Your EC2 Instance

After building the network stack, you have to assign an Amazon Machine Image (AMI) to your VM. An *AMI*, which is a "snapshot" of a disk, is used as a template to prevent having to install the operating system on EC2 instances from scratch. You need to find an existing AMI that suits your needs: you need an AMI that can support a Windows Server 2016 instance, so first you need to find the name of that instance. Enumerate all of the available instances with the **`Get-EC2ImageByName`** command, and you should see an image called `WINDOWS_2016_BASE`. Perfect.

Now that you know the image name, use `Get-EC2ImageByName` again, and this time, specify the image you'd like to use. Doing so will tell the command to return the image object you need, as you can see in Listing 13-16.

```
PS> $ami = Get-EC2ImageByName -Name 'WINDOWS_2016_BASE'
PS> $ami

Architecture        : x86_64
BlockDeviceMappings : {/dev/sda1, xvdca, xvdcb, xvdcc...}
CreationDate        : 2019-08-15T02:27:20.000Z
Description         : Microsoft Windows Server 2016...
EnaSupport          : True
Hypervisor          : xen
ImageId             : ami-0b7b74ba8473ec232
```

```
ImageLocation      : amazon/Windows_Server-2016-English-Full-Base-2019.08.15
ImageOwnerAlias    : amazon
ImageType          : machine
KernelId           :
Name               : Windows_Server-2016-English-Full-Base-2019.08.15
OwnerId            : 801119661308
Platform           : Windows
ProductCodes       : {}
Public             : True
RamdiskId          :
RootDeviceName     : /dev/sda1
RootDeviceType     : ebs
SriovNetSupport    : simple
State              : available
StateReason        :
Tags               : {}
VirtualizationType : hvm
```

Listing 13-16: Finding the AMI

Your image is stored and ready to go. Finally, you can create your EC2 instance. All you need is the instance type; unfortunately, you can't get a list of them with a PowerShell cmdlet, but you can find them at *https://aws.amazon.com/ec2/instance-types/*. Let's use the free one: `t2.micro`. Load up your parameters—the image ID, whether you want to associate with a public IP, the instance type, and subnet ID—and run the `New-EC2Instance` command (Listing 13-17).

```
PS> $params = @{
>>      ImageId = $ami.ImageId
>>      AssociatePublicIp = $false
>>      InstanceType = 't2.micro'
>>      SubnetId = $sn.SubnetId
}
PS> New-EC2Instance @params

GroupNames    : {}
Groups        : {}
Instances     : {}
OwnerId       : 013223035658
RequesterId   :
ReservationId : r-05aa0d9b0fdf2df4f
```

Listing 13-17: Creating an EC2 instance

It's done! You should see a brand-new EC2 instance in your AWS Management Console, or you can use the `Get-EC2Instance` command to return your newly created instance.

Wrapping Up

You nailed down the code to create the EC2 instance, but, as is, the code is cumbersome to use. Let's make this code easier to use over and over again.

Chances are, creating an EC2 instance will be a frequent occurrence, so you'll create a custom function to avoid doing everything one step at a time. At a high level, this function works the same way as the one you created in Chapter 12 in Azure; I won't go through the specifics of the function here, but the script can be found in the book's resources, and I highly recommend you try to build the function on your own.

When the script is called and all dependencies already exist *except* for the EC2 instance itself, you'll see output similar to Listing 13-18 when you run it with the Verbose parameter.

```
PS> $parameters = @{
>>     VpcCidrBlock = '10.0.0.0/16'
>>     EnableDnsSupport = $true
>>     SubnetCidrBlock = '10.0.1.0/24'
>>     OperatingSystem = 'Windows Server 2016'
>>     SubnetAvailabilityZone = 'us-east-1d'
>>     InstanceType = 't2.micro'
>>     Verbose = $true
}
PS> New-CustomEC2Instance @parameters

VERBOSE: Invoking Amazon Elastic Compute Cloud operation 'DescribeVpcs' in region 'us-east-1'
VERBOSE: A VPC with the CIDR block [10.0.0.0/16] has already been created.
VERBOSE: Enabling DNS support on VPC ID [vpc-03ba701f5633fcfac]...
VERBOSE: Invoking Amazon EC2 operation 'ModifyVpcAttribute' in region 'us-east-1'
VERBOSE: Invoking Amazon EC2 operation 'ModifyVpcAttribute' in region 'us-east-1'
VERBOSE: Invoking Amazon Elastic Compute Cloud operation 'DescribeInternetGateways' in region
         'us-east-1'
VERBOSE: An internet gateway is already attached to VPC ID [vpc-03ba701f5633fcfac].
VERBOSE: Invoking Amazon Elastic Compute Cloud operation 'DescribeRouteTables' in region
         'us-east-1'
VERBOSE: Route table already exists for VPC ID [vpc-03ba701f5633fcfac].
VERBOSE: A default route has already been created for route table ID [rtb-0b4aa3a0e1801311f
         rtb-0aed41cac6175a94d].
VERBOSE: Invoking Amazon Elastic Compute Cloud operation 'DescribeSubnets' in region 'us-east-1'
VERBOSE: A subnet has already been created and registered with VPC ID [vpc-03ba701f5633fcfac].
VERBOSE: Invoking Amazon EC2 operation 'DescribeImages' in region 'us-east-1'
VERBOSE: Creating EC2 instance...
VERBOSE: Invoking Amazon EC2 operation 'RunInstances' in region 'us-east-1'

GroupNames    : {}
Groups        : {}
Instances     : {}
OwnerId       : 013223035658
RequesterId   :
ReservationId : r-0bc2437cfbde8e92a
```

Listing 13-18: Running the custom EC2 instance creation function

You now have the tools you need to automate the boring task of creating EC2 instances in AWS!

Deploying an Elastic Beanstalk Application

Much like Microsoft Azure's Web App service, AWS has a web app service of its own. *Elastic Beanstalk (EB)* is a service that allows you to upload web packages to be hosted on the AWS infrastructure. In this section, you'll see what it takes to create an EB application and then deploy a package to one. This process requires five steps:

1. Create the application.
2. Create the environment.
3. Upload the package to make it available to the application.
4. Create a new version of the application.
5. Deploy the new version to the environment.

Let's start by creating a new application.

Creating the Application

To create a new application, use the `New-EBApplication` command, which provides the application's name. Let's call it `AutomateWorkflow`. Run the command, and you should see something like Listing 13-19.

```
PS> $ebApp = New-EBApplication -ApplicationName 'AutomateWorkflow'
PS> $ebSApp

ApplicationName         : AutomateWorkflow
ConfigurationTemplates  : {}
DateCreated             : 9/19/2019 11:43:56 AM
DateUpdated             : 9/19/2019 11:43:56 AM
Description             :
ResourceLifecycleConfig : Amazon.ElasticBeanstalk.Model
                          .ApplicationResourceLifecycleConfig
Versions                : {}
```

Listing 13-19: Creating a new Elastic Beanstalk application

The next step is creating the *environment*, which is the infrastructure the application will be hosted on. The command to create a new environment is `New-EBEnvironment`. Unfortunately, creating the environment isn't quite as straightforward as creating the application. A couple of the parameters, such as the application name and name of the environment, are up to you, but you need to know the `SolutionStackName`, `Tier_Type`, and `Tier_Name`. Let's look at these a little more closely.

You use the `SolutionStackName` to specify the operating system and IIS version you'd like your app to run under. For a list of available solution stacks, run the `Get-EBAvailableSolutionStackList` command and inspect the `SolutionStackDetails` property, as shown in Listing 13-20.

```
PS> (Get-EBAvailableSolutionStackList).SolutionStackDetails

PermittedFileTypes SolutionStackName
------------------ -----------------
{zip}              64bit Windows Server Core 2016 v1.2.0 running IIS 10.0
{zip}              64bit Windows Server 2016 v1.2.0 running IIS 10.0
{zip}              64bit Windows Server Core 2012 R2 v1.2.0 running IIS 8.5
{zip}              64bit Windows Server 2012 R2 v1.2.0 running IIS 8.5
{zip}              64bit Windows Server 2012 v1.2.0 running IIS 8
{zip}              64bit Windows Server 2008 R2 v1.2.0 running IIS 7.5
{zip}              64bit Amazon Linux 2018.03 v2.12.2 runni...
{jar, zip}         64bit Amazon Linux 2018.03 v2.7.4 running Java 8
{jar, zip}         64bit Amazon Linux 2018.03 v2.7.4 running Java 7
{zip}              64bit Amazon Linux 2018.03 v4.5.3 running Node.js
{zip}              64bit Amazon Linux 2015.09 v2.0.8 running Node.js
{zip}              64bit Amazon Linux 2015.03 v1.4.6 running Node.js
{zip}              64bit Amazon Linux 2014.03 v1.1.0 running Node.js
{zip}              32bit Amazon Linux 2014.03 v1.1.0 running Node.js
{zip}              64bit Amazon Linux 2018.03 v2.8.1 running PHP 5.4
--snip--
```

Listing 13-20: Finding available solution stacks

As you can see, you have a lot of options. For this example, choose 64-bit Windows Server Core 2012 R2 running IIS 8.5.

Now let's look at the `Tier_Type`. The `Tier_Type` specifies the kind of environment your web service will be running under. The `Standard` type is required if you'll be using this environment to host a website.

And finally, for the `Tier_Name` parameter, you have the options of `WebServer` and `Worker`. Choose `WebServer` here because you'd like to host a website (`Worker` would be required if you were creating an API).

Now that your parameters are all figured out, let's run `New-EBEnvironment`. Listing 13-21 shows the command and the output.

```
PS> $parameters = @{
>>      ApplicationName = 'AutomateWorkflow'
>>      EnvironmentName = 'Testing'
>>      SolutionStackName = '64bit Windows Server Core 2012 R2 running IIS 8.5'
>>      Tier_Type = 'Standard'
>>      Tier_Name = 'WebServer'
}
PS> New-EBEnvironment @parameters

AbortableOperationInProgress : False
ApplicationName              : AutomateWorkflow
CNAME                        :
DateCreated                  : 9/19/2019 12:19:36 PM
DateUpdated                  : 9/19/2019 12:19:36 PM
Description                  :
EndpointURL                  :
EnvironmentArn               : arn:aws:elasticbeanstalk:...
EnvironmentId                : e-wkba2k4kcf
```

```
EnvironmentLinks              : {}
EnvironmentName               : Testing
Health                        : Grey
HealthStatus                  :
PlatformArn                   : arn:aws:elasticbeanstalk...
Resources                     :
SolutionStackName             : 64bit Windows Server Core 2012 R2 running IIS 8.5
Status                        : Launching
TemplateName                  :
Tier                          : Amazon.ElasticBeanstalk.Model.EnvironmentTier
VersionLabel                  :
```

Listing 13-21: Creating an Elastic Beanstalk application

You'll notice that the status shows `Launching`. This means the app isn't available yet, so you may have to wait a bit for the environment to come up. You can periodically check on the status of the app by running **`Get-EBEnvironment -ApplicationName 'AutomateWorkflow' -EnvironmentName 'Testing'`**. The environment may stay in a `Launching` state for a few minutes.

When you see the `Status` property turn to `Ready`, the environment is up, and it's time to deploy a package to the site.

Deploying a Package

Let's deploy. The package you'll deploy should contain any files you want your website to host. You can put whatever you'd like in there—for our purposes, it doesn't matter. All you have to make sure of is that it's in a ZIP file. Use the `Compress-Archive` command to zip up whatever files you want to deploy:

```
PS> Compress-Archive -Path 'C:\MyPackageFolder\*' -DestinationPath 'C:\package.zip'
```

With your package nice and zipped up, you need to put it somewhere the application can find. You could put it in a couple of places, but for this example, you'll put it in an Amazon S3 bucket, a common way to store data in AWS. But to put it in an Amazon S3 bucket, you first need an Amazon S3 bucket! Let's make one in PowerShell. Go ahead and run **`New-S3Bucket -BucketName 'automateworkflow'`**.

With your S3 bucket up and waiting for contents, upload the ZIP file by using the `Write-S3Object` command, as shown in Listing 13-22.

```
PS> Write-S3Object -BucketName 'automateworkflow' -File 'C:\package.zip'
```

Listing 13-22: Uploading the package to S3

Now you have to point the application to the S3 key you just created and specify a version label for it. The version label can be anything, but typically, you use a unique number based on the time. So let's use the number of ticks representing the current date and time. Once you have the version label, run `New-EBApplicationVersion` with a few more parameters, as shown in Listing 13-23.

```
PS> $verLabel = [System.DateTime]::Now.Ticks.ToString()
PS> $newVerParams = @{
>>      ApplicationName       = 'AutomateWorkflow'
>>      VersionLabel          = $verLabel
>>      SourceBundle_S3Bucket = 'automateworkflow'
>>      SourceBundle_S3Key    = 'package.zip'
}
PS> New-EBApplicationVersion @newVerParams

ApplicationName        : AutomateWorkflow
BuildArn               :
DateCreated            : 9/19/2019 12:35:21 PM
DateUpdated            : 9/19/2019 12:35:21 PM
Description            :
SourceBuildInformation :
SourceBundle           : Amazon.ElasticBeanstalk.Model.S3Location
Status                 : Unprocessed
VersionLabel           : 636729573206374337
```

Listing 13-23: Creating a new application version

Your application version has now been created! It's time to deploy this version to your environment. Do that by using the `Update-EBEnvironment` command, as shown in Listing 13-24.

```
PS> Update-EBEnvironment -ApplicationName 'AutomateWorkflow'  -EnvironmentName
'Testing' -VersionLabel $verLabel -Force

AbortableOperationInProgress : True
ApplicationName              : AutomateWorkflow
CNAME                        : Testing.3u2ukxj2ux.us-ea...
DateCreated                  : 9/19/2019 12:19:36 PM
DateUpdated                  : 9/19/2019 12:37:04 PM
Description                  :
EndpointURL                  : awseb-e-w-AWSEBL...
EnvironmentArn               : arn:aws:elasticbeanstalk...
EnvironmentId                : e-wkba2k4kcf
EnvironmentLinks             : {}
EnvironmentName              : Testing
Health                       : Grey
HealthStatus                 :
PlatformArn                  : arn:aws:elasticbeanstalk:...
Resources                    :
SolutionStackName            : 64bit Windows Server Core 2012 R2 running IIS 8.5
Status                       : ❶Updating
TemplateName                 :
Tier                         : Amazon.ElasticBeanstalk.Model.EnvironmentTier
VersionLabel                 : 636729573206374337
```

Listing 13-24: Deploying the application to the EB environment

You can see that the status has gone from `Ready` to `Updating` ❶. Again, you need to wait a bit until the status turns back to `Ready` as you can see in Listing 13-25.

```
PS> Get-EBEnvironment -ApplicationName 'AutomateWorkflow'
-EnvironmentName 'Testing'

AbortableOperationInProgress : False
ApplicationName              : AutomateWorkflow
CNAME                        : Testing.3u2ukxj2ux.us-e...
DateCreated                  : 9/19/2019 12:19:36 PM
DateUpdated                  : 9/19/2019 12:38:53 PM
Description                  :
EndpointURL                  : awseb-e-w-AWSEBL...
EnvironmentArn               : arn:aws:elasticbeanstalk...
EnvironmentId                : e-wkba2k4kcf
EnvironmentLinks             : {}
EnvironmentName              : Testing
Health                       : Green
HealthStatus                 :
PlatformArn                  : arn:aws:elasticbeanstalk:...
Resources                    :
SolutionStackName            : 64bit Windows Server Core 2012 R2 running IIS 8.5
Status                       : ❶Ready
TemplateName                 :
Tier                         : Amazon.ElasticBeanstalk.Model.EnvironmentTier
VersionLabel                 :
```

Listing 13-25: Confirming the application is ready

As you check in, the status is Ready again ❶. Everything looks good!

Creating a SQL Server Database in AWS

As an AWS administrator, you may need to set up different types of relational databases. AWS provides the Amazon Relational Database Service (Amazon RDS), which allows for administrators to easily provision a few types of databases. There a few options, but for now, you'll stick with SQL.

In this section, you'll create a blank Microsoft SQL Server database in RDS. The main command you'll use is `New-RDSDBInstance`. Like `New-AzureRmSqlDatabase`, `New-RDSDBInstance` has *a lot* of parameters, more than I can possibly cover in this section. If you're curious about other ways to provision RDS instances, I encourage you to review the help contents for `New-RDSDBInstance`.

For our purposes, though, you need the following information:

- The name of the instance
- The database engine (SQL Server, MariaDB, MySQL, and so on)
- The instance class that specifies the type of resources the SQL Server runs on
- The master username and password
- The size of the database (in GB)

A few of these things you can figure out easily: the name, username/password, and size. The others require further investigation.

Let's start with the engine version. You can get a list of all available engines and their versions by using the `Get-RDSDBEngineVersion` command. When run with no parameters, this command returns a lot of information—too much for what you're doing. You can use the `Group-Object` command to group all the objects by engine, which will provide a list of all engine versions grouped by the engine name. As you can see in Listing 13-26, you now have a more manageable output that shows all the available engines you can use.

```
PS> Get-RDSDBEngineVersion | Group-Object -Property Engine

Count Name                     Group
----- ----                     -----
    1 aurora-mysql             {Amazon.RDS.Model.DBEngineVersion}
    1 aurora-mysql-pq          {Amazon.RDS.Model.DBEngineVersion}
    1 neptune                  {Amazon.RDS.Model.DBEngineVersion}
--snip--
   16 sqlserver-ee             {Amazon.RDS.Model.DBEngineVersion,
                               Amazon.RDS.Model.DBEngineVersion,
                               Amazon.RDS.Model.DBEngineVersion,
                               Amazon.RDS.Mo...

   17 sqlserver-ex             {Amazon.RDS.Model.DBEngineVersion,
                               Amazon.RDS.Model.DBEngineVersion,
                               Amazon.RDS.Model.DBEngineVersion,
                               Amazon.RDS.Mo...

   17 sqlserver-se             {Amazon.RDS.Model.DBEngineVersion,
                               Amazon.RDS.Model.DBEngineVersion,
                               Amazon.RDS.Model.DBEngineVersion,
                               Amazon.RDS.Mo...

   17 sqlserver-web            {Amazon.RDS.Model.DBEngineVersion,
                               Amazon.RDS.Model.DBEngineVersion,
                               Amazon.RDS.Model.DBEngineVersion,
                               Amazon.RDS.Mo...
--snip--
```

Listing 13-26: Investigating RDS DB engine versions

You have four `sqlserver` entries, representing SQL Server Express, Web, Standard Edition, and Enterprise Edition. Since this is just an example, you'll go with SQL Server Express; it's a no-frills database engine and, most important, it's free, which allows you to tune and tweak it if necessary. Select the SQL Server Express engine by using **`sqlserver-ex`**.

After picking an engine, you have to specify a version. By default, `New-RDSDBInstance` provisions the latest version (which you'll be using), but you can specify a different version by using the `EngineVersion` parameter. To see all the available versions, you'll run `Get-RDSDBEngineVersion` again, limit the search to `sqlserver-ex`, and return only the engine versions (Listing 13-27).

```
PS> Get-RDSDBEngineVersion -Engine 'sqlserver-ex' |
Format-Table -Property EngineVersion

EngineVersion
-------------
10.50.6000.34.v1
10.50.6529.0.v1
10.50.6560.0.v1
11.00.5058.0.v1
11.00.6020.0.v1
11.00.6594.0.v1
11.00.7462.6.v1
12.00.4422.0.v1
12.00.5000.0.v1
12.00.5546.0.v1
12.00.5571.0.v1
13.00.2164.0.v1
13.00.4422.0.v1
13.00.4451.0.v1
13.00.4466.4.v1
14.00.1000.169.v1
14.00.3015.40.v1
```

Listing 13-27: Finding SQL Server Express engine versions

The next parameter value you need to provide to `New-RDSDBInstance` is the instance class. The instance class represents the performance of the underlying infrastructure—memory, CPU, and so forth—that the database will be hosted on. Unfortunately, there's no PowerShell command to easily find all available instance class options, but you can check out this link to get a full rundown: *https://docs.aws.amazon.com/AmazonRDS/latest/UserGuide/Concepts.DBInstanceClass.html.*

When selecting an instance class, it's important to verify that it's supported by the engine you chose. Here, you'll use the `db2.t2.micro` instance class to create your RDS DB, but many of the other options will not work. For a full breakdown on which instance classes are supported under which RDS DB, refer to the AWS RDS FAQs (*https://aws.amazon.com/rds/faqs/*). If you choose an instance class that's not supported by the engine you're using, you'll receive an error as in Listing 13-28.

```
New-RDSDBInstance : RDS does not support creating a DB instance with the
following combination: DBInstanceClass=db.t1.micro, Engine=sqlserver-ex,
EngineVersion=14.00.3015.40.v1, LicenseModel=license-included. For supported
combinations of instance class and database engine version, see the
documentation.
```

Listing 13-28: Error when specifying an invalid instance configuration

Once you've selected a (supported) instance class, you have to decide on a username and password. Note that AWS will not accept any old password: you cannot have a slash, `@` sign, comma, or space in your password, or you will receive an error message like the one in Listing 13-29.

```
New-RDSDBInstance : The parameter MasterUserPassword is not a valid password.
Only printable ASCII characters besides '/', '@', '"', ' ' may be used.
```

Listing 13-29: Specifying an invalid password with `New-RDSDBInstance`

With that, you have all the parameters needed to fire off `New-RDSDBInstance`! You can see the expected output in Listing 13-30.

```
PS> $parameters = @{
>>      DBInstanceIdentifier = 'Automating'
>>      Engine = 'sqlserver-ex'
>>      DBInstanceClass = 'db.t2.micro'
>>      MasterUsername = 'sa'
>>      MasterUserPassword = 'password'
>>      AllocatedStorage = 20
}
PS> New-RDSDBInstance @parameters

AllocatedStorage                        : 20
AutoMinorVersionUpgrade                 : True
AvailabilityZone                        :
BackupRetentionPeriod                   : 1
CACertificateIdentifier                 : rds-ca-2015
CharacterSetName                        :
CopyTagsToSnapshot                      : False
--snip--
```

Listing 13-30: Provisioning a new RDS database instance

Congratulations! Your AWS should have a shiny, new RDS database.

Summary

This chapter covered the basics of using AWS with PowerShell. You looked at AWS authentication and then went through several common AWS tasks: creating EC2 instances, deploying Elastic Beanstalk web applications, and provisioning an Amazon RDS SQL database.

After this chapter and the preceding one, you should have a good sense of how to use PowerShell to work with the cloud. Of course, there's much more to learn—more than I could ever cover in this book—but for now, you'll be moving on to the next part of this book: creating your own fully functional PowerShell module.

14

CREATING A SERVER INVENTORY SCRIPT

So far in this book, you've focused on learning PowerShell as a language, getting familiar with its syntax and commands. But more than a language, PowerShell is a tool. Now that you have a grip on the ins and outs of PowerShell, it's time for the fun stuff!

The real power of PowerShell lies in its tool-making abilities. In this context, a *tool* refers to a PowerShell script, a module, a function, or something that helps you perform a management task. Whether that task is creating a report, gathering information about a computer, creating a company user account, or something more complex, you'll learn how to automate it with PowerShell.

In this chapter, I'll show you how to collect data with PowerShell so you can make more-informed decisions. Specifically, you'll build a server inventory project. You'll learn to create a script with parameters, feed it server names, and discover a wealth of information to peruse: operating system specs as well as hardware information including storage size, free storage, memory, and more.

Prerequisites

Before you begin this chapter, you need to have a domain-joined Windows computer, read permission to Active Directory computer objects, an Active Directory organizational unit (OU) of computer accounts, and the Remote Server Administration Toolkit (RSAT) software package, which you can download from *https://www.microsoft.com/en-us/download/details.aspx?id=45520.*

Creating the Project Script(s)

Since you'll be building scripts in this chapter and not just executing code at the console, you first need to create a new PowerShell script. Create a script called *Get-ServerInformation.ps1*. I've put mine in *C:*. You'll be adding code to this script throughout the chapter.

Defining the Final Output

Before you start coding, it's good practice to make a "back of the napkin" plan of what you want the output to look like when you're done. This simple sketch is a great way to measure progress, especially when building large scripts.

For this server inventory script, we'll say that when the script ends, you'd like output to the PowerShell console that looks like this:

```
ServerName IPAddress OperatingSystem AvailableDriveSpace (GB) Memory (GB) UserProfilesSize (MB) StoppedServices
MYSERVER   x.x.x.x   Windows....     10                       4           50.4                  service1,service2,service3
```

Now that you know what you want to see, let's make it happen.

Discovery and Script Input

The first step is deciding how to tell your script what to query. You'll be collecting information from multiple servers. As stated in the "Prerequisites" section, you'll use Active Directory to find your server names.

Of course, you could query server names from text files, from an array of server names stored in a PowerShell script, from the Registry, from a Windows Management Instrumentation (WMI) repository, from databases—it doesn't matter. As long as somehow, some way, your script ends up with an array of strings representing server names, you're good to go. For this project, however, you'll use servers from Active Directory.

In this example, all the servers are in a single OU. If you try this on your own and you find that they're not, that's okay; you'll just have to loop through your OUs and read the computer objects in each. But here, your first task is reading all the computer objects in the OU. In this environment, all the servers are in the `Servers` OU. Your domain is called `powerlab.local`. To retrieve computer objects from AD, use the Get-ADComputer command, as shown in Listing 14-1. This command should return all the AD computer objects for the servers you're interested in.

```
PS> $serversOuPath = 'OU=Servers,DC=powerlab,DC=local'
PS> $servers = Get-ADComputer -SearchBase $serversOuPath -Filter *
PS> $servers

DistinguishedName : CN=SQLSRV1,OU=Servers,DC=Powerlab,DC=local
DNSHostName       : SQLSRV1.Powerlab.local
Enabled           : True
Name              : SQLSRV1
ObjectClass       : computer
ObjectGUID        : c288d6c1-56d4-4405-ab03-80142ac04b40
SamAccountName    : SQLSRV1$
SID               : S-1-5-21-763434571-1107771424-1976677938-1105
UserPrincipalName :

DistinguishedName : CN=WEBSRV1,OU=Servers,DC=Powerlab,DC=local
DNSHostName       : WEBSRV1.Powerlab.local
Enabled           : True
Name              : WEBSRV1
ObjectClass       : computer
ObjectGUID        : 3bd2da11-4abb-4eb6-9c71-7f2c58594a98
SamAccountName    : WEBSRV1$
SID               : S-1-5-21-763434571-1107771424-1976677938-1106
UserPrincipalName :
```

Listing 14-1: Using Get-AdComputer to return server data

Notice that instead of directly setting the SearchBase parameter argument, you define a variable. You should get used to doing this. In fact, every time you have a specific configuration like this, it's always a good idea to put it into a variable, because you never know when you'll need to use that value again. You also return the output of Get-ADComputer to a variable. Since you'll be working with these servers later, you want to have the names to reference.

The Get-ADComputer command returns the whole AD objects, but you're looking for just the server names. You can narrow this down by using Select -Object to return only the Name property:

```
PS> $servers = Get-ADComputer -SearchBase $serversOuPath -Filter * |
Select-Object -ExpandProperty Name
PS> $servers
SQLSRV1
WEBSRV1
```

Now that you have a basic idea of how to query an individual server, let's look at how to query all of them.

Querying Each Server

To query each server, you need to make a loop that'll make it possible to query every server in your array exactly once.

It's never a good idea to assume that your code will work immediately (it usually doesn't). Instead, I like to start slow and test each piece as I'm building it. In this case, instead of trying to do everything in one go, use `Write-Host` to ensure that the script is returning the server names you expect:

```
foreach ($server in $servers) {
    Write-Host $server
}
```

By now, you should have a script called *Get-ServerInformation.ps1* that looks like Listing 14-2.

```
$serversOuPath = 'OU=Servers,DC=powerlab,DC=local'
$servers = Get-ADComputer -SearchBase $serversOuPath -Filter * | Select-Object -ExpandProperty Name
foreach ($server in $servers) {
    Write-Host $server
}
```

Listing 14-2: Your script so far

Once you run the script, you get a few server names. Your output may look different, depending on which servers you used:

```
PS> C:\Get-ServerInformation.ps1
SQLSRV1
WEBSRV1
```

Great! You have a loop setup that iterates over each server name in your array. Your first task is complete.

Thinking Ahead: Combining Different Types of Information

One of the keys to success with PowerShell is good planning and organization. Part of this is knowing what to expect. For many beginners, who don't have much experience with the kinds of results PowerShell will give, this is a problem: they know what they want to happen (hopefully), but they don't know what *could* happen. As a result, they create scripts that zigzag among data sources, getting data from one, and then the other, and then the first, and then the third, linking them all together, and doing it all again. There are easier ways to do things, and I would be doing you a disservice if I didn't pause to explain them.

Looking at the output in Listing 14-1, you can see that you'll need a few commands to pull information from various sources (WMI, the filesystem, Windows services). Each source will return a different kind of object, and you'll have an absolute mess if you try to combine them thoughtlessly.

Jumping ahead a little, let's get a glimpse of what the output would look like if you tried to pull the service name and memory without any formatting or output attention. You might get something like this:

```
Status   Name               DisplayName
------   ----               -----------
Running  wuauserv           Windows Update

__GENUS              : 2
__CLASS              : Win32_PhysicalMemory
__SUPERCLASS         : CIM_PhysicalMemory
__DYNASTY            : CIM_ManagedSystemElement
__RELPATH            : Win32_PhysicalMemory.Tag="Physical Memory 0"
__PROPERTY_COUNT     : 30
__DERIVATION         : {CIM_PhysicalMemory, CIM_Chip, CIM_PhysicalComponent, CIM_PhysicalElement...}
__SERVER             : DC
__NAMESPACE          : root\cimv2
__PATH               : \\DC\root\cimv2:Win32_PhysicalMemory.Tag="Physical Memory 0"
```

Here, you're querying a service and trying to get memory from a server at the same time. The objects are different, the properties on those objects are different, and if you merge all the output and dump it, it looks terrible.

Let's see how to avoid this kind of output. Since you'll be combining different kinds of output, and you need something that fits our exact specifications, you have to create your own type of output. Don't worry, this isn't as complicated as you might think. In Chapter 2, you learned how to create `PSCustomObject` types. These generic objects in PowerShell allow you to add your own properties—perfect for what you're doing here.

You know the headers of the output you need (and, as I'm sure you know by now, these "headers" will always be object properties). Let's create a custom object with the properties you'd like to see in the output. For obvious reasons, I've called this object `$output`; you'll return it after you populate its properties:

```
$output = [pscustomobject]@{
    'ServerName'                 = $null
    'IPAddress'                  = $null
    'OperatingSystem'            = $null
    'AvailableDriveSpace (GB)'   = $null
    'Memory (GB)'                = $null
    'UserProfilesSize (MB)'      = $null
    'StoppedServices'            = $null
}
```

You'll notice that the hashtable keys are surrounded by single quotes. This isn't mandatory if there's no space in the key. However, because I am using spaces in some key names, I decided to standardize on single quotes across all of the keys. It's generally not recommended to use spaces in object property names in lieu of using custom formatting, but that is outside the scope of this book. For more information on custom formatting, refer to the *about_Format.ps1xml* help topic.

If you copy this to the console, and return it with the formatting cmdlet, `Format-Table`, you can see the headers you're looking for:

```
PS> $output | Format-Table -AutoSize

ServerName IPAddress OperatingSystem AvailableDriveSpace (GB) Memory (GB) UserProfilesSize (MB) StoppedServices
```

The `Format-Table` command is one of a few format commands in PowerShell that are meant to be used as the last command in the pipeline. They transform current output and display it differently. In this instance, you're telling PowerShell to transform your object output into a table format and autosize the rows based on the width of the console.

Once you define your custom output object, you can go back to your loop and make sure each server is returned in this format. Since you already know the server name, you can set that property right away, as in Listing 14-3.

```
$serversOuPath = 'OU=Servers,DC=powerlab,DC=local'
$servers = Get-ADComputer -SearchBase $serversOuPath -Filter * | Select-Object -ExpandProperty Name
foreach ($server in $servers) {
    $output = @{
        'ServerName'                  = $server
        'IPAddress'                   = $null
        'OperatingSystem'             = $null
        'AvailableDriveSpace (GB)'    = $null
        'Memory (GB)'                 = $null
        'UserProfilesSize (MB)'       = $null
        'StoppedServices'             = $null
    }
    [pscustomobject]$output
}
```

Listing 14-3: Putting your output object in your loop and setting the server name

Notice that you created `output` as a hashtable and cast it as a `PSCustomObject` only after you filled it with data. You do this because it's simpler to keep the property values in a hashtable than in a `PSCustomObject`; you care about `output` being an object of that type only when it's being output so that when you bring in other sources of information, they will all be the same object type.

You can see all the property names that your `PSCustomObject` has, along with the names of the servers you're querying, with this code:

```
PS> C:\Get-ServerInformation.ps1 | Format-Table -AutoSize

ServerName UserProfilesSize (MB) AvailableDriveSpace (GB) OperatingSystem StoppedServices IPAddress Memory (GB)
---------- --------------------- ------------------------ --------------- --------------- --------- -----------
SQLSRV1
WEBSRV1
```

As you can see, you have data. It may not seem like much, but you're well on your way!

Querying Remote Files

Now that you know how you're going to store your data, you just need to get it. This means pulling the information you need from each server and returning only the properties you care about. Let's start with the value for `UserProfileSize` (MB). To do this, let's figure out a way to find out how much space is being consumed by all these profiles located in the *C:\Users* folder on each server.

Because of the way you set up the loop, you need to figure out how to do this for only one server. Since you know the folder path is *C:\Users*, let's first see if you can query all the files under all the server's user profile folders.

When you run `Get-ChildItem -Path \\WEBSRV1\c$\Users -Recurse -File` and have access to that file share, you can immediately see it's returning all the files and folders in all user profiles, but you don't see anything related to size. Let's pipe the output to `Select-Object` to return all properties:

```
PS> Get-ChildItem -Path \\WEBSRV1\c$\Users -Recurse -File | Select-Object -Property *

PSPath            : Microsoft.PowerShell.Core\FileSystem::\WEBSRV1\c$\Users\Adam\file.log
PSParentPath      : Microsoft.PowerShell.Core\FileSystem::\\WEBSRV1\c$\Users\Adam
PSChildName       : file.log
PSProvider        : Microsoft.PowerShell.Core\FileSystem
PSIsContainer     : False
Mode              : -a----
VersionInfo       : File:             \\WEBSRV1\c$\Users\Adam\file.log
                    InternalName:
                    OriginalFilename:
                    FileVersion:
                    FileDescription:
                    Product:
                    ProductVersion:
                    Debug:            False
                    Patched:          False
                    PreRelease:       False
                    PrivateBuild:     False
                    SpecialBuild:     False
                    Language:

BaseName          : file
Target            :
LinkType          :
Name              : file.log
Length            : 8926
DirectoryName     : \\WEBSRV1\c$\Users\Adam
--snip--
```

The `Length` property shows how large the file is in bytes. Knowing this, you'll have to figure out how to add up the `Length` values of each file in the server's *C:\Users* folder. Luckily, PowerShell makes this easy with one of its cmdlets: `Measure-Object`. This cmdlet accepts input from the pipeline and automatically adds up the values of a specific property:

```
PS> Get-ChildItem -Path '\\WEBSRV1\c$\Users\' -File | Measure-Object -Property Length -Sum

Count    : 15
Average  :
Sum      : 600554
Maximum  :
Minimum  :
Property : Length
```

You now have a property (`Sum`) that you can use to represent the total user profile size in your output. At this point, it's just a matter of incorporating the code into your loop and setting the appropriate property in your `$output` hashtable. Since you need only the `Sum` property from the object returned by `Measure-Object`, you'll enclose the command in parentheses and reference the `Sum` property as in Listing 14-4.

```
Get-ServerInformation.ps1
-------------------
$serversOuPath = 'OU=Servers,DC=powerlab,DC=local'
$servers = Get-ADComputer -SearchBase $serversOuPath -Filter * | Select-Object -ExpandProperty Name
foreach ($server in $servers) {
    $output = @{
        'ServerName'                  = $null
        'IPAddress'                   = $null
        'OperatingSystem'             = $null
        'AvailableDriveSpace (GB)'    = $null
        'Memory (GB)'                 = $null
        'UserProfilesSize (MB)'       = $null
        'StoppedServices'             = $null
    }
    $output.ServerName = $server
    $output.'UserProfilesSize (MB)' = (Get-ChildItem -Path "\\$server\c$\Users\" -File |
    Measure-Object -Property Length -Sum).Sum
    [pscustomobject]$output
}
```

Listing 14-4: Updating your script to store `UserProfilesSize`

If you run the script, you get the following:

```
PS> C:\Get-ServerInformation.ps1 | Format-Table -AutoSize

ServerName UserProfilesSize (MB) AvailableDriveSpace (GB) OperatingSystem StoppedServices IPAddress Memory (GB)
---------- --------------------- ------------------------ --------------- --------------- --------- -----------
SQLSRV1                   636245
WEBSRV1                   600554
```

As you can see, you now have the total size of the user profiles—but it's not in megabytes. You calculated the sum of `Length`, and `Length` is in bytes. PowerShell makes conversions like this easy: if you simply divide the number by `1MB`, you'll have your number. You might see the resulting values represented with decimal points. You can take a final step and ensure that you have a whole number by casting the output to an integer, which will "round" the number to a whole megabyte value:

```
$userProfileSize = (Get-ChildItem -Path "\\$server\c$\Users\" -File |
Measure-Object -Property Length -Sum).Sum
$output.'UserProfilesSize (MB)' = [int]($userProfileSize / 1MB)
```

Querying Windows Management Instrumentation

You have five more values to fill. For four of them, you'll use a built-in Microsoft feature called *Windows Management Instrumentation (WMI)*. Based on the industry standard Common Information Model (CIM), WMI is a repository containing real-time information about thousands of attributes relating to the operating system and the hardware it's running on. The information is separated into various namespaces, classes, and properties. If you're looking for information about a computer, chances are, you'll be using WMI a lot.

For this particular script, you'll pull information about hard drive space, the operating system version, the server's IP address, and the amount of memory the server contains.

PowerShell has two commands to query WMI: `Get-WmiObject` and `Get-CimInstance`. The `Get-WmiObject` command is older and not as flexible as `Get-CimInstance` (if you want the technical details: this is mainly because `Get-WmiObject` uses only DCOM to connect to remote computers, while `Get-CimInstance`, by default, uses WSMAN and can optionally use DCOM as well). As of right now, Microsoft appears to be putting all its effort into `Get-CimInstance`, so that's the command you'll use. For a detailed breakdown of CIM versus WMI, check out this blog post: *https://blogs.technet.microsoft.com/heyscriptingguy/2016/02/08/should-i-use-cim-or-wmi-with-windows-powershell/*.

The hardest part of querying WMI is figuring out where the information you're looking for is hidden. Normally, you'd do this research on your own (and I encourage you to try it here), but for time's sake, let me offer you the answer sheet to this script: all storage resource usage is in `Win32_LogicalDisk`, information about the operating system is in `Win32_OperatingSystem`, Windows services are all represented in `Win32_Service`, any network adapter information is in `Win32_NetworkAdapterConfiguration`, and memory information is in `Win32_PhysicalMemory`.

Now let's see how to use `Get-CimInstance` to query these WMI classes for the properties you're looking for.

Disk Free Space

Let's start with the available hard drive space, found in `Win32_LogicalDisk`. As with `UserProfilesSize`, you'll start with one server and then generalize in your loop. Here, you can see that you lucked out; you don't even need to use `Select-Object` to dig into all the properties—`FreeSpace` is right there:

```
PS> Get-CimInstance -ComputerName sqlsrv1 -ClassName Win32_LogicalDisk

DeviceID DriveType ProviderName VolumeName Size        FreeSpace   PSComputerName
-------- --------- ------------ ---------- ----        ---------   --------------
C:       3                                 42708496384 34145906688 sqlsrv1
```

Knowing that `Get-CimInstance` returns an object, you can simply access the property that you need to get only the amount of free space:

```
PS> (Get-CimInstance -ComputerName sqlsrv1 -ClassName Win32_LogicalDisk).FreeSpace
34145906688
```

You have the value but, like last time, it's in bytes (this is a common thing in WMI). You can do the same conversion trick as before, except now you want gigabytes so you'll divide by `1GB`. When you update the script by dividing the `FreeSpace` property by `1GB`, you get output that looks something like this:

```
PS> C:\Get-ServerInformation.ps1 | Format-Table -AutoSize

ServerName UserProfilesSize (MB) AvailableDriveSpace (GB) OperatingSystem StoppedServices IPAddress Memory (GB)
---------- --------------------- ------------------------ --------------- --------------- --------- -----------
SQLSRV1                   636245         31.800853729248
WEBSRV1                   603942        34.5973815917969
```

You don't need to see the free space out to 12 digits, so you can do a little rounding by using the `Round()` method on the `[Math]` class, making the output look much better:

```
$output.'AvailableDriveSpace (GB)' = [Math]::Round(((Get-CimInstance -ComputerName $server
-ClassName Win32_LogicalDisk).FreeSpace / 1GB),1)

ServerName UserProfilesSize (MB) AvailableDriveSpace (GB) OperatingSystem StoppedServices IPAddress Memory (GB)
---------- --------------------- ------------------------ --------------- --------------- --------- -----------
SQLSRV1                   636245                     31.8
WEBSRV1                   603942                     34.6
```

Now the values are much easier to read. Three down, four to go.

Operating System Information

By now you should see the general pattern: query a single server, find the appropriate property, and add the query to your `foreach` loop.

From now on, you'll simply add lines to your `foreach` loop. The process of narrowing down the class, class property, and the property value is the same for any value you'll be querying from WMI. Just follow this same general pattern:

```
$output.'PropertyName' = (Get-CimInstance -ComputerName ServerName
-ClassName WMIClassName).WMIClassPropertyName
```

Adding the next value gives you a script that looks like Listing 14-5.

```
Get-ServerInformation.ps1
-------------------
$serversOuPath = 'OU=Servers,DC=powerlab,DC=local'
$servers = Get-ADComputer -SearchBase $serversOuPath -Filter * |
Select-Object -ExpandProperty Name
foreach ($server in $servers) {
    $output = @{
        'ServerName'                  = $null
        'IPAddress'                   = $null
        'OperatingSystem'             = $null
        'AvailableDriveSpace (GB)'    = $null
        'Memory (GB)'                 = $null
        'UserProfilesSize (MB)'       = $null
        'StoppedServices'             = $null
    }
    $output.ServerName = $server
    $output.'UserProfilesSize (MB)' = (Get-ChildItem -Path "\\$server\c$\
    Users\" -File | Measure-Object -Property Length -Sum).Sum / 1MB
    $output.'AvailableDriveSpace (GB)' = [Math]::Round(((Get-CimInstance
    -ComputerName $server -ClassName Win32_LogicalDisk).FreeSpace / 1GB),1)
    $output.'OperatingSystem' = (Get-CimInstance -ComputerName $server
    -ClassName Win32_OperatingSystem).Caption
    [pscustomobject]$output
}
```

Listing 14-5: Your script updated to include a query for `OperatingSystem`

Now run your script:

```
PS> C:\Get-ServerInformation.ps1 | Format-Table -AutoSize

ServerName UserProfilesSize (MB) AvailableDriveSpace (GB) OperatingSystem                          StoppedServices IPAddress Memory (GB)
---------- --------------------- ------------------------ ---------------                          --------------- --------- -----------
SQLSRV1                   636245         31.8005790710449 Microsoft Windows Server 2016 Standard
WEBSRV1                   603942         34.5973815917969 Microsoft Windows Server 2012 R2 Standard
```

You've gotten some useful OS information. Let's take the next step and figure out how to query some information on memory.

Memory

Moving onto the next piece of information to gather (`Memory`), you'll use the `Win32_PhysicalMemory` class. Testing your query on a single server again gives the information you're looking for. In this case, the memory information you need is stored in Capacity:

```
PS> Get-CimInstance -ComputerName sqlsrv1 -ClassName Win32_PhysicalMemory

Caption              : Physical Memory
Description          : Physical Memory
InstallDate          :
Name                 : Physical Memory
Status               :
CreationClassName    : Win32_PhysicalMemory
Manufacturer         : Microsoft Corporation
Model                :
OtherIdentifyingInfo :
--snip--
Capacity             : 2147483648
--snip--
```

Each instance under Win32_PhysicalMemory represents a *bank* of RAM. You can think of a bank as a physical stick of RAM in a server. It just so happens that my SQLSRV1 server has only one bank of memory. However, you will undoubtedly find servers with many more.

Since you're looking for total memory in a server, you'll have to follow the same routine you used to get profile size. You'll have to add up the value of Capacity across all the instances. Lucky for us, the Measure-Object cmdlet works across any number of object types. As long as the property is a number, it can add them all up.

Again, since Capacity was represented in bytes, you'll convert it to the appropriate label:

```
PS> (Get-CimInstance -ComputerName sqlsrv1 -ClassName Win32_PhysicalMemory |
Measure-Object -Property Capacity -Sum).Sum /1GB
2
```

As you can see in Listing 14-6, your script grows and grows!

```
Get-ServerInformation.ps1
-------------------
$serversOuPath = 'OU=Servers,DC=powerlab,DC=local'
$servers = Get-ADComputer -SearchBase $serversOuPath -Filter * | Select-Object
-ExpandProperty Name
foreach ($server in $servers) {
    $output = @{
        'ServerName'                = $null
        'IPAddress'                 = $null
        'OperatingSystem'           = $null
        'AvailableDriveSpace (GB)'  = $null
        'Memory (GB)'               = $null
        'UserProfilesSize (MB)'     = $null
        'StoppedServices'           = $null
    }
```

```
    $output.ServerName = $server
    $output.'UserProfilesSize (MB)' = (Get-ChildItem -Path "\\$server\c$\
    Users\" -File | Measure-Object -Property Length -Sum).Sum / 1MB
    $output.'AvailableDriveSpace (GB)' = [Math]::Round(((Get-CimInstance
    -ComputerName $server -ClassName Win32_LogicalDisk).FreeSpace / 1GB),1)
    $output.'OperatingSystem' = (Get-CimInstance -ComputerName $server
    -ClassName Win32_OperatingSystem).Caption
    $output.'Memory (GB)' = (Get-CimInstance -ComputerName $server -ClassName
    Win32_PhysicalMemory | Measure-Object -Property Capacity -Sum).Sum /1GB
    [pscustomobject]$output
}
```

Listing 14-6: Your script with the query for Memory

Let's look at the output so far:

```
PS> C:\Get-ServerInformation.ps1 | Format-Table -AutoSize

ServerName UserProfilesSize (MB) AvailableDriveSpace (GB) OperatingSystem                            StoppedServices IPAddress Memory (GB)
---------- --------------------- ------------------------ ---------------                            --------------- --------- -----------
SQLSRV1                   636245                     31.8 Microsoft Windows Server 2016 Standard                                         2
WEBSRV1                   603942                     34.6 Microsoft Windows Server 2012 R2 Standard                                      2
```

With that, you have only two fields left to fill!

Network Information

The final piece of WMI information is the IP address, which you'll grab from Win32_NetworkAdapterConfiguration. I saved the task of finding the IP address for last because, unlike the other data entries, finding the IP address of the server isn't as cut and dried as finding a value and then adding it to your $output hashtable. You'll have to do some filtering to narrow it down.

Let's first see what the output looks like using the same method you've used so far:

```
PS> Get-CimInstance -ComputerName SQLSRV1 -ClassName Win32_NetworkAdapterConfiguration

ServiceName    DHCPEnabled    Index    Description    PSComputerName
-----------    -----------    -----    -----------    --------------
kdnic          True           0        Microsoft...   SQLSRV1
netvsc         False          1        Microsoft...   SQLSRV1
tunnel         False          2        Microsoft...   SQLSRV1
```

You'll see right away that the default output doesn't show the IP address, not that that has stopped you before. But, somewhat trickier, here the command doesn't return a single instance. This server has three network adapters on it. How do you select the one that has the IP address you're looking for?

First, you have to see all the properties by using Select-Object. Using Get-CimInstance -ComputerName SQLSRV1 -ClassName Win32_NetworkAdapter Configuration | Select-Object -Property *, you can scroll through the (substantial) output. Depending on the network adapters installed on the server, you may notice fields that don't have anything for the IPAddress property. This is common because network adapters do not have an IP address. However, when you do find one with an IP address bound to it, it should look similar to the following code, where you can see the IPAddress property ❶ has (in this instance) an IPv4 address of 192.168.0.40 and a couple of IPv6 addresses:

```
DHCPLeaseExpires              :
Index                         : 1
Description                   : Microsoft Hyper-V Network Adapter
DHCPEnabled                   : False
DHCPLeaseObtained             :
DHCPServer                    :
DNSDomain                     : Powerlab.local
DNSDomainSuffixSearchOrder    : {Powerlab.local}
DNSEnabledForWINSResolution   : False
DNSHostName                   : SQLSRV1
DNSServerSearchOrder          : {192.168.0.100}
DomainDNSRegistrationEnabled  : True
FullDNSRegistrationEnabled    : True
❶ IPAddress                   : {192.168.0.40...
IPConnectionMetric            : 20
IPEnabled                     : True
IPFilterSecurityEnabled       : False
--snip--
```

The script needs to be dynamic and support lots of network adapter configurations. It's important that the script is able to handle other types of network adapters other than the Microsoft Hyper-V Network Adapter you're working with here. You'll need to find a standard criterion to filter on so that it can apply to all servers.

The IPEnabled property is the key. When this property is set to True, the TCP/IP protocol is bound to this network adapter, which is a prerequisite to having an IP address. If you can narrow down the NIC that has the IPEnabled property set to True, you'll have the adapter you're looking for.

When filtering WMI instances, it's always best to use the Filter parameter on Get-CimInstance. There's a saying in the PowerShell community: *filter left*. Basically, it means that if you can, always filter output as far to the left as possible—meaning filter as early as possible so that you're not sending unnecessary objects through the pipeline. Don't use Where-Object unless you have to. The performance will be much faster instead if the pipeline isn't clogged with unneeded objects.

The Filter parameter on Get-CimInstance uses *Windows Query Language (WQL)*, which is a small subset of *Structured Query Language (SQL)*. The Filter parameter accepts the same WHERE clause syntax that WQL does. Take this example: if, in WQL, you want all the Win32_NetworkAdapterConfiguration class instances with the IPEnabled property set to True, you could use SELECT * FROM Win32_NetworkAdapterConfiguration WHERE IPEnabled = 'True'. Since you're already specifying the class name for the ClassName parameter argument in Get-CimInstance, you need to specify IPEnabled = 'True' for Filter:

```
Get-CimInstance -ComputerName SQLSRV1 -ClassName Win32_NetworkAdapterConfiguration
-Filter "IPEnabled = 'True'" | Select-Object -Property *
```

This should return only network adapters that are IPEnabled (meaning they have an IP address).

Now that you have a single WMI instance, and now that you know the property you're looking for (IPAddress), let's see what it looks like when querying a single server. You'll use the same *object.property* syntax you've been using:

```
PS> (Get-CimInstance -ComputerName SQLSRV1 -ClassName Win32_NetworkAdapterConfiguration
-Filter "IPEnabled = 'True'").IPAddress

192.168.0.40
fe80::e4e1:c511:e38b:4f05
2607:fcc8:acd9:1f00:e4e1:c511:e38b:4f05
```

Ouch! Looks like it has IPv4 and IPv6 references in there. You'll have to filter out more elements. Because WQL can't filter deeper than the property value, you'll need to parse out the IPv4 address.

Doing some investigation, you can see that all the addresses are enclosed with curly brackets separated by a comma:

```
IPAddress : {192.168.0.40, fe80::e4e1:c511:e38b:4f05, 2607:fcc8:acd9:1f00:e4e1:c511:e38b:4f05}
```

This is a good indication that this property isn't stored as one big string but rather as an array. To confirm that this is an array, you can try using an index to see whether you can get only the IPv4 address:

```
PS> (Get-CimInstance -ComputerName SQLSRV1 -ClassName Win32_NetworkAdapterConfiguration
-Filter "IPEnabled = 'True'").IPAddress[0]

192.168.0.40
```

You're in luck! The IPAddress property *is* an array. At this point, you have your value, and you can add your full command to your script, as shown in Listing 14-7.

```
Get-ServerInformation.ps1
-------------------
$serversOuPath = 'OU=Servers,DC=powerlab,DC=local'
$servers = Get-ADComputer -SearchBase $serversOuPath -Filter * |
Select-Object -ExpandProperty Name
foreach ($server in $servers) {
    $output = @{
        'ServerName'                = $null
        'IPAddress'                 = $null
```

```
        'OperatingSystem'             = $null
        'AvailableDriveSpace (GB)'    = $null
        'Memory (GB)'                 = $null
        'UserProfilesSize (MB)'       = $null
        'StoppedServices'             = $null
    }
    $output.ServerName = $server
    $output.'UserProfilesSize (MB)' = (Get-ChildItem -Path "\\$server\c$\
    Users\" -File | Measure-Object -Property Length -Sum).Sum / 1MB
    $output.'AvailableDriveSpace (GB)' = [Math]::Round(((Get-CimInstance
    -ComputerName $server -ClassName Win32_LogicalDisk).FreeSpace / 1GB),1)
    $output.'OperatingSystem' = (Get-CimInstance -ComputerName $server
    -ClassName Win32_OperatingSystem).Caption
    $output.'Memory (GB)' = (Get-CimInstance -ComputerName $server -ClassName
    Win32_PhysicalMemory | Measure-Object -Property Capacity -Sum).Sum /1GB
    $output.'IPAddress' = (Get-CimInstance -ComputerName $server -ClassName
    Win32_NetworkAdapterConfiguration -Filter "IPEnabled = 'True'").IPAddress[0]
    [pscustomobject]$output
}
```

Listing 14-7: Updated code that now handles `IPAddress`

Now you run this:

```
PS> C:\Get-ServerInformation.ps1 | Format-Table -AutoSize

ServerName UserProfilesSize (MB) AvailableDriveSpace (GB) OperatingSystem                          StoppedServices IPAddress    Memory (GB)
---------- --------------------- ------------------------ ---------------                          --------------- ---------    -----------
SQLSRV1                   636245                     31.8 Microsoft Windows Server 2016 Standard                   192.168.0.40 2
WEBSRV1                   603942                     34.6 Microsoft Windows Server 2012 R2 Standard                192.168.0.70 2
```

Now that you have all the WMI information you need, there's only one thing left to do.

Windows Services

The last piece of data to gather is a list of the services on the server that are stopped. You'll follow our basic algorithm, testing on a single server first. To do that, you'll use the `Get-Service` command on the server, which will return all of the services being used. You'll then pipe that output to a `Where-Object` command that will filter only for services that have a status of `Stopped`. All in all, the command will look like this: `Get-Service -ComputerName sqlsrv1 | Where-Object { $_.Status -eq 'Stopped' }`.

This command is returning whole objects with all their properties. But you're just looking for service names, so you'll use the same technique you've been using—referencing the property name—and return a list of only service names.

```
PS> (Get-Service -ComputerName sqlsrv1 | Where-Object { $_.Status -eq 'Stopped' }).DisplayName
Application Identity
Application Management
AppX Deployment Service (AppXSVC)
--snip--
```

Adding this to your script, you get Listing 14-8.

```
Get-ServerInformation.ps1
-------------------
$serversOuPath = 'OU=Servers,DC=powerlab,DC=local'
$servers = Get-ADComputer -SearchBase $serversOuPath -Filter * |
Select-Object -ExpandProperty Name
foreach ($server in $servers) {
    $output = @{
        'ServerName'                  = $null
        'IPAddress'                   = $null
        'OperatingSystem'             = $null
        'AvailableDriveSpace (GB)'    = $null
        'Memory (GB)'                 = $null
        'UserProfilesSize (MB)'       = $null
        'StoppedServices'             = $null
    }
    $output.ServerName = $server
    $output.'UserProfilesSize (MB)' = (Get-ChildItem -Path "\\$server\c$\
    Users\" -File | Measure-Object -Property Length -Sum).Sum / 1MB
    $output.'AvailableDriveSpace (GB)' = [Math]::Round(((Get-CimInstance
    -ComputerName $server -ClassName Win32_LogicalDisk).FreeSpace / 1GB),1)
    $output.'OperatingSystem' = (Get-CimInstance -ComputerName $server
    -ClassName Win32_OperatingSystem).Caption
    $output.'Memory (GB)' = (Get-CimInstance -ComputerName $server -ClassName
    Win32_PhysicalMemory | Measure-Object -Property Capacity -Sum).Sum /1GB
    $output.'IPAddress' = (Get-CimInstance -ComputerName $server -ClassName
    Win32_NetworkAdapterConfiguration -Filter "IPEnabled = 'True'").IPAddress[0]
    $output.StoppedServices = (Get-Service -ComputerName $server |
    Where-Object { $_.Status -eq 'Stopped' }).DisplayName
    [pscustomobject]$output
}
```

Listing 14-8: Updating and using your script to print the stopped services

Run the following code to test your script:

```
PS> C:\Get-ServerInformation.ps1 | Format-Table -AutoSize

ServerName UserProfilesSize (MB) AvailableDriveSpace (GB) OperatingSystem                              StoppedServices
---------- --------------------- ------------------------ ---------------                              ---------------
SQLSRV1                   636245                     31.8 Microsoft Windows Server 2016 Standard       {Application Identity,
                                                                                                        Application Management,
                                                                                                        AppX Deployment Servi...
WEBSRV1                   603942                     34.6 Microsoft Windows Server 2012 R2 Standard {Application Experience,
                                                                                                        Application Management,
                                                                                                        Background Intellig...
```

As far as stopped services go, everything looks okay—but where did the other properties go? At this point, the console window has no room left. Removing the `Format-Table` reference allows you to see all the values:

```
PS> C:\Get-ServerInformation.ps1 | Format-Table -AutoSize

ServerName                : SQLSRV1
UserProfilesSize (MB)     : 636245
AvailableDriveSpace (GB) : 31.8
OperatingSystem           : Microsoft Windows Server 2016 Standard
StoppedServices           : {Application Identity, Applic...
IPAddress                 : 192.168.0.40
Memory (GB)               : 2

ServerName                : WEBSRV1
UserProfilesSize (MB)     : 603942
AvailableDriveSpace (GB) : 34.6
OperatingSystem           : Microsoft Windows Server 2012 R2 Standard
StoppedServices           : {Application Experience, Application Management,
                            Background Intelligent Transfer Service, Computer
                            Browser...}
IPAddress                 : 192.168.0.70
Memory (GB)               : 2
```

Looks good!

Script Cleanup and Optimization

Rather than declare victory and move on, let's reflect a little. Writing code is an iterative process. It's entirely possible that you start out with a goal, accomplish that goal, and still end up with bad code—there's more to a good program than simply doing what needs to be done. The script does exactly what you want it to do now, but you could do it in a better way. How?

Recall the DRY method: *don't repeat yourself*. You can see a lot of repetition in this script. You have lots of `Get-CimInstance` references where you're using the same parameters over and over again. You're also making a lot of calls to WMI for the same server. These look like good places to make the code more efficient.

First of all, the CIM cmdlets have a `CimSession` parameter. This parameter allows you to create a single CIM session once and then reuse it. Rather than creating a temporary session, using it, and tearing it down again, you can create a single session, use it all you want, and then tear it down, as shown in Listing 14-9. The concept is similar to the `Invoke-Command` command's `Session` parameter that we covered in Chapter 8.

```
Get-ServerInformation.ps1
-------------------
$serversOuPath = 'OU=Servers,DC=powerlab,DC=local'
$servers = Get-ADComputer -SearchBase $serversOuPath -Filter * |
Select-Object -ExpandProperty Name
foreach ($server in $servers) {
```

```
    $output = @{
        'ServerName'                  = $null
        'IPAddress'                   = $null
        'OperatingSystem'             = $null
        'AvailableDriveSpace (GB)'    = $null
        'Memory (GB)'                 = $null
        'UserProfilesSize (MB)'       = $null
        'StoppedServices'             = $null
    }
    $cimSession = New-CimSession -ComputerName $server
    $output.ServerName = $server
    $output.'UserProfilesSize (MB)' = (Get-ChildItem -Path "\\$server\c$\
    Users\" -File | Measure-Object -Property Length -Sum).Sum
    $output.'AvailableDriveSpace (GB)' = [Math]::Round(((Get-CimInstance
    -CimSession $cimSession -ClassName Win32_LogicalDisk).FreeSpace / 1GB),1)
    $output.'OperatingSystem' = (Get-CimInstance -CimSession $cimSession
    -ClassName Win32_OperatingSystem).Caption
    $output.'Memory (GB)' = (Get-CimInstance -CimSession $cimSession
    -ClassName Win32_PhysicalMemory | Measure-Object -Property Capacity -Sum)
    .Sum /1GB
    $output.'IPAddress' = (Get-CimInstance -CimSession $cimSession -ClassName
    Win32_NetworkAdapterConfiguration -Filter "IPEnabled = 'True'").IPAddress[0]
    $output.StoppedServices = (Get-Service -ComputerName $server |
    Where-Object { $_.Status -eq 'Stopped' }).DisplayName
    Remove-CimSession -CimSession $cimSession
    [pscustomobject]$output
}
```

Listing 14-9: Updating your code to create, and reuse, a single session

Now you're reusing a single CIM session rather than multiple ones. But you're still referencing it a lot in different commands' parameters. To make this even better, you can create a hashtable and assign it a key called `CIMSession` and a value of the CIM session you just created. Once you have a common set of parameters saved in a hashtable, you can reuse it across all `Get-CimInstance` references.

This technique is known as *splatting*, and you can do it by specifying the hashtable you just created while calling each of the `Get-CimInstance` references via the `@` symbol followed by the hashtable name, as shown in Listing 14-10.

```
Get-ServerInformation.ps1
-------------------
$serversOuPath = 'OU=Servers,DC=powerlab,DC=local'
$servers = Get-ADComputer -SearchBase $serversOuPath -Filter * |
Select-Object -ExpandProperty Name
foreach ($server in $servers) {
    $output = @{
        'ServerName'                  = $null
        'IPAddress'                   = $null
        'OperatingSystem'             = $null
        'AvailableDriveSpace (GB)'    = $null
        'Memory (GB)'                 = $null
        'UserProfilesSize (MB)'       = $null
        'StoppedServices'             = $null
```

```
    }
    $getCimInstParams = @{
        CimSession = New-CimSession -ComputerName $server
    }
    $output.ServerName = $server
    $output.'UserProfilesSize (MB)' = (Get-ChildItem -Path "\\$server\c$\
    Users\" -File | Measure-Object -Property Length -Sum).Sum
    $output.'AvailableDriveSpace (GB)' = [Math]::Round(((Get-CimInstance
    @getCimInstParams -ClassName Win32_LogicalDisk).FreeSpace / 1GB),1)
    $output.'OperatingSystem' = (Get-CimInstance @getCimInstParams -ClassName
    Win32_OperatingSystem).Caption
    $output.'Memory (GB)' = (Get-CimInstance @getCimInstParams -ClassName
    Win32_PhysicalMemory | Measure-Object -Property Capacity -Sum).Sum /1GB
    $output.'IPAddress' = (Get-CimInstance @getCimInstParams -ClassName
    Win32_NetworkAdapterConfiguration -Filter "IPEnabled = 'True'").IPAddress[0]
    $output.StoppedServices = (Get-Service -ComputerName $server |
    Where-Object { $_.Status -eq 'Stopped' }).DisplayName
    Remove-CimSession -CimSession $cimSession
    [pscustomobject]$output
}
```

Listing 14-10: Creating the `CIMSession` parameter to reuse

At this point, you're probably used to passing parameters to commands in the dash*<parameter name> <parameter value>* format. This works but it becomes inefficient, especially if you're passing the same parameters to commands over and over again. Instead, you can use splatting as you've done here, by creating a hashtable and then simply passing that single hashtable to each command that requires the same parameter.

Now you've eliminated the `$cimSession` variable altogether.

Summary

In this chapter, you've taken essential information from all the previous chapters and applied it to a situation you might find in the real world. A script that queries information is one of the first types of scripts I usually recommend creating. It teaches you a lot about PowerShell, and there's little chance of screwing anything up!

You moved iteratively through this chapter, going from a goal to a solution to an even better solution. This is a process you'll follow over and over again as you work with PowerShell. Define your goal, start small, get your framework laid out (a `foreach` loop, in this case), and start adding code piece by piece, overcoming one obstacle at a time until it all comes together.

Once you finish your script, keep in mind that you haven't really finished until you review your code: see how to make it more efficient, use fewer resources, and get faster. Experience will make optimizing easier. You'll build the perspective you need until optimizing becomes second nature. When you're finished optimizing, sit back, bask in your success, and get ready to start your next project!

PART III

BUILDING YOUR OWN MODULE

By now, you should have a firm grasp on what makes PowerShell *PowerShell*. We've covered the syntax of the language, as well as a few specific modules you may use in your day-to-day automation work. But up until the preceding chapter, we've been doing things only in pieces: a little syntax here, a little syntax there, nothing major. In Chapter 14, with the server inventory script, you got your first taste of working on a prolonged PowerShell project. In Part III, we're going to go bigger: you're going to build your own PowerShell module.

PowerLab

PowerLab is a single PowerShell module that contains the functions you need to provision Windows servers from scratch. You'll build PowerLab brick by brick; if you want to see the final result, you can find it in this GitHub repository: *https://github.com/adbertram/PowerLab.*

The process of provisioning a Windows server from scratch will look something like this:

- Create a virtual machine.
- Install a Windows operating system.
- Install a server service (Active Directory, SQL Server, or IIS).

This means you'll need your PowerLab module to do five things:

- Create Hyper-V virtual machines
- Install a Windows server
- Create an Active Directory forest
- Provision SQL servers
- Provision IIS web servers

To accomplish these tasks, you'll use three primary commands:

- `New-PowerLabActiveDirectoryForest`
- `New-PowerLabSqlServer`
- `New-PowerLabWebServer`

Of course, you're going to use more than three commands. You'll build each of these commands with multiple helper commands that will take care of behind-the-scenes functionality, including creating the virtual machine and installing the operating system. But we'll go through all of that in the chapters ahead.

Prerequisites

You'll need a few things to build PowerLab:

- A Windows 10 Professional client computer in a workgroup. A Windows 10 machine joined to a domain may work but was not tested.
- A Hyper-V host in a workgroup running Windows Server 2012 R2 (at least) on the same network as the client—although the host could be joined to a domain as well, but this scenario was not tested.
- ISO files for Windows Server 2016, located on your Hyper-V host. Windows Server 2019 was not tested. You can download evaluation versions of Windows Server from *https://www.microsoft.com/en-us/evalcenter/evaluate-windows-server-2016?filetype=ISO.*
- Remote Server Administration Tools (RSAT) enabled on the client computer (download from *https://www.microsoft.com/en-us/download/details.aspx?id=45520*).
- The latest version of the Pester PowerShell module installed on your client computer.

You also need to be logged in as a member of the local administrators group on the client computer, and have the PowerShell execution policy set to unrestricted. (You can run **`Set-ExecutionPolicy Unrestricted`** to change the execution policy, but I recommend changing this back to `AllSigned` or `RemoteSigned` when the lab setup is complete.)

Setting Up PowerLab

When providing something like PowerLab to consumers, you want to make setup as painless as possible. One way to do this is by providing a script that handles the installation and configuration of your module with minimal user input.

I've already written the installation script for PowerLab. It can be found in the PowerLab GitHub repository: *https://raw.githubusercontent.com/adbertram/PowerLab/master/Install-PowerLab.ps1*. That link will provide the raw source code for the script. You could copy and paste it into a new text file and save it as *Install-PowerLab.ps1*, but this is a PowerShell book, so let's try running the following command:

```
PS> Invoke-WebRequest -Uri 'http://bit.ly/powerlabinstaller' -OutFile 'C:\Install-PowerLab.ps1'
```

Be warned: when you run the script, you'll have to answer some questions. You'll need the hostname of the Hyper-V host, the IP address of the Hyper-V host, the local administrator username and password for the Hyper-V host, and the product keys (if not using a Windows Server evaluation copy) for each operating system you want to install.

Once you have all the information on hand, run the install script with the following command:

```
PS> C:\Install-PowerLab.ps1

Name of your HYPERV host: HYPERVSRV
IP address of your HYPERV host: 192.168.0.200
Enabling PS remoting on local computer...
Adding server to trusted computers...
PS remoting is already enabled on [HYPERVSRV]
Setting firewall rules on Hyper-V host...
Adding the ANONYMOUS LOGON user to the local machine and host server
Distributed COM Users group for Hyper-V manager
Enabling applicable firewall rules on local machine...
Adding saved credential on local computer for Hyper-V host...
Ensure all values in the PowerLab configuration file are valid and close the
ISE when complete.
Enabling the Microsoft-Hyper-V-Tools-All features...
Lab setup is now complete.
```

If you'd like to inspect what this script does, you can always download it via the book's resources and check it out. However, know that it's meant to get us both to the same infrastructure, not necessarily show you what the script is doing; it may be over your head at this time. This script is meant to enable you to follow along with me.

Demo Code

All the code you will write in the following chapters can be found at *https://github.com/adbertram/PowerShellForSysadmins/tree/master/Part%20III*. In addition to all the PowerLab code, you'll find necessary data files and the Pester scripts to test the module and verify that your environment meets all the expected prerequisites. Before starting each chapter, I *strongly* suggest that you use the `Invoke-Pester` command to run the *Prerequisites.Tests.ps1* Pester script found in each chapter's files. Doing so will save you from many headache-inducing bugs down the line.

Summary

You should have everything you need to start building PowerLab. We'll cover a lot of ground in the following chapters, and draw on many areas of PowerShell, so don't be surprised if you see something you don't recognize. Plenty of online resources can help you through thorny syntax, and if you don't understand something, you can always reach out to me on Twitter at @adbertram or reach out to others on the internet.

With that, let's get started!

15

PROVISIONING A VIRTUAL ENVIRONMENT

PowerLab is a final, massive project using all the concepts you've learned and more. It's a project that automates the provisioning of Hyper-V virtual machines (VMs) all the way up to installing and configuring services including SQL and IIS. Imagine being able to run a single command such as `New-PowerLabSqlServer`, `New-PowerLabIISServer`, or even `New-PowerLab`, wait a few minutes, and have a fully configured machine (or machines) pop out. That's what you're going to get if you stick with me throughout the rest of the book.

The purpose of the PowerLab project is to remove all the repetitive, time-consuming tasks required to bring up a test environment or a lab. When you're done, you should have just a handful of commands to build an entire Active Directory forest from nothing but a Hyper-V host and a few ISO files.

I've purposefully not covered *everything* that's going into PowerLab in Parts I and II. Instead, I challenge you to notice these areas and come up with unique solutions on your own. After all, in programming there are always lots of ways to accomplish the same task. If you get stuck, please feel free to reach out to me on Twitter at @adbertram.

By building a project of this scale, you will not only cover hundreds of PowerShell topics, but also see just how powerful a scripting language can be and come away with a substantial time-saving utility.

In this chapter, you'll get PowerLab started by creating the bare-bones `PowerLab` module. Then you'll add the ability to automate the creation of a virtual switch, VM, and virtual hard disk (VHD).

PowerLab Module Prerequisites

To follow along with all the code examples you'll work with in Part III, you need to meet a few prerequisites. Each chapter in this part has a "Prerequisites" section. This is to ensure that you always know what to expect.

For the project in this chapter, you need a Hyper-V host with the following configuration:

- A network adapter
- IP: 10.0.0.5 (optional, but to follow along exactly, you need this IP)
- Subnet mask: 255.255.255.0
- A workgroup
- At least 100GB of available storage
- Windows Server 2016 with a full GUI

To create a Hyper-V server, you need to install the Hyper-V role on the Windows server you intend to use. You can expedite the setup process by downloading and running the Hyper-V *Setup.ps1* script in the book's resources at *https://github.com/adbertram/PowerShellForSysadmins/*. This will set up Hyper-V and create a few necessary folders.

NOTE *If you're planning on following along word for word, please run the associated chapter's Pester prerequisite script* (Prerequisites.Tests.ps1) *to confirm that your Hyper-V server is set up as expected. These tests will confirm that your lab environment is set up exactly as mine is. Run* `Invoke-Pester`*, passing it the prerequisite script, as in Listing 15-1. For the rest of the book, all code will be executed on the Hyper-V host itself.*

```
PS> Invoke-Pester -Path 'C:\PowerShellForSysadmins\Part III\Automating Hyper-V\Prerequisites
.Tests.ps1'

Describing Automating Hyper-V Chapter Prerequisites
 [+] Hyper-V host server should have the Hyper-V Windows feature installed 2.23s
 [+] Hyper-V host server is Windows Server 2016 147ms
 [+] Hyper-V host server should have at least 100GB of available storage 96ms
 [+] has a PowerLab folder at the root of C 130ms
 [+] has a PowerLab\VMs folder at the root of C 41ms
```

```
 [+] has a PowerLab\VHDs folder at the root of C 47ms
Tests completed in 2.69s
Passed: 5 Failed: 0 Skipped: 0 Pending: 0 Inconclusive: 0
```

Listing 15-1: Running Pester prerequisite checks for Hyper-V work

If you have successfully set up your environment, the output should confirm five passes. Once you've confirmed that your environment is all set up and ready go, you can get started on the project!

Creating the Module

Because you know that you'll need to automate a potentially large number of tasks that all relate to one another, you should create a PowerShell module. As you learned in Chapter 7, a PowerShell module is a great way to combine lots of like-functions into one unit; that way, you can easily manage all the code necessary to perform the tasks surrounding a specific purpose. PowerLab is no different. There's no reason to think about everything at once, so start small—add functionality, test, and repeat.

Creating a Blank Module

First, you need to create a blank module. To do that, remote-desktop to your soon-to-be Hyper-V host and log in as the local administrator—or any account in the local administrators group. You'll build this module directly on the Hyper-V host to ease VM creation and administration. This means you'll use an RDP session to connect to your Hyper-V host's console session. Then you'll create the module folder, the module itself (the *.psm1* file), and the optional manifest (the *.psd1* file).

Since you're logged in via the local administrator account and may one day allow others to use your PowerLab module, create the module in the *All Users* location of *C:\Files*. This will allow you to access the module when logged in as any administrative user on the host.

Next, open a PowerShell console and choose **Run as Administrator**. Then, create a PowerLab module folder by using the following:

```
PS> New-Item -Path C:\Program Files\WindowsPowerShell\Modules\PowerLab -ItemType Directory
```

Next, create a blank text file called *PowerLab.psm1*. Use the `New-Item` command:

```
PS> New-Item -Path 'C:\Program Files\WindowsPowerShell\Modules\PowerLab\PowerLab.psm1'
```

Creating a Module Manifest

Now, create a module manifest. To create a module manifest, use the handy `New-ModuleManifest` command. This command creates a template manifest, which you can then open in a text editor and tweak after the initial file is built, if necessary. Here are the parameters I used to build the template manifest:

```
PS> New-ModuleManifest -Path 'C:\Program Files\WindowsPowerShell\Modules\PowerLab\PowerLab.psd1'
-Author 'Adam Bertram'
-CompanyName 'Adam the Automator, LLC'
-RootModule 'PowerLab.psm1'
-Description 'This module automates all tasks to provision entire environments of a domain
controller, SQL server and IIS web server from scratch.'
```

Feel free to modify the parameter values to suit your needs.

Using Built-In Prefixes for Function Names

A function doesn't necessarily need a specific name. However, when you're building a module that is typically a group of related functions, it's always a good idea to preface the noun part of the function with the same label. For example, your project is called *PowerLab*. In this project, you'll build functions that all relate to that common theme. To differentiate the functions in PowerLab from the functions in other modules you may have loaded, you can add the name of the module before the actual noun portion of the name. This means that most functions' nouns will start with the term *PowerLab*.

However, not all functions will start with the name of the module. Examples include helper functions that only assist other functions and will never be called by a user.

When you're sure you want all function nouns to use the same prefix without having to explicitly define it in the function name, the module manifest has an option called `DefaultCommandPrefix`. This option will force PowerShell to preface the noun with a particular string. For example, if you define the `DefaultCommandPrefix` key in a manifest and create a function inside the module called `New-Switch`, when the module is imported, the function won't be available for use as `New-Switch` but as `New-PowerLabSwitch`:

```
# Default prefix for commands exported from this modul...
# DefaultCommandPrefix = ''
```

I prefer *not* to go with this approach because it forcefully prefaces *all* function name nouns inside the module with that string.

Importing the New Module

Now that you've built the manifest, you're ready to see whether it imports successfully. Since you haven't written any functions yet, the module won't be able to do anything, but it's important to see whether PowerShell can see the module. If you see the following result, you're good to go.

```
PS> Get-Module -Name PowerLab -ListAvailable

    Directory: C:\Program Files\WindowsPowerShell\Modules

ModuleType Version    Name                                ExportedCommands
---------- -------    ----                                ----------------
Script     1.0        PowerLab
```

If the PowerLab module doesn't appear at the bottom of the output, return to the previous steps. In addition, check to ensure that you have the PowerLab folder created under *C:\Program Files\WindowsPowerShell\Modules* with *PowerLab.psm1* and *PowerLab.psd1* files inside.

Automating Virtual Environment Provisioning

Now that you have built the module's structure, you can begin to add functionality to it. Since the task of creating a server, such as SQL or IIS, has various steps that depend on one another, you'll first work on automating the creation of a virtual switch, virtual machine, and virtual disk. Then you'll automate deploying the operating system to these VMs, and finally, you'll install SQL Server and IIS on these VMs.

Virtual Switches

Before you can begin automating the creation of VMs, you need to ensure that a virtual switch is set up on the Hyper-V host. *Virtual switches* allow VMs to communicate with client machines and other VMs built on a host.

Creating a Virtual Switch Manually

Your virtual switch will be an *external* switch, called `PowerLab`. Chances are, a switch with this name isn't already on the Hyper-V host, but just to be sure, list all the virtual switches on the host. You'll never regret checking first.

To see all of the switches set up on your Hyper-V host, use the **`Get-VmSwitch`** command. Once you confirm that the PowerLab switch doesn't exist, create a new virtual switch with the `New-VmSwitch` command, specifying the name (`PowerLab`) and the type of switch:

```
PS> New-VMSwitch -Name PowerLab -SwitchType External
```

Since you need your VMs to be able to communicate with hosts outside Hyper-V, you pass the value `External` to the `SwitchType` parameter. Whoever you share this project with will also need to create an external switch.

With your switch created, it's now time to create the PowerLab module's first function.

Automating VM Switch Creation

The first PowerLab function, called `New-PowerLabSwitch`, creates the Hyper-V switch. This function isn't too complicated. In fact, without it, you would simply need to execute a single command at the prompt—that is, `New-VmSwitch`. But if you wrap that Hyper-V command inside a custom function, you will have the ability to perform other work: adding any kind of default configuration to the switch, for example.

I am a big fan of *idempotency*, which is a fancy word that means "regardless of the state in which the command executes, it performs the same task every time." In this example, if the task of creating the switch were not idempotent, then running `New-VmSwitch` would result in an error if the switch already existed.

To remove the requirement to manually check whether the switch is created before attempting to create a switch, you can use the `Get-VmSwitch` command. This command checks whether the switch has been created. Then, if—and only if—the switch doesn't exist will you attempt to create a new switch. This allows you to run `New-PowerLabSwitch` in any environment and know that it will always create the virtual switch without returning an error—regardless of the state of the Hyper-V host.

Open the *C:\Program Files\WindowsPowerShell\Modules\PowerLab\PowerLab.psm1* file and create the `New-PowerLabSwitch` function, as shown in Listing 15-2.

```
function New-PowerLabSwitch {
    param(
        [Parameter()]
        [string]$SwitchName = 'PowerLab',

        [Parameter()]
        [string]$SwitchType = 'External'
    )

    if (-not (Get-VmSwitch -Name $SwitchName -SwitchType $SwitchType -ErrorAction
    SilentlyContinue)) { ❶
        $null = New-VMSwitch -Name $SwitchName -SwitchType $SwitchType ❷
    } else {
        Write-Verbose -Message "The switch [$($SwitchName)] has already been created." ❸
    }
}
```

Listing 15-2: `New-PowerLabSwitch` function in the `PowerLab` module

This function first checks to see whether the switch is already created ❶. If it isn't, the function creates it ❷. If the switch is already created, the function will simply return a verbose message to the console ❸.

Save the module and then force it to import again by using **`Import-Module -Name PowerLab -Force`**.

Because you previously imported the module, PowerShell hadn't loaded any functions into the session. When you add new functions to the module, you must import the module again. If a module is already imported, you must use the `Force` parameter with `Import-Module` to force

PowerShell to import it again. Otherwise, PowerShell will see that the module has already been imported and skip it.

Once you've imported the module again, the `New-PowerLabSwitch` function should be available to you. Run this command:

```
PS> New-PowerLabSwitch -Verbose
VERBOSE: The switch [PowerLab] has already been created.
```

Notice that you don't receive an error, but instead, a useful verbose message saying the switch has already been created. This is because you passed the optional `Verbose` parameter to the function. Defaults were chosen for the `SwitchName` and `SwitchType` parameters, since these will usually be the same.

Creating Virtual Machines

Now that you've set up a virtual switch, it's time to create a VM. For this demo, you'll create a generation 2 VM, called LABDC, with 2GB attached to the virtual switch you just built in the *C:\PowerLab\VMs* folder on the Hyper-V host. I've chosen *LABDC* as the name because this will eventually be our Active Directory domain controller. This VM will eventually be the domain controller you'll use for your fully built lab.

First, take a look at all the existing VMs and ensure that one doesn't already exist with the same name. Since you already know the name of the VM you want to create, pass that value to the `Name` parameter of `Get-Vm`:

```
PS> Get-Vm -Name LABDC
Get-Vm : A parameter is invalid. Hyper-V was unable to find a virtual machine with name LABDC.
At line:1 char:1
+ Get-Vm -Name LABDC
+ ~~~~~~~~~~~~~~~~~~~~~~~~~~~~~~~~~~~~~~~~~~~~~~~
    + CategoryInfo          : InvalidArgument: (LABDC:String) [Get-VM],
                              VirtualizationInvalidArgumentException
    + FullyQualifiedErrorId : InvalidParameter,Microsoft.HyperV.PowerShell.Commands.GetVMCommand
```

The `Get-Vm` command returns an error when it can't find the VM with the specified name. Because you're just checking whether it exists, and it doesn't necessarily matter to us whether it does or doesn't at this point, use the `ErrorAction` parameter with the `SilentlyContinue` value to ensure that the command returns nothing if the VM doesn't exist in your automation script later. You're not using a `try/catch` here for simplicity's sake.

This technique works only if the command returns a nonterminating error. If the command returns a terminating error, you'll have to either look into returning all the objects and filtering them with `Where-Object` or enclosing the command in a `try/catch` block.

Creating a VM Manually

The VM doesn't exist, which means you need to create it. To create a VM, you need to run the `Get-Vm` command and pass it the values that you defined at the start of this section.

```
PS> New-VM -Name 'LABDC' -Path 'C:\PowerLab\VMs'
-MemoryStartupBytes 2GB -Switch 'PowerLab' -Generation 2

Name    State CPUUsage(%) MemoryAssigned(M) Uptime   Status             Version
----    ----- ----------- ----------------- ------   ------             -------
LABDC   Off   0           0                 00:00:00 Operating normally 8.0
```

You should now have a VM, but confirm this by running **Get-Vm** again.

Automating VM Creation

To automate creating a simple VM, you again need to add another function. This function will follow the same pattern as that used to create a new virtual switch: make an idempotent function that performs a task regardless of the state of the Hyper-V host.

Enter the New-PowerLabVm function, as shown in Listing 15-3, into your *PowerLab.psm1* module.

```
function New-PowerLabVm {
    param(
        [Parameter(Mandatory)]
        [string]$Name,

        [Parameter()]
        [string]$Path = 'C:\PowerLab\VMs',

        [Parameter()]
        [string]$Memory = 4GB,

        [Parameter()]
        [string]$Switch = 'PowerLab',

        [Parameter()]
        [ValidateRange(1, 2)]
        [int]$Generation = 2
    )

  ❶ if (-not (Get-Vm -Name $Name -ErrorAction SilentlyContinue)) {
      ❷ $null = New-VM -Name $Name -Path $Path -MemoryStartupBytes $Memory
          -Switch $Switch -Generation $Generation
    } else {
      ❸ Write-Verbose -Message "The VM [$($Name)] has already been created."
    }
}
```

Listing 15-3: New-PowerLabVm function in the PowerLab module

This function checks whether the VM already exists ❶. If it doesn't, the function will create one ❷. If it does, the function will display a verbose message to the console ❸.

Save *PowerLab.psm1* and execute your new function at the prompt:

```
PS> New-PowerLabVm -Name 'LABDC' -Verbose
VERBOSE: The VM [LABDC] has already been created.
```

Again, when you run this command, you can create a VM with the specified parameter values—whether that VM already exists (after you force the module to be imported again) or not.

Virtual Hard Disks

You now have a VM attached to a switch, but a VM isn't any good without storage attached to it. To take care of that, you need to create a local virtual hard disk (VHD) and connect it to a VM.

NOTE *In Chapter 16, you'll use a community script that converts an ISO file into a VHD. Therefore, you don't need to create a VHD. But if you aren't planning on automating the operating system deployment, or if you need to automate the VHD creation as part of another script, I still recommend that you complete this section.*

Creating a VHD Manually

To create a VHD file, you need only a single command: `New-Vhd`. In this section, you'll create a VHD that's capable of growing to 50GB in size; and to save space, you'll set the VHD to dynamically size.

You first need to create a folder on the Hyper-V host at *C:\PowerLab\VHDs* to place the VHD. Be sure to name your VHD with the same name as the VM you intend to attach it to in order to keep things simple.

Create the VHD with `New-Vhd`:

```
PS> New-Vhd ❶-Path 'C:\PowerLab\VHDs\MYVM.vhdx' ❷-SizeBytes 50GB ❸-Dynamic

ComputerName            : HYPERVSRV
Path                    : C:\PowerLab\VHDs\LABDC.vhdx
VhdFormat               : VHDX
VhdType                 : Dynamic
FileSize                : 4194304
Size                    : 53687091200
MinimumSize             :
LogicalSectorSize       : 512
PhysicalSectorSize      : 4096
BlockSize               : 33554432
ParentPath              :
DiskIdentifier          : 3FB5153D-055D-463D-89F3-BB733B9E69BC
FragmentationPercentage : 0
Alignment               : 1
Attached                : False
DiskNumber              :
Number                  :
```

You pass New-Vhd the path ❶ and the VHD size ❷, and, finally, indicate that you want it to dynamically size ❸.

Confirm that you successfully created the VHD on your Hyper-V host with the Test-Path command. If Test-Path returns True, you were successful:

```
PS> Test-Path -Path 'C:\PowerLab\VHDs\MYVM.vhdx'
True
```

Now you need to attach the VHD to the VM you created earlier. To do this, you use the Add-VMHardDiskDrive command. But because you're *not* going to be attaching a VHD to LABDC—the OS deployment automation, in Chapter 16, will do that—create another VM, called MYVM, to attach to the VHD:

```
PS> New-PowerLabVm -Name 'MYVM'
PS> ❶Get-VM -Name MYVM | Add-VMHardDiskDrive -Path 'C:\PowerLab\VHDs\MYVM.vhdx'
PS> ❷Get-VM -Name MYVM | Get-VMHardDiskDrive

VMName ControllerType ControllerNumber ControllerLocation DiskNumber Path
------ -------------- ---------------- ------------------ ---------- ----
MYVM   SCSI           0                0                             C:\PowerLab\VHDs\LABDC.vhdx
```

The Add-VMHardDiskDrive command accepts the object type that the Get-VM command returns for its pipeline input so you can pass the VM directly from Get-VM to Add-VMHardDiskDrive—specifying the path to the VHD on the Hyper-V host ❶.

Immediately after, use Get-VMHardDiskDrive to confirm that the VHDX was added successfully ❷.

Automating VHD Creation

You can add another function to your module to automate the process of creating a VHD and attaching it to a VM. When you create scripts or functions, accounting for various configurations is important.

Listing 15-4 defines the New-PowerLabVhd function, which creates a VHD and attaches a VM to it.

```
function New-PowerLabVhd {
    param
    (
        [Parameter(Mandatory)]
        [string]$Name,

        [Parameter()]
        [string]$AttachToVm,

        [Parameter()]
        [ValidateRange(512MB, 1TB)]
        [int64]$Size = 50GB,
```

```
        [Parameter()]
        [ValidateSet('Dynamic', 'Fixed')]
        [string]$Sizing = 'Dynamic',

        [Parameter()]
        [string]$Path = 'C:\PowerLab\VHDs'
    )

    $vhdxFileName = "$Name.vhdx"
    $vhdxFilePath = Join-Path -Path $Path -ChildPath "$Name.vhdx"

    ### Ensure we don't try to create a VHD when there's already one there
    if (-not (Test-Path -Path $vhdxFilePath -PathType Leaf)) { ❶
        $params = @{
            SizeBytes = $Size
            Path      = $vhdxFilePath
        }
        if ($Sizing -eq 'Dynamic') { ❷
            $params.Dynamic = $true
        } elseif ($Sizing -eq 'Fixed') {
            $params.Fixed = $true
        }

        New-VHD @params
        Write-Verbose -Message "Created new VHD at path [$($vhdxFilePath)]"
    }

    if ($PSBoundParameters.ContainsKey('AttachToVm')) {
        if (-not ($vm = Get-VM -Name $AttachToVm -ErrorAction SilentlyContinue)) { ❸
            Write-Warning -Message "The VM [$($AttachToVm)] does not exist. Unable to attach VHD."
        } elseif (-not ($vm | Get-VMHardDiskDrive | Where-Object { $_.Path -eq $vhdxFilePath })) { ❹
            $vm | Add-VMHardDiskDrive -Path $vhdxFilePath
            Write-Verbose -Message "Attached VHDX [$($vhdxFilePath)] to VM [$($AttachToVM)]."
        } else { ❺
            Write-Verbose -Message "VHDX [$($vhdxFilePath)] already attached to VM [$($AttachToVM)]."
        }
    }
}
```

Listing 15-4: `New-PowerLabVhd` *function in the* `PowerLab` *module*

This function supports both dynamic and fixed sizing ❷, and it accounts for four individual states:

- The VHD already exists ❶.
- The VM to attach the VHD to doesn't exist ❸.
- The VM to attach the VHD to exists, but the VHD hasn't been connected yet ❹.
- The VM to attach the VHD to exists, and the VHD has already been attached ❺.

Function design is a whole other matter entirely. It takes years of coding and practice to be able to create a script or function that's resilient across many scenarios. It's an art that has never truly been perfected, but if you're able to think through as many different ways a problem may occur and account for those up front, your function will be that much better off. However, don't go *too* overboard and spend hours on a function or script making sure *every* detail is covered! This is just code. You can change it later.

Executing the New-PowerLabVhd Function

You can execute this code in various states and account for each state. Let's test multiple states to ensure that this automation script works in each situation:

```
PS> New-PowerLabVhd -Name MYVM -Verbose -AttachToVm MYVM

VERBOSE: VHDX [C:\PowerLab\VHDs\MYVM.vhdx] already attached to VM [MYVM].

PS> Get-VM -Name MYVM | Get-VMHardDiskDrive | Remove-VMHardDiskDrive
PS> New-PowerLabVhd -Name MYVM -Verbose -AttachToVm MYVM

VERBOSE: Attached VHDX [C:\PowerLab\VHDs\MYVM.vhdx] to VM [MYVM].
PS> New-PowerLabVhd -Name MYVM -Verbose -AttachToVm NOEXIST

WARNING: The VM [NOEXIST] does not exist. Unable to attach VHD.
```

Here, you're not quite testing in the formal sense. Instead, you're putting your new function through its paces by forcing it to run through each of the code paths you defined.

Testing the New Functions with Pester

You should now be able to automate the creation of a Hyper-V VM, but you should always build Pester tests for everything you create in order to make sure everything works as you expect, as well as monitor your automation over time. You'll build Pester tests for all the work you do in the rest of the book. You can find the Pester tests in this book's resources at *https://github.com/adbertram/PowerShellForSysadmins/*.

In this chapter, you accomplished four things:

- Created a virtual switch
- Created a VM
- Created a VHDX
- Attached the VHDX to the VM

I broke the Pester tests for this chapter into sections that correspond to the four accomplishments. Breaking tests into stages like this helps keep your tests organized.

Let's run the test against the code you wrote in this chapter. To run the test script, make sure you downloaded the *Automating-Hyper-V.Tests.ps1* script from the book's resources. In the following code, the test script is located in the root of *C:*, but your path may be different depending on where you downloaded the resource files.

```
PS> Invoke-Pester 'C:\Automating-Hyper-V.Tests.ps1'
Describing Automating Hyper-V Chapter Demo Work
   Context Virtual Switch
    [+] created a virtual switch called PowerLab 195ms
   Context Virtual Machine
    [+] created a virtual machine called LABDC 62ms
   Context Virtual Hard Disk
    [+] created a VHDX called MYVM at C:\PowerLab\VHDs 231ms
    [+] attached the MYVM VHDX to the MYVM VM 194ms
Tests completed in 683ms
Passed: 4 Failed: 0 Skipped: 0 Pending: 0 Inconclusive: 0
```

All four tests pass, so you're good to move on to the next chapter.

Summary

You created the foundation for your first real-world PowerShell automation project! I hope you're already seeing just how much time you can save by automating with PowerShell! By using a freely available PowerShell module from Microsoft, you were able to run just a few commands to quickly create a virtual switch, VM, and disk drive. Microsoft gave you the commands, but it was up to you to build the logic around them to make everything flow seamlessly.

You might now see that it's possible to build scripts on the fly that work, but by thinking ahead and adding conditional logic, your scripts can account for more situations.

In the next chapter, you'll take the VM you just created and automate deploying an operating system to it with little more than an ISO file.

16

INSTALLING AN OPERATING SYSTEM

In the preceding chapter, you set up your PowerLab module so that it's ready to go. Now, you'll take the next step in your automation journey: learning to automate installation of the operating system. Since you have a VM created with a VHD attached, you need to install Windows. To do this, you'll use a Windows Server ISO file, the *Convert-WindowsImage.ps1* PowerShell script, and a whole lot of scripting to create a hands-off, completely automated deployment of Windows!

Prerequisites

I'm assuming that you followed along from the preceding chapter and have those prerequisites met. Here, you'll need a few more things in order to keep up. First, since you'll be deploying an operating system, you need a Windows Server 2016 ISO. A free trial is available at *http://bit.ly/2r5TPRP* once you log in with a free Microsoft account.

From the preceding chapter, I'm expecting that you have a *C:\PowerLab* folder created on your Hyper-V server. Now you should make an ISOs subfolder, *C:\PowerLab\ISOs*, containing your Windows Server 2016 ISO. At the time of this writing, the ISO filename is *en_windows_server_2016_x64_dvd_9718492.iso*. You'll use this file path in your scripts, so if yours is different, make sure to update the script code accordingly.

You also need to have the *Convert-WindowsImage.ps1* PowerShell script in your PowerLab module folder. If you downloaded the book's resources, this script will come with the chapter's resources.

A few more things: I'm expecting you to have the LABDC VM that you made in the preceding chapter on the Hyper-V server. You'll use this as the place to associate your newly created virtual disk.

And finally, you need the unattended XML answer file (also available via the chapter's downloadable resources) called *unattend.xml* in the PowerLab module folder.

As always, go ahead and run the chapter's associated *Prerequisites.Tests.ps1* Pester test script to ensure that you meet all the prerequisites ahead of time.

OS Deployments

When it comes to automating OS deployments, you'll work with three basic components:

- An ISO file containing the bits for the OS
- An answer file providing all the input you'd normally enter manually during install time
- Microsoft's PowerShell script that converts the ISO file to a VHDX

Your job is to figure out a way to stitch all these components together. Most of the heavy lifting is done by the answer file and the ISO conversion script. What you need to do is create a small script ensuring that the conversion script gets called with the appropriate parameters and attaches the newly created VHD to the appropriate VM.

You can follow along with this script called *Install-LABDCOperatingSystem.ps1* in the downloaded resources.

Creating the VHDX

The LABDC VM will have a 40GB, dynamic, VHDX disk-partitioned GUID Partition Table (GPT) running Windows Server 2016 Standard Core. The conversion script will need this information. It will also need to know the path to the source ISO, and the path to the unattended answer file.

First, define the paths to the ISO file and the prefilled answer file:

```
$isoFilePath = 'C:\PowerLab\ISOs\en_windows_server_2016_x64_dvd_9718492.iso'
$answerFilePath = 'C:\PowerShellForSysAdmins\PartII\Automating Operating System Installs\LABDC.xml'
```

Next, you'll build all the parameters for the conversion script. Using PowerShell's splatting technique, you can create a single hashtable and define all these parameters as one. This method of defining and passing parameters to commands is much cleaner than typing out every parameter on a single line:

```
$convertParams = @{
    SourcePath          = $isoFilePath
    SizeBytes           = 40GB
    Edition             = 'ServerStandardCore'
    VHDFormat           = 'VHDX'
    VHDPath             = 'C:\PowerLab\VHDs\LABDC.vhdx'
    VHDType             = 'Dynamic'
    VHDPartitionStyle = 'GPT'
    UnattendPath        = $answerFilePath
}
```

Once all the parameters are defined for the conversion script, you'll dot source the *Convert-WindowsImage.ps1* script. You don't want to call this conversion script directly because it contains a function also called `Convert-WindowsImage`. If you were to simply execute the *Convert-WindowsImage.ps1* script, nothing would happen because it would just be loading the function inside the script.

Dot sourcing is a way to load the function into memory to use it for later; it loads all functions defined in the script in the current session but doesn't actually execute them. Here's how to dot source the *Convert-WindowsImage.pst1* script:

```
. "$PSScriptRoot\Convert-WindowsImage.ps1"
```

Take a look at this code. There's a new variable: `$PSScriptRoot`. This is an automatic variable representing the folder path in which the script resides. In this example, since the *Convert-WindowsImage.ps1* script is in the same folder as the PowerLab module, you're referencing that script in the PowerLab module.

Once the conversion script has been dot sourced into the session, you have the ability to call the functions that were inside it, including `Convert-WindowsImage`. This function will do all the dirty work for you: it'll open the ISO file, appropriately format a new virtual disk, set a boot volume, inject the answer file you provided it, and end up with a VHDX file that has a fresh copy of Windows ready for you to boot up!

```
Convert-WindowsImage @convertParams

Windows(R) Image to Virtual Hard Disk Converter for Windows(R) 10
Copyright (C) Microsoft Corporation.  All rights reserved.
Version 10.0.9000.0.amd64fre.fbl_core1_hyp_dev(mikekol).141224-3000 Beta

INFO   : Opening ISO en_windows_server_2016_x64_dvd_9718492.iso...
INFO   : Looking for E:\sources\install.wim...
```

```
INFO   : Image 1 selected (ServerStandardCore)...
INFO   : Creating sparse disk...
INFO   : Attaching VHDX...
INFO   : Disk initialized with GPT...
INFO   : Disk partitioned
INFO   : System Partition created
INFO   : Boot Partition created
INFO   : System Volume formatted (with DiskPart)...
INFO   : Boot Volume formatted (with Format-Volume)...
INFO   : Access path (F:\) has been assigned to the System Volume...
INFO   : Access path (G:\) has been assigned to the Boot Volume...
INFO   : Applying image to VHDX. This could take a while...
INFO   : Applying unattend file (LABDC.xml)...
INFO   : Signing disk...
INFO   : Image applied. Making image bootable...
INFO   : Drive is bootable. Cleaning up...
INFO   : Closing VHDX...

INFO   : Closing Windows image...
INFO   : Closing ISO...

INFO   : Done.
```

Using community scripts such as *Convert-WindowsImage.ps1* is a great way to speed up development. The script saves considerable time, and since it was created by Microsoft, you can trust it. If you're ever curious about what this script does, feel free to open it. It's doing a lot, and I, for one, am glad we have a resource like this to automate operating system installations.

Attaching the VM

When the conversion script is complete, you should have a *LABDC.vhdx* file located in *C:\PowerLab\VHDs* that's ready to boot. But you're not done just yet. As is, this virtual disk isn't attached to a VM. You have to attach this virtual disk to an existing VM (you'll use the LABDC VM created earlier).

Just as you did in the preceding chapter, use the `Add-VmHardDiskDrive` function to attach the virtual disk to your VM:

```
$vm = Get-Vm -Name 'LABDC'
Add-VMHardDiskDrive -VMName 'LABDC' -Path 'C:\PowerLab\VHDs\LABDC.vhdx'
```

You need to boot from this disk, so let's make sure it's in the proper boot order. You can discover the existing boot order by using the `Get-VMFirmware` command and looking at the `BootOrder` property:

```
$bootOrder = (Get-VMFirmware -VMName 'LABDC').Bootorder
```

Notice that the boot order has a network boot as the first boot device. This isn't what you want. You want the VM to boot from the disk you just created.

```
$bootOrder.BootType

BootType
------
Network
```

To set the VHDX you just created as the first boot device, use the `Set-VMFirmware` command and the `FirstBootDevice` parameter:

```
$vm | Set-VMFirmware -FirstBootDevice $vm.HardDrives[0]
```

At this point, you should have a VM called LABDC with a virtual disk attached that will boot into Windows. Fire up the VM with **`Start-VM -Name LABDC`** and ensure that it boots into Windows successfully. If so, you're finished!

Automating OS Deployments

So far, you've successfully created a VM called LABDC that boots into Windows. Now it's important to realize that the script you were using was specifically tailored to your single VM. In the real world, you're rarely afforded that luxury. A great script is reusable and portable, meaning that it doesn't need to be changed for every specific input, but instead works around a set of ever-changing parameter values.

Let's take a look at the `Install-PowerLabOperatingSystem` function in the PowerLab module, found in this chapter's downloadable resources. This function gives a good example of how to turn the *Install-LABDCOperatingSystem.ps1* script you were using into one that can be used to deploy operating systems across multiple virtual disks, all by simply changing parameter values.

I won't cover the whole script in this section since we covered most of the functionality in the previous section, but I do want to point out a few differences. First, notice that you're using more variables. Variables allow your script to be more flexible. They provide placeholders for values rather than hardcoding things directly into the code.

Notice, also, the conditional logic in the script. Take a look at the code in Listing 16-1. This is a `switch` statement that finds an ISO file path based on an operating system name. You didn't need this in the previous script because everything was hardcoded into the script.

Because the `Install-PowerLabOperatingSystem` function has an `OperatingSystem` parameter, you have the flexibility needed to install different operating systems. You just need a way to account for all those operating systems. One great way to do that is a `switch` statement, which lets you easily add another condition.

```
switch ($OperatingSystem) {
    'Server 2016' {
        $isoFilePath = "$IsoBaseFolderPath\en_windows_server_2016_x64_dvd_9718492.iso"
    }
    default {
```

```
        throw "Unrecognized input: [$_]"
    }
}
```

Listing 16-1: Using the PowerShell `switch` *logic*

You can see how you moved hardcoded values into parameters. I can't stress this point enough: parameters are key to building reusable scripts. Avoid hardcoding as much as you can, and always keep an eye out for values that you'll have to change at runtime (and then use a parameter for them!). But, you might wonder, what if you want to change the value of something only some of the time? Next, you can see that multiple parameters have default values. This allows you to statically set the "typical" values and then override as necessary.

```
param
(
    [Parameter(Mandatory)]
    [string]$VmName,

    [Parameter()]
    [string]$OperatingSystem = 'Server 2016',

    [Parameter()]
    [ValidateSet('ServerStandardCore')]
    [string]$OperatingSystemEdition = 'ServerStandardCore',

    [Parameter()]
    [string]$DiskSize = 40GB,

    [Parameter()]
    [string]$VhdFormat = 'VHDX',

    [Parameter()]
    [string]$VhdType = 'Dynamic',

    [Parameter()]
    [string]$VhdPartitionStyle = 'GPT',

    [Parameter()]
    [string]$VhdBaseFolderPath = 'C:\PowerLab\VHDs',

    [Parameter()]
    [string]$IsoBaseFolderPath = 'C:\PowerLab\ISOs',

    [Parameter()]
    [string]$VhdPath
)
```

Using the `Install-PowerLabOperatingSystem` function, you can turn all that stuff into a single line that supports dozens of configurations. You now have a single, cohesive unit of code that you can call in many ways, all without changing a single line of the script!

Storing Encrypted Credentials on Disk

You'll finish up this stage of the project soon enough, but before going any further, you need to take a slight detour. This is because you're about to be doing things with PowerShell that require credentials. It's common enough when scripting to have sensitive information (for example, username/password combos) stored in plaintext inside the script itself. And likewise, it's not uncommon to think that if this is being done in a test environment, it's no big deal—but it sets a dangerous precedent. It's important to be conscious of security measures even when you're testing so that you can build good security habits for when you're moving out of testing and into production.

A simple way to avoid having plaintext passwords in your script is to encrypt them in a file. When you need them, your script can decrypt them and use them. Thankfully, PowerShell provides a way to natively do this: the Windows Data Protection API. This API is used under the hood of the `Get-Credential` command, a command that returns a `PSCredential` object.

`Get-Credential` creates an encrypted form of the password known as a *secure string*. Once in the secure string format, the whole credential object can be saved to the disk by using the `Export-CliXml` command; inversely, you can read the `PSCredential` object by using the `Import-CliXml` command. These commands make a handy password management system.

When handling credentials in PowerShell, you want to store `PSCredential` objects, the types of objects most `Credential` parameters accept. In previous chapters, you were either interactively typing in the username and password or storing them in plaintext. But now that you've gotten your feet wet, let's do it for real and add protection for your credentials.

Saving a `PSCredential` object in an encrypted format to disk requires the `Export-CliXml` command. Using the `Get-Credential` command, you can create a prompt for username and password and prompt the result into `Export-CliXml`, which takes the path to save the XML file as shown in Listing 16-2.

```
Get-Credential | Export-CliXml  -Path C:\DomainCredential.xml
```

Listing 16-2: Exporting a credential to a file

If you open the XML file, it should look something like this:

```
<TN RefId="0">
  <T>System.Management.Automation.PSCredential</T>
  <T>System.Object</T>
  </TN>
  <ToString>System.Management.Automation.PSCredential</ToString>
  <Props>
  <S N="UserName">userhere</S>
  <SS N="Password">ENCRYPTEDTEXTHERE</SS>
  </Props>
  </Obj>
</Objs>
```

Now that the credential has been saved to the disk, let's see how to get it in PowerShell. Use the `Import-CliXml` command to interpret the XML file and create a `PSCredential` object:

```
$cred = Import-Clixml -Path C:\DomainCredential.xml
$cred | Get-Member


   TypeName: System.Management.Automation.PSCredential

Name                 MemberType Definition
----                 ---------- ----------
Equals               Method     bool Equals(System.Object obj)
GetHashCode          Method     int GetHashCode()
GetNetworkCredential Method     System.Net.NetworkCredential
                                GetNetworkCredential()
GetObjectData        Method     void GetObjectData(System.Runtime...
GetType              Method     type GetType()
ToString             Method     string ToString()
Password             Property   securestring Password {get;}
UserName             Property   string UserName {get;}
```

You set the code up so that you simply need to pass `$cred` to any `Credential` parameter on a command. Now the code will work just as if you interactively typed it in. This method is short and sweet, but you wouldn't generally use it in a production environment because the user that encrypted the text must also be the one that decrypts it (not how encryption is supposed to work!). The one-user requirement won't scale well at all. But all that said, in a test environment, it works great!

PowerShell Direct

Now, back to our project. Typically, when you run commands against remote computers in PowerShell, you're forced to use PowerShell remoting. This, obviously, depends on network connectivity between your local host and a remote host. Wouldn't it be nice if you could simplify this setup and not have to worry about network connectivity at all? Well, you can!

Because you're running all your automation on a Windows Server 2016 Hyper-V host, you have a useful feature at your disposal: PowerShell Direct. *PowerShell Direct* is a newer feature of PowerShell that allows you to run commands on any VMs hosted on the Hyper-V server *without network connectivity*. There's no need to set up the network adapters on the VMs ahead of time (although you already did this with the unattend XML file).

For convenience's sake, rather than use the full network stack, you'll use PowerShell Direct quite a bit. If you didn't, because you're in a workgroup environment, you'd have to configure PowerShell remoting in a workgroup environment—no easy task (see the guide at *http://bit.ly/2D3deUX*). It's always a good idea to choose your battles in PowerShell, and here, I'll choose the easiest one!

PowerShell Direct is nearly identical to PowerShell remoting. It's a way to run commands on remote computers. Typically, this requires network connectivity, but with PowerShell Direct, there's no need. To initiate a command on a remote computer via PowerShell remoting, you'd usually use the `Invoke-Command` with the `ComputerName` and `ScriptBlock` parameters:

```
Invoke-Command -ComputerName LABDC -ScriptBlock { hostname }
```

When using PowerShell Direct, though, the `ComputerName` parameter turns into `VMName`, and a `Credential` parameter is added. The exact same command will run via PowerShell Direct as in the previous code, but only from the Hyper-V host itself. To make things easy, let's first store a `PSCredential` object on disk so you don't have to keep prompting for a credential in the future.

For this example, use the username `powerlabuser` and the password `P@$$w0rd12`:

```
Get-Credential | Export-CliXml -Path C:\PowerLab\VMCredential.xml
```

Now that you have saved the credential to disk, you'll decrypt it and pass it to `Invoke-Command`. Let's read the credential saved in *VMCredential.xml* and then use that credential to execute code on the LABDC VM:

```
$cred = Import-CliXml -Path C:\PowerLab\VMCredential.xml
Invoke-Command -VMName LABDC -ScriptBlock { hostname } -Credential $cred
```

A lot more is going on under the covers to make PowerShell Direct work, but I'm not going to go into the details here. For a full breakdown of how PowerShell Direct works, I recommend taking a look at the Microsoft blog post announcing the feature (*https://docs.microsoft.com/en-us/virtualization/hyper-v-on-windows/user-guide/powershell-direct*).

Pester Tests

It's now time for the most important part of the chapter: let's bring it all together with the Pester tests! You'll follow the same pattern as in the preceding chapter, but here I'd like to point out one piece of the tests. In this chapter's Pester tests, you'll use the `BeforeAll` and `AfterAll` blocks (Listing 16-3).

As their names suggest, the `BeforeAll` block contains code that's executed before all the tests, and the `AfterAll` block contains code that's executed after. You use these blocks because you'll need to connect to your LABDC server multiple times via PowerShell Direct. PowerShell remoting and PowerShell Direct both support the concept of a session, which you learned about in Part I (Chapter 8). Rather than having `Invoke-Command` build and tear down multiple sessions, it's better to define a single session ahead of time and reuse it.

```
BeforeAll {
    $cred = Import-CliXml -Path C:\PowerLab\VMCredential.xml
    $session = New-PSSession -VMName 'LABDC' -Credential $cred
}

AfterAll {
    $session | Remove-PSSession
}
```

Listing 16-3: Tests.ps1—*BeforeAll and AfterAll blocks*

You'll notice that you're decrypting your saved credential from disk inside the `BeforeAll` block. Once you create the credential, you pass it and the name of the VM to the `New-PSSession` command. This is the same `New-PSSession` covered in Part I (Chapter 8), but here you can see that instead of using `ComputerName` as a parameter, you're using `VMName`.

This will create a single remote session that you can reuse throughout the tests. After all the tests are done, Pester will look in the `AfterAll` block and remove the session. This approach is much more efficient than repeatedly creating a session, especially if you have dozens or hundreds of tests that need to run code remotely.

The rest of the script in the chapter resources is straightforward and follows the same pattern you've been using. As you can see, all the Pester tests come back positive, which means you're still on the right track!

```
PS> Invoke-Pester 'C:\PowerShellForSysadmins\Part II\Automating Operating
System Installs\Automating Operating System Installs.Tests.ps1'
Describing Automating Operating System Installs
   Context Virtual Disk
    [+] created a VHDX called LABDC in the expected location 305ms
    [+] attached the virtual disk to the expected VM 164ms
    [+] creates the expected VHDX format 79ms
    [+] creates the expected VHDX partition style 373ms
    [+] creates the expected VHDX type 114ms
    [+] creates the VHDDX of the expected size 104ms
   Context Operating System
    [+] sets the expected IP defined in the unattend XML file 1.07s
    [+] deploys the expected Windows version 65ms
Tests completed in 2.28s
Passed: 8 Failed: 0 Skipped: 0 Pending: 0 Inconclusive: 0
```

Summary

In this chapter, you went a little deeper into our real-world project. You used the existing VM you built in the preceding chapter and, both manually and automatically, deployed an operating system to it. At this point, you have a fully functioning Windows VM ready for the next stage in your journey.

In the next chapter, you'll set up Active Directory (AD) on your LABDC VM. Setting up AD will create a new AD forest and domain to which, by the end of the session, you'll have joined even more servers.

17

DEPLOYING ACTIVE DIRECTORY

In this chapter, you'll take what you've learned over the last few chapters of Part II and begin deploying services on top of your virtual machines. Because so many other services depend on Active Directory, you must first deploy an Active Directory forest and domain. The AD forest and domain will support your authentication and authorization needs for the remaining chapters.

Assuming that you already read through and provisioned the LABDC VM in the preceding chapter, you'll be using that to fully automate provisioning an Active Directory forest, and populating it with some test users and groups.

Prerequisites

You'll use what you made in Chapter 16, so I'm assuming that you have a LABDC VM set up, built using the unattended XML, and booted up running Windows Server 2016. If so, you're good to go! If not, you can still mine this chapter for examples of how to automate Active Directory, but fair warning: you won't be able to completely follow along.

As always, run the associated prerequisite Pester test to ensure that you meet all the prerequisites for this chapter.

Creating an Active Directory Forest

The good news is that, all things considered, creating an AD forest with PowerShell is pretty easy. When it comes down to it, you're essentially running just two commands: `Install-WindowsFeature` and `Install-ADDSForest`. With these two commands, you can build a single forest, build a domain, and provision a Windows server as a domain controller.

Because you'll use this forest in a lab environment, you'll also be creating some organizational units, users, and groups. Being in a lab environment means you don't have any production objects to work with. Without going through the hassle of attempting to sync production AD objects with your lab, you can, instead, create many objects that mimic production and give you some objects to work with.

Building the Forest

The first thing you need to do when creating a new AD forest is to promote a *domain controller*, the lowest common denominator in Active Directory. To have a functioning AD environment, you must have at least one domain controller.

Since this is a lab environment, you'll use a single domain controller. In a real-world situation, you'd want at least two domain controllers for redundancy. However, because you have no data in your lab environment and the ability to quickly re-create it from scratch, you'll use only one here. Before doing anything, you need to install the `AD-Domain-Services` Windows feature on your LABDC server. The command to install a Windows feature is `Install-WindowsFeature`:

```
PS> $cred = Import-CliXml -Path C:\Files.xml
PS> Invoke-Command -VMName 'LABDC' -Credential $cred -ScriptBlock
{ Install-windowsfeature -Name AD-Domain-Services }
PSComputerName : LABDC RunspaceId : 33d41d5e-50f3-475e-a624-4cc407858715
Success : True RestartNeeded : No FeatureResult : {Active Directory Domain
Services, Remote Server Administration Tools, Active Directory module for
Windows PowerShell, AD DS and AD LDS Tools...} ExitCode : Success ```
```

After providing a credential to connect to the server, you use `Invoke-Command` to remotely run the `Install-WindowsFeature` commands on the remote server.

Once the feature is installed, you can create the forest by using the `Install-ADDSForest` command. This command is part of the `ActiveDirectory` PowerShell module, which was installed on LABDC as part of the feature installation.

The `Install-ADDSForest` command is the only command you need to create a forest. It takes a few parameters, which you'll fill in using code but are usually filled in using a GUI. This forest will be called `powerlab.local`. Since the domain controller is Windows Server 2016, you'll set the domain mode and forest mode both to `WinThreshold`. For a full breakdown of all the available `DomainMode` and `ForestMode` values, refer to the *Install-ADDSForest* Microsoft documentation page (*http://bit.ly/2rrgUi6*).

Saving Secure Strings to Disk

In Chapter 16, when you needed credentials, you saved `PSCredential` objects and reused them in your commands. This time around, you don't need a `PSCredential` object. Instead, you need only a single encrypted string.

In this section, you'll see that you need to pass a safe mode administrator password to a command. As with any piece of sensitive information, you want to use encryption. As you did in the preceding chapter, you'll use `Export-CliXml` and `Import-CliXml` to save and retrieve PowerShell objects from the filesystem. Here, though, instead of calling `Get-Credential`, you'll create a secure string by using `ConvertTo-SecureString` and then save that object to a file.

To save an encrypted password to a file, you pass the plaintext password to `ConvertTo-SecureString` and then export that secure string object to `Export -CliXml`, creating a file you can reference later:

```
PS> 'P@$$w0rd12' | ConvertTo-SecureString -Force -AsPlainText
| Export-Clixml -Path C:\PowerLab\SafeModeAdministratorPassword.xml
```

As you can see, after you have the safe mode administrator password saved to disk, you can read it with `Import-CliXml` and pass in all the other parameters that `Install-ADDSForest` needs to run. You do this with the following code:

```
PS> $safeModePw = Import-CliXml -Path C:\PowerLab\
SafeModeAdministratorPassword.xml
PS> $cred = Import-CliXml -Path C:\PowerLab\VMCredential.xml
PS> $forestParams = @{
>>> DomainName                    = 'powerlab.local' ❶
>>> DomainMode                    = 'WinThreshold' ❷
>>> ForestMode                    = 'WinThreshold'
>>> Confirm                       = $false ❸
>>> SafeModeAdministratorPassword = $safeModePw ❹
>>> WarningAction                 = 'Ignore ❺
>>>}
PS> Invoke-Command -VMName 'LABDC' -Credential $cred -ScriptBlock { $null =
Install-ADDSForest @using:forestParams }
```

Here, you're creating a forest and domain called *powerlab.local* ❶ running at a Windows Server 2016 functional level (`WinThreshold`) ❷, bypassing all confirmations ❸, passing your safe mode administrator password ❹, and ignoring the irrelevant warning messages that typically come up ❺.

Automating Forest Creation

Now that you've done it manually, let's build a function in your PowerLab module that will handle AD forest creation for you. Once you have a function, you'll be able to use it across numerous environments.

In the PowerLab module included with this chapter's resources, you'll see a function called `New-PowerLabActiveDirectoryForest`, as shown in Listing 17-1.

```
function New-PowerLabActiveDirectoryForest {
    param(
        [Parameter(Mandatory)]
        [pscredential]$Credential,

        [Parameter(Mandatory)]
        [string]$SafeModePassword,

        [Parameter()]
        [string]$VMName = 'LABDC',

        [Parameter()]
        [string]$DomainName = 'powerlab.local',

        [Parameter()]
        [string]$DomainMode = 'WinThreshold',

        [Parameter()]
        [string]$ForestMode = 'WinThreshold'
    )

    Invoke-Command -VMName $VMName -Credential $Credential -ScriptBlock {

        Install-windowsfeature -Name AD-Domain-Services

        $forestParams = @{
            DomainName                    = $using:DomainName
            DomainMode                    = $using:DomainMode
            ForestMode                    = $using:ForestMode
            Confirm                       = $false
            SafeModeAdministratorPassword = (ConvertTo-SecureString
                                            -AsPlainText -String $using:
                                            SafeModePassword -Force)
            WarningAction                 = 'Ignore'
        }
        $null = Install-ADDSForest @forestParams
    }
}
```

Listing 17-1: The `New-PowerLabActiveDirectoryForest` function

As in the preceding chapter, you simply define several parameters you'll use to pass to the ActiveDirectory module's Install-ADDSForest command. Notice that you define two Mandatory parameters for the credentials and password. As its name suggests, these are parameters the user needs to pass in (because the other parameters have default values, the user does not necessarily need to pass them in). You'll use this function by reading in your saved administrator password and credential, and then passing the two into the function:

```
PS> $safeModePw = Import-CliXml -Path C:\PowerLab\SafeModeAdministratorPassword.xml
PS> $cred = Import-CliXml -Path C:\PowerLab\VMCredential.xml
PS> New-PowerLabActiveDirectoryForest -Credential $cred -SafeModePassword $safeModePw
```

After running this code, you'll have a fully working Active Domain forest! Well, you should, anyway—let's figure out a way to confirm that the forest is up and running. A good test is to query all the default user accounts in the domain. To do so, however, you need to create another PSCredential object stored on disk; because LABDC is a domain controller now, you need a domain user account (not a local user account). You'll create and save a credential with the username of powerlab.local\administrator and a password of P@$$w0rd12 to the *C:\PowerLab\DomainCredential.xml* file. Remember that you need to do this only once. Then, you can use the new domain credential to connect to LABDC:

```
PS> Get-Credential | Export-CliXml -Path C:\PowerLab\DomainCredential.xml
```

Once the domain credential is created, you'll create another function in your PowerLab module called Test-PowerLabActiveDirectoryForest. Right now, this function just gathers all the users in a domain, but because you have this functionality wrapped in a function, you can customize this test to your liking:

```
function Test-PowerLabActiveDirectoryForest {
    param(
        [Parameter(Mandatory)]
        [pscredential]$Credential,

        [Parameter()]
        [string]$VMName = 'LABDC'
    )

    Invoke-Command -Credential $Credential -ScriptBlock {Get-AdUser -Filter * }
}
```

Try executing the Test-PowerLabActiveDirectoryForest function by using the domain credential and a VMName of LABDC. If you're shown a few user accounts, congrats! You're done! You've now successfully set up a domain controller and stored credentials for connecting to VMs in a workgroup (and any future domain-joined VMs).

Populating the Domain

In the preceding section, you set up a domain controller in your PowerLab. Now let's create some test objects. Since this is a test lab, you want to create various objects (OUs, users, groups, and so on) so that you cover all your bases. You could run the required command to create each individual object, but because you have so many objects to create, that wouldn't be practical. It'll be a much better use of your time to define everything in one file, read in each object, and create them all in one go.

Handling Your Object Spreadsheet

Here, you'll use an Excel spreadsheet as your input file to define everything you need as input. This Excel spreadsheet is available via the chapter's downloadable resources. When you open it, you'll see it has two worksheets: Users (Figure 17-1) and Groups (Figure 17-2).

	A	B	C	D	E
1	OUName	UserName	FirstName	LastName	MemberOf
2	PowerLab Users	jjones	Joe	Jones	Accounting
3	PowerLab Users	abertram	Adam	Bertram	Accounting
4	PowerLab Users	jhicks	Jeff	Hicks	Accounting
5	PowerLab Users	dtrump	Donald	Trump	Human Resources
6	PowerLab Users	alincoln	Abraham	Lincoln	Human Resources
7	PowerLab Users	bobama	Barack	Obama	Human Resources
8	PowerLab Users	tjefferson	Thomas	Jefferson	IT
9	PowerLab Users	bclinton	Bill	Clinton	IT
10	PowerLab Users	gbush	George	Bush	IT
11	PowerLab Users	rreagan	Ronald	Reagan	IT

Figure 17-1: The Users spreadsheet

	A	B	C
1	OUName	GroupName	Type
2	PowerLab Groups	Accounting	DomainLocal
3	PowerLab Groups	Human Resources	DomainLocal
4	PowerLab Groups	IT	DomainLocal

Figure 17-2: The Groups spreadsheet

Each row of these worksheets corresponds to a user or group that needs to be created, containing information you'll read into PowerShell. As you saw in Chapter 10, native PowerShell cannot handle Excel spreadsheets without significant work. With the help of a popular community module, however, you can make this much easier. Using the `ImportExcel` module, you can read Excel spreadsheets just as easily as you can natively read CSV files. To get `ImportExcel`, you can download it from the PowerShell Gallery by using **`Install-Module -Name ImportExcel`**. After a few security prompts, you should have the module downloaded and ready to use.

Now let's use the `Import-Excel` command to parse in the rows from the worksheet:

```
PS> Import-Excel -Path 'C:\Program Files\WindowsPowerShell\Modules\PowerLab\
ActiveDirectoryObjects.xlsx' -WorksheetName Users | Format-Table -AutoSize
```

```
OUName         UserName    FirstName LastName  MemberOf
------         --------    --------- --------  --------
PowerLab Users jjones      Joe       Jones     Accounting
PowerLab Users abertram    Adam      Bertram   Accounting
PowerLab Users jhicks      Jeff      Hicks     Accounting
PowerLab Users dtrump      Donald    Trump     Human Resources
PowerLab Users alincoln    Abraham   Lincoln   Human Resources
PowerLab Users bobama      Barack    Obama     Human Resources
PowerLab Users tjefferson  Thomas    Jefferson IT
PowerLab Users bclinton    Bill      Clinton   IT
PowerLab Users gbush       George    Bush      IT
PowerLab Users rreagan     Ronald    Reagan    IT

PS> Import-Excel -Path 'C:\Program Files\WindowsPowerShell\Modules\PowerLab\
ActiveDirectoryObjects.xlsx' -WorksheetName Groups | Format-Table -AutoSize

OUName          GroupName       Type
------          ---------       ----
PowerLab Groups Accounting      DomainLocal
PowerLab Groups Human Resources DomainLocal
PowerLab Groups IT              DomainLocal
```

Using the Path and WorksheetName parameters, you can easily pull out the data you need. Notice that here, you're using the Format-Table command. This is a useful command that forces PowerShell to display the output in a table format. The AutoSize parameter tells PowerShell to try to squeeze each row into one line in the console.

Creating a Plan

You now have a way to read the data from the Excel spreadsheet. The next step is figuring out what to do with it. You'll build a function in your PowerLab module that reads each row and performs the action it requires. All code covered here is available via the New-PowerLabActiveDirectoryTestObject function in the associated PowerLab module.

This function is a little more complicated than our previous scripts, so let's break it down in an informal way—this way, you have something to refer back to. This step may not sound important, but as you make bigger functions, you'll find that planning them out at the start will save you a lot of work in the long run. In this function, you need to do the following:

1. Read both worksheets in an Excel spreadsheet and retrieve all user and group rows.
2. Read each row in both worksheets and first confirm whether the OU that the user or group is supposed to be a part of exists.
3. If the OU does not exist, create the OU.
4. If the user/group does not exist, create the user or group.
5. For users only: add the user as a member of the specified group.

Now that you have this informal outline, let's get down to coding.

Creating the AD Objects

For the first pass through, you want to keep it simple: let's focus on handling a single object. No need to complicate things now by worrying about all of them. You installed the `AD-Domain-Services` Windows feature on LABDC earlier, so now you have the `ActiveDirectory` module installed. This module provides a large set of useful commands (as you saw in Chapter 11). Recall that many of the commands follow the same naming convention of `Get/Set/New-AD`.

Let's open a blank *.ps1* script and get to work. Start by writing out all the commands you need (Listing 17-2) based on the previous outline:

```
Get-ADOrganizationalUnit -Filter "Name -eq 'OUName'" ❶
New-ADOrganizationalUnit -Name OUName ❷

Get-ADGroup -Filter "Name -eq 'GroupName'" ❸
New-ADGroup -Name GroupName -GroupScope GroupScope -Path "OU=OUName,DC=powerlab,DC=local" ❹

Get-ADUser -Filter "Name -eq 'UserName'" ❺
New-ADUser -Name $user.UserName -Path "OU=$($user.OUName),DC=powerlab,DC=local" ❻

UserName -in (Get-ADGroupMember -Identity GroupName).Name ❼
Add-ADGroupMember -Identity GroupName -Members UserName ❽
```

Listing 17-2: Figuring out code to check for and create new users and groups

Recall from our plan that you first need to check whether an OU exists ❶, and then create one if it doesn't ❷. You do the same thing with each group: check whether it exists ❸ and create one if it doesn't ❹. And do the same thing for each user: check ❺ and create ❻. Lastly, for your users, check whether they are a member of the group specified in the spreadsheet ❼, and add them to it if they are not ❽.

All you're missing here is the conditional structure, which you add in Listing 17-3.

```
if (-not (Get-ADOrganizationalUnit -Filter "Name -eq 'OUName'")) {
    New-ADOrganizationalUnit -Name OUName
}

if (-not (Get-ADGroup -Filter "Name -eq 'GroupName'")) {
    New-ADGroup -Name GroupName -GroupScope GroupScope -Path "OU=OUName,DC=powerlab,DC=local"
}

if (-not (Get-ADUser -Filter "Name -eq 'UserName'")) {
    New-ADUser -Name $user.UserName -Path "OU=OUName,DC=powerlab,DC=local"
}

if (UserName -notin (Get-AdGroupMember -Identity GroupName).Name) {
    Add-ADGroupMember -Identity GroupName -Members UserName
}
```

Listing 17-3: Creating users and groups only if they don't already exist

Now that you have the code to do what you want for an individual user or group, you need to figure out how to do it for all of them. First, though, you need to read in the worksheets. You've already seen which commands to use; now you need to store all those rows in variables. This isn't technically required, but it keeps your code more explicit and self-documenting. You'll use `foreach` loops to read all users and groups, as shown in Listing 17-4.

```
$users = Import-Excel -Path 'C:\Program Files\WindowsPowerShell\Modules\
PowerLab\ActiveDirectoryObjects.xlsx' -WorksheetName Users
$groups = Import-Excel -Path 'C:\Program Files\WindowsPowerShell\Modules\
PowerLab\ActiveDirectoryObjects.xlsx' -WorksheetName Groups

foreach ($group in $groups) {

}

foreach ($user in $users) {

}
```

Listing 17-4: Building the code structure to iterate over each Excel worksheet row

Now that you have a structure to loop through every row, let's use our individual code to handle the rows, as shown in Listing 17-5.

```
$users = Import-Excel -Path 'C:\Program Files\WindowsPowerShell\Modules\PowerLab\
ActiveDirectoryObjects.xlsx' -WorksheetName Users
$groups = Import-Excel -Path 'C:\Program Files\WindowsPowerShell\Modules\PowerLab\
ActiveDirectoryObjects.xlsx' -WorksheetName Groups

foreach ($group in $groups) {
    if (-not (Get-ADOrganizationalUnit -Filter "Name -eq '$($group.OUName)'")) {
        New-ADOrganizationalUnit -Name $group.OUName
    }
    if (-not (Get-ADGroup -Filter "Name -eq '$($group.GroupName)'")) {
        New-ADGroup -Name $group.GroupName -GroupScope $group.Type
        -Path "OU=$($group.OUName),DC=powerlab,DC=local"
    }
}

foreach ($user in $users) {
    if (-not (Get-ADOrganizationalUnit -Filter "Name -eq '$($user.OUName)'")) {
        New-ADOrganizationalUnit -Name $user.OUName
    }
    if (-not (Get-ADUser -Filter "Name -eq '$($user.UserName)'")) {
        New-ADUser -Name $user.UserName -Path "OU=$($user.OUName),DC=powerlab,DC=local"
    }
    if ($user.UserName -notin (Get-ADGroupMember -Identity $user.MemberOf).Name) {
        Add-ADGroupMember -Identity $user.MemberOf -Members $user.UserName
    }
}
```

Listing 17-5: Performing tasks on all users and groups

You're almost done! The script is all ready to go, but now you need to run it on the LABDC server. Since you're not running this code directly on the LABDC VM itself yet, you have to wrap all this up into a scriptblock and have `Invoke-Command` run it remotely on LABDC for you. Since you want to create and populate the forest in one go, you'll take all your "scratch" code and move it into your `New-PowerLabActiveDirectoryTestObject` function. You can download a copy of this fully created function in the chapter's resources.

Building and Running Pester Tests

You have all the code you need to create a new AD forest and populate it. Now you'll build some Pester tests to confirm that everything is working as planned. You have quite a bit to test, so the Pester tests are going to be more complicated than before. Just as you did before creating the *New-PowerLab ActiveDirectoryTestObject.ps1* script, first create a Pester test script, and then start thinking of test cases. If you need a refresher about Pester, check out Chapter 9. I've also included all Pester tests for this chapter in the book's resources.

What do you need to test? In this chapter, you did the following:

- Created a new AD forest
- Created a new AD domain
- Created AD users
- Created AD groups
- Created AD organizational units

After determining that they exist, you need to make sure that your objects have the correct attributes (the attributes you passed in as parameters to the commands that created them). These are the attributes you're looking for:

Table 17-1: AD Attributes

Object	Attributes
AD forest	`DomainName`, `DomainMode`, `ForestMode`, safe mode administrator password
AD user	OU path, name, group member
AD group	OU path, name
AD organizational unit	Name

With that, you have a good back-of-the-napkin plan for what you're looking for with your Pester tests. If you take a look at the *Creating an Active Directory Forest.Tests.ps1* script, you'll see that I've chosen to break down each of these entities into contexts and test all the associated attributes inside as individual tests.

To give you an idea of how these tests are created, Listing 17-6 has a snippet of the test code.

```
context 'Domain' {
❶ $domain = Invoke-Command -Session $session -ScriptBlock { Get-AdDomain }
  $forest = Invoke-Command -Session $session -ScriptBlock { Get-AdForest }

❷ it "the domain mode should be Windows2016Domain" {
      $domain.DomainMode | should be 'Windows2016Domain'
  }

  it "the forest mode should be WinThreshold" {
      $forest.ForestMode | should be 'Windows2016Forest'
  }

  it "the domain name should be powerlab.local" {
      $domain.Name | should be 'powerlab'
  }
}
```

Listing 17-6: Some of the Pester test code

For this context, you want to make sure that the AD domain and forest are created properly. So you first create the domain and forest ❶; then you verify that the domain and forest have the attributes you expect ❷.

Running the whole test should give you something like this:

```
Describing Active Directory Forest
   Context Domain
    [+] the domain mode should be Windows2016Domain 933ms
    [+] the forest mode should be WinThreshold 25ms
    [+] the domain name should be powerlab.local 41ms
   Context Organizational Units
    [+] the OU [PowerLab Users] should exist 85ms
    [+] the OU [PowerLab Groups] should exist 37ms
   Context Users
    [+] the user [jjones] should exist 74ms
    [+] the user [jjones] should be in the [PowerLab Users] OU 35ms
    [+] the user [jjones] should be in the [Accounting] group 121ms
    [+] the user [abertram] should exist 39ms
    [+] the user [abertram] should be in the [PowerLab Users] OU 30ms
    [+] the user [abertram] should be in the [Accounting] group 80ms
    [+] the user [jhicks] should exist 39ms
    [+] the user [jhicks] should be in the [PowerLab Users] OU 32ms
    [+] the user [jhicks] should be in the [Accounting] group 81ms
    [+] the user [dtrump] should exist 45ms
    [+] the user [dtrump] should be in the [PowerLab Users] OU 40ms
    [+] the user [dtrump] should be in the [Human Resources] group 84ms
    [+] the user [alincoln] should exist 41ms
    [+] the user [alincoln] should be in the [PowerLab Users] OU 40ms
    [+] the user [alincoln] should be in the [Human Resources] group 125ms
    [+] the user [bobama] should exist 44ms
    [+] the user [bobama] should be in the [PowerLab Users] OU 27ms
    [+] the user [bobama] should be in the [Human Resources] group 92ms
```

```
  [+] the user [tjefferson] should exist 58ms
  [+] the user [tjefferson] should be in the [PowerLab Users] OU 33ms
  [+] the user [tjefferson] should be in the [IT] group 73ms
  [+] the user [bclinton] should exist 47ms
  [+] the user [bclinton] should be in the [PowerLab Users] OU 29ms
  [+] the user [bclinton] should be in the [IT] group 84ms
  [+] the user [gbush] should exist 50ms
  [+] the user [gbush] should be in the [PowerLab Users] OU 33ms
  [+] the user [gbush] should be in the [IT] group 78ms
  [+] the user [rreagan] should exist 56ms
  [+] the user [rreagan] should be in the [PowerLab Users] OU 30ms
  [+] the user [rreagan] should be in the [IT] group 78ms
 Context Groups
  [+] the group [Accounting] should exist 71ms
  [+] the group [Accounting] should be in the [PowerLab Groups] OU 42ms
  [+] the group [Human Resources] should exist 48ms
  [+] the group [Human Resources] should be in the [PowerLab Groups] OU 29ms
  [+] the group [IT] should exist 51ms
  [+] the group [IT] should be in the [PowerLab Groups] OU 31ms
```

Summary

In this chapter, you took the next step in the creation of your PowerLab and added an Active Directory forest before populating it with several objects. You did this both manually and automatically, and in the process, reviewed some of what you had learned about Active Directory in previous chapters. Lastly, you dived a little deeper into Pester testing, taking a closer look at how to build custom tests that suit your needs. In the next chapter, you'll continue with the PowerLab project and learn how to automate installing and configuring a SQL server.

18

CREATING AND CONFIGURING A SQL SERVER

So far, you've created a module that can create a VM, attach a VHD to it, install Windows, and create (and populate) an Active Directory forest. Let's add one more thing to that list: deploying a SQL server. With a VM provisioned, an OS installed, and a domain controller set up, you've done most of the hard work! Now you just need to leverage your existing functions and, with a few tweaks, you'll be able to install a SQL server.

Prerequisites

Throughout this chapter, I'm assuming that you've been following along in Part III and have created at least one VM called LABDC that's running on your Hyper-V host. This VM will be a domain controller, and since you'll again be connecting to multiple VMs via PowerShell Direct, you'll need the domain credential saved to the Hyper-V host (check out Chapter 17 to see how we did this).

You'll use a script called *ManuallyCreatingASqlServer.ps1* (found in this chapter's resources) to explain how to properly automate the deploying of a SQL server. This script contains all the rough steps covered in this chapter and will be a great resource to reference as you progress through this chapter.

As always, please run the Prerequisites test script included with this chapter to ensure you meet all the expected prerequisites.

Creating the Virtual Machine

When you think *SQL Server*, you probably think about things like databases, jobs, and tables. But before you can even get there, a ton of background work has to be done: for starters, every SQL database must exist on a server, every server needs an operating system, and every operating system needs a physical or virtual machine to be installed on. Luckily, you've spent the past few chapters setting up the exact environment you need to create a SQL server.

A good automator starts every project by breaking down all the required dependencies. They automate around those dependencies, and then on top of them. This process results in a modular, decoupled architecture that has the flexibility to be changed at any time with relative ease.

What you're ultimately looking for is a single function that uses a standard configuration to bring up any number of SQL servers. But to get there, you have to think about this project in layers. The first layer is the virtual machine. Let's handle that first.

Since you already have a function in your PowerLab module that'll build a VM, you'll use that. Because all lab environments you build are going to be the same, and because you defined many of the parameters needed to provision a new VM as default parameter values in the `New-PowerLabVM` function, the only value you need to pass to this function is the VM name:

```
PS> New-PowerLabVm -Name 'SQLSRV'
```

Installing the Operating System

Just like that, you have a VM ready to go. That was easy. Let's do it again. Use the command you wrote in Chapter 16 to install Windows on your VM:

```
PS> Install-PowerLabOperatingSystem -VmName 'SQLSRV'
Get-Item : Cannot find path 'C:\Program Files\WindowsPowerShell\Modules\
powerlab\SQLSRV.xml' because it does not exist.
At C:\Program Files\WindowsPowerShell\Modules\powerlab\PowerLab.psm1:138 char:16
+     $answerFile = Get-Item -Path "$PSScriptRoot\$VMName.xml"
+                   ~~~~~~~~~~~~~~~~~~~~~~~~~~~~~~~~~~~~~~~~~~~~
    + CategoryInfo          : ObjectNotFound: (C:\Program File...rlab\SQLSRV
                              .xml:String) [Get-Item], ItemNotFoundException
```

Oops! You used the existing `Install-PowerLabOperatingSystem` function in the PowerLab module to install the operating system on the soon-to-be SQL server, but it failed because it was referencing a file called *SQLSRV.xml* in the module folder. When you built this function, you assumed there would be an *.xml* file in the module folder. Problems like path discrepancies and files that don't exist are common when building large automation projects like this. You'll have many dependencies that you must address. The only way to flush out all these bugs is to execute the code as many times as possible in as many scenarios as possible.

Adding a Windows Unattended Answer File

The `Install-PowerLabOperatingSystem` function was assuming there would always be a file called *.xml* in the PowerLab module folder. This means that before you deploy a new server, you have to first ensure that you have this file in the right place. Luckily, now that you created the LABDC unattended answer file, this should be easy. The first thing you have to do is copy the already-existing *LABDC.xml* file and call it *SQLSRV.xml*:

```
PS> Copy-Item -Path 'C:\Program Files\WindowsPowerShell\Modules\PowerLab\LABDC.xml' -Destination
'C:\Program Files\WindowsPowerShell\Modules\PowerLab\SQLSRV.xml'
```

Once you've made a copy, you have to make a few tweaks: the name of the host and the IP address. Since you haven't deployed a DHCP server, you'll use static IP addresses and have to change them (otherwise you'd have to change just the server name).

Open *C:\Program Files\WindowsPowerShell\Modules\SQLSRV.xml* and look for the spot that defines the hostname. Once you find it, change the `ComputerName` value. It should look similar to this:

```
<component name="Microsoft-Windows-Shell-Setup" processorArchitecture="amd64"
publicKeyToken="31bf3856ad364e35" language="neutral" versionScope="nonSxS"
    xmlns:wcm="http://schemas.microsoft.com/WMIConfig/2002/State"
    xmlns:xsi="http://www.w3.org/2001/XMLSchema-instance">
    <ComputerName>SQLSRV</ComputerName>
    <ProductKey>XXXXXXXXXXXXX</ProductKey>
</component>
```

Next, look for the `UnicastIPAddress` node. It will look like the following code. Note I'm using a 10.0.0.0/24 network and have chosen to make my SQL server have the IP address of 10.0.0.101:

```
<UnicastIpAddresses>
    <IpAddress wcm:action="add" wcm:keyValue="1">10.0.0.101</IpAddress>
</UnicastIpAddresses>
```

Save the *SQLSRV.xml* file and try running the `Install-PowerLabOperatingSystem` command again. At this time, your command should run successfully and should deploy Windows Server 2016 to your SQLSRV VM.

Adding the SQL Server to a Domain

You just installed the operating system, so now you need to start up the VM. This is easy enough using the Start-VM cmdlet:

```
PS> Start-VM -Name SQLSRV
```

Now you have to wait for the VM to come online—this could take a while. How long? That depends; there are a lot of variables. One thing you can do is use a while loop to continually check whether you can connect to the VM.

Let's walk though how to do this. In Listing 18-1, you're grabbing the locally saved credential for the VM. Once you have that, you can create a while loop that keeps executing the Invoke-Command until something is returned.

Notice that you're using the Ignore value for the ErrorAction parameter. You have to do this because without it, when Invoke-Command can't connect to a computer, it will return a nonterminating error message. To avoid having your console flood with expected errors (since you know that it might not connect and are OK with it), you're ignoring the error messages.

```
$vmCred = Import-CliXml -Path 'C:\PowerLab\VMCredential.xml'
while (-not (Invoke-Command -VmName SQLSRV -ScriptBlock { 1 } -Credential
$vmCred -ErrorAction Ignore)) {
    Start-Sleep -Seconds 10
    Write-Host 'Waiting for SQLSRV to come up...'
}
```

Listing 18-1: Checking to see whether the server is alive, and ignoring the error messages

Once the VM finally comes up, it's time to add it to the domain you created in the preceding chapter. The command that adds a computer to a domain is Add-Computer. Since you're running all commands from the Hyper-V host itself, and aren't depending on network connectivity, you need to wrap the Add-Computer command in a scriptblock and execute it via PowerShell Direct to run it directly on SQLSRV itself.

Notice that in Listing 18-2, you have to use both the local user account for the VM and a domain account. To do so, you first make a connection to the SQLSRV server itself by using Invoke-Command. Once you are connected, you'll pass the domain credential to the domain controller to get authenticated, which will let you add the computer account.

```
$domainCred = Import-CliXml -Path 'C:\PowerLab\DomainCredential.xml'
$addParams = @{
    DomainName = 'powerlab.local'
    Credential = $domainCred
    Restart    = $true
    Force      = $true
}
Invoke-Command -VMName SQLSRV -ScriptBlock { Add-Computer ❶@using:addParams } -Credential $vmCred
```

Listing 18-2: Retrieving the credentials and adding the computer to the domain

Notice that you're using the $using keyword ❶. This keyword allows you to pass the local variable $addParams to the remote session on your SQLSRV server.

Since you used the Restart switch parameter on Add-Computer, the VM will restart as soon as it gets added to the domain. Again, because you have further work to do, you need to wait for this to happen. However, this time, you need to wait for it to go down *and* come back up (Listing 18-3) because the script is so fast that if you don't wait for it to go down first, you risk the script continuing because it detected that it was up when it didn't even go down yet!

```
❶ while (Invoke-Command -VmName SQLSRV -ScriptBlock { 1 } -Credential $vmCred
  -ErrorAction Ignore) {
    ❷ Start-Sleep -Seconds 10
    ❸ Write-Host 'Waiting for SQLSRV to go down...'
  }

❶ while (-not (Invoke-Command -VmName SQLSRV -ScriptBlock { 1 } -Credential
  $domainCred -ErrorAction Ignore)) {
    ❷ Start-Sleep -Seconds 10
    ❸ Write-Host 'Waiting for SQLSRV to come up...'
  }
```

Listing 18-3: Waiting for the server to reboot

You first check whether SQLSRV has been powered down by simply returning the number 1 on SQLSRV ❶. If it receives output, this means that PowerShell remoting is available and thus SQLSRV has not been powered down yet. If output is returned, you then pause for 10 seconds ❷, write a message to the screen ❸, and try again.

You then do the opposite when testing to see when SQLSRV comes back up. Once the script releases control of the console, SQLSRV should now be up and added to your Active Directory domain.

Installing the SQL Server

Now that you've created a VM with Windows Server 2016, you can install SQL Server 2016 to it. This is new code! Up until now, you simply leveraged existing code; now you're back blazing new trails.

Installing SQL Server via PowerShell consists of a few steps:

1. Copying, and tweaking, a SQL Server answer file
2. Copying the SQL Server ISO file to the soon-to-be SQL server
3. Mounting the ISO file on the soon-to-be SQL server
4. Running the SQL Server installer
5. Dismounting the ISO file
6. Cleaning up any temporary copied files on the SQL server

Copying Files to the SQL Server

As per our plan, the first thing to do is to get a few files on the soon-to-be SQL server. You need the unattended answer file that the SQL Server installer needs, and you also need the ISO file that contains the SQL Server installation content. Since we're assuming that you have no network connectivity from the Hyper-V host to the VMs, you'll again use PowerShell Direct to copy these files. To use PowerShell Direct to copy files, you first need to create a session on the remote VM. In the following code, you're using the `Credential` parameter to authenticate to SQLSRV. If your server were in the same Active Directory domain as the computer you're currently working on, the `Credential` parameter would not be necessary.

```
$session = New-PSSession -VMName 'SQLSRV' -Credential $domainCred
```

Next, make a copy of the template *SQLServer.ini* file found in the PowerLab module:

```
$sqlServerAnswerFilePath = "C:\Program Files\WindowsPowerShell\Modules\
PowerLab\SqlServer.ini"
$tempFile = Copy-Item -Path $sqlServerAnswerFilePath -Destination "C:\Program
Files\WindowsPowerShell\Modules\PowerLab\temp.ini" -PassThru
```

Once that's done, you'll modify the file to match the configuration you need. Recall that earlier, when you needed to change some values, you manually opened the unattended XML file. This was more work than you needed to do—believe it or not, you can automate this step as well!

In Listing 18-4, you're reading in the contents of the copied template file, looking for the strings `SQLSVCACCOUNT=`, `SQLSVCPASSWORD=`, and `SQLSYSADMINACCOUNTS=` and replacing those strings with specific values. When you're finished, rewrite the copied template file with your new changed strings.

```
$configContents = Get-Content -Path $tempFile.FullName -Raw
$configContents = $configContents.Replace('SQLSVCACCOUNT=""', 'SQLSVCACCOUNT="PowerLabUser"')
$configContents = $configContents.Replace('SQLSVCPASSWORD=""', 'SQLSVCPASSWORD="P@$$w0rd12"')
$configContents = $configContents.Replace('SQLSYSADMINACCOUNTS=""', 'SQLSYSADMINACCOUNTS=
"PowerLabUser"')
Set-Content -Path $tempFile.FullName -Value $configContents
```

Listing 18-4: Replacing the strings

Once you have the answer file, and have copied that file and the SQL Server ISO file to the soon-to-be SQL server, the installer will be ready to go:

```
$copyParams = @{
    Path        = $tempFile.FullName
    Destination = 'C:\'
    ToSession   = $session
}
Copy-Item @copyParams
Remove-Item -Path $tempFile.FullName -ErrorAction Ignore
Copy-Item -Path 'C:\PowerLab\ISOs\en_sql_server_2016_standard_x64_dvd_8701871.iso'
-Destination 'C:\' -Force -ToSession $session
```

Running the SQL Server Installer

You're finally ready to install SQL Server. Listing 18-5 contains the code to do so:

```
$icmParams = @{
    Session      = $session
    ArgumentList = $tempFile.Name
    ScriptBlock  = {
        $image = Mount-DiskImage -ImagePath 'C:\en_sql_server_2016_standard_x64_dvd_8701871
        .iso' -PassThru ❶
        $installerPath = "$(($image | Get-Volume).DriveLetter):"
        $null = & "$installerPath\setup.exe" "/CONFIGURATIONFILE=C:\$($using:tempFile.Name)" ❷
        $image | Dismount-DiskImage ❸
    }
}
Invoke-Command @icmParams
```

Listing 18-5: Using `Invoke-Command` to mount, install, and dismount the image

First, you mount the copied ISO file on the remote machine ❶; then you execute the installer, assigning the output to `$null` ❷ as you don't need it; lastly, when you're all done, you dismount the image ❸. In Listing 18-5, you're using `Invoke-Command` and PowerShell Direct to remotely execute these commands.

When SQL Server has been installed, do some cleanup work to ensure that you remove all the temporary copied files, as shown in Listing 18-6.

```
$scriptBlock = { Remove-Item -Path 'C:\en_sql_server_2016_standard_x64_dvd
_8701871.iso', "C:\$($using:tempFile.Name)" -Recurse -ErrorAction Ignore }
Invoke-Command -ScriptBlock $scriptBlock -Session $session
$session | Remove-PSSession
```

Listing 18-6: Cleaning up the temporary files

At this point, the SQL Server will be set up and ready to go! In just 64 lines of PowerShell, you created a Microsoft SQL Server from nothing but a Hyper-V host. This is great progress, but you can make it even better.

Automating the SQL Server

You've done most of the heavy lifting already. By now, you have a script that does everything you need it to do. What you want next is to roll all that functionality into a few functions in your PowerLab module: the `New-PowerLabSqlServer` and `Install-PowerLabOperatingSystem` functions.

You'll follow the basic automation pattern established in the previous chapters: build functions around all the common actions and call them instead of using hardcoded values in many places. The result will be a single function the user can call. In Listing 18-7, you use existing functions to create the VM and VHD, and create a second `Install-PowerLabSQLServer` function to house the code for installing the SQL Server:

```
function New-PowerLabSqlServer {
    [CmdletBinding()]
    param
    (
        [Parameter(Mandatory)]
        [string]$Name,

        [Parameter(Mandatory)]
        [pscredential]$DomainCredential,

        [Parameter(Mandatory)]
        [pscredential]$VMCredential,

        [Parameter()]
        [string]$VMPath = 'C:\PowerLab\VMs',

        [Parameter()]
        [int64]$Memory = 2GB,

        [Parameter()]
        [string]$Switch = 'PowerLab',

        [Parameter()]
        [int]$Generation = 2,

        [Parameter()]
        [string]$DomainName = 'powerlab.local',

        [Parameter()]
        [string]$AnswerFilePath = "C:\Program Files\WindowsPowerShell\Modules\PowerLab
        \SqlServer.ini"
    )

    ## Build the VM
    $vmparams = @{
        Name       = $Name
        Path       = $VmPath
        Memory     = $Memory
        Switch     = $Switch
        Generation = $Generation
    }
    New-PowerLabVm @vmParams
    Install-PowerLabOperatingSystem -VmName $Name
    Start-VM -Name $Name
    Wait-Server -Name $Name -Status Online -Credential $VMCredential
    $addParams = @{
        DomainName = $DomainName
        Credential = $DomainCredential
        Restart    = $true
        Force      = $true
```

```
    Invoke-Command -VMName $Name -ScriptBlock { Add-Computer @using:addParams } -Credential
    $VMCredential
    Wait-Server -Name $Name -Status Offline -Credential $VMCredential
    Wait-Server -Name $Name -Status Online -Credential $DomainCredential
    $tempFile = Copy-Item -Path $AnswerFilePath
    -Destination "C:\Program Files\WindowsPowerShell\Modules\PowerLab\temp.ini" -PassThru

    Install-PowerLabSqlServer -ComputerName $Name -AnswerFilePath $tempFile.FullName
}
```

Listing 18-7: The `New-PowerLabSqlServer` function

You should recognize most of this code: it's the exact same code we covered just a bit ago, here wrapped in a function for easy reuse! I used the same code body but instead of using hardcoded values, I parameterized many attributes, allowing you to install SQL Server with different parameters without changing the code itself.

Turning specific scripts into a general function preserves the functionality of your code and allows greater flexibility if at some point in the future you want to change the behavior of how you deploy SQL servers.

Let's take a look at the important pieces of the `Install-PowerLabSqlServer` code in Listing 18-8.

```
function Install-PowerLabSqlServer {
❶ param
    (
        [Parameter(Mandatory)]
        [string]$ComputerName,

        [Parameter(Mandatory)]
        [pscredential]$DomainCredential,

        [Parameter(Mandatory)]
        [string]$AnswerFilePath,

        [Parameter()]
        [string]$IsoFilePath = 'C:\PowerLab\ISOs\en_sql_server_2016_standard
        _x64_dvd_8701871.iso'
    )

    try {
        --snip--

      ❷ ## Test to see if SQL Server is already installed
        if (Invoke-Command -Session $session
        -ScriptBlock { Get-Service -Name 'MSSQLSERVER' -ErrorAction Ignore }) {
            Write-Verbose -Message 'SQL Server is already installed'
        } else {

          ❸ PrepareSqlServerInstallConfigFile -Path $AnswerFilePath
```

```
        --snip--
    } catch {
        $PSCmdlet.ThrowTerminatingError($_)
    }
}
```

Listing 18-8: The `Install-PowerLabSqlServer` PowerLab module function

You parameterize all the types of input you need to install SQL Server ❶ and add an error-handling step ❷ to check whether SQL Server is already installed. This allows you to run the function over and over again; if SQL Server is already installed, the function will simply skip over it.

Notice that you call a function you haven't seen before: `PrepareSqlServerInstallConfigFile` ❸. This is a *helper function*: a small function that captures some bit of functionality you're likely to use again and again (helper functions are usually hidden from the user and used behind the scenes). Although not required by any means, breaking out small bits of functionality like this makes code more readable. As a general rule, functions should only do one "thing." *Thing* here is, of course, a highly relative term, but the more you program, the more you'll have an intuitive sense for when a function is doing too many things at once.

Listing 18-9 is the code for the `PrepareSqlServerInstallConfigFile` function.

```
function PrepareSqlServerInstallConfigFile {
    [CmdletBinding()]
    param
    (
        [Parameter(Mandatory)]
        [string]$Path,

        [Parameter()]
        [string]$ServiceAccountName = 'PowerLabUser',

        [Parameter()]
        [string]$ServiceAccountPassword = 'P@$$w0rd12',

        [Parameter()]
        [string]$SysAdminAccountName = 'PowerLabUser'
    )

    $configContents = Get-Content -Path $Path -Raw
    $configContents = $configContents.Replace('SQLSVCACCOUNT=""',
    ('SQLSVCACCOUNT="{0}"' -f $ServiceAccountName))
    $configContents = $configContents.Replace('SQLSVCPASSWORD=""',
    ('SQLSVCPASSWORD="{0}"' -f $ServiceAccountPassword))
    $configContents = $configContents.Replace('SQLSYSADMINACCOUNTS=""',
    ('SQLSYSADMINACCOUNTS="{0}"' -f $SysAdminAccountName))
    Set-Content -Path $Path -Value $configContents
}
```

Listing 18-9: The `PrepareSqlServerInstallConfigFile` helper function

You'll recognize this code from Listing 18-4; it hasn't changed much. You added the parameters `Path`, `ServiceAccountName`, `ServiceAccountPassword`, and `SysAdminAccountName` to represent each attribute instead of the hardcoded values used earlier.

Now that you have all your functions in a row, bringing up an SQL server from scratch is just a few commands away. Run the following code to bring up a SQL server from scratch!

```
PS> $vmCred = Import-CliXml -Path 'C:\PowerLab\VMCredential.xml'
PS> $domainCred = Import-CliXml -Path 'C:\PowerLab\DomainCredential.xml'
PS> New-PowerLabSqlServer -Name SQLSRV -DomainCredential $domainCred -VMCredential $vmCred
```

Running Pester Tests

It's that time again: let's run some Pester tests to test the new changes you implemented. For this chapter, you installed SQL Server on the existing SQLSRV VM. You didn't do too much configuring when you installed, and accepted most of the installation defaults, so you'll have only a few Pester tests: you have to make sure that SQL Server is installed, and you have to make sure that during installation it read the unattended configuration file you supplied it. You can do this by verifying that `PowerLabUser` holds a server sysadmin role and that SQL Server is running under the `PowerLabUser` account:

```
PS> Invoke-Pester 'C:\PowerShellForSysAdmins\Part II\Creating and Configuring
SQL Servers\Creating and Configuring SQL Servers.Tests.ps1'

Describing SQLSRV
   Context SQL Server installation
    [+] SQL Server is installed 4.33s
   Context SQL Server configuration
    [+] PowerLabUser holds the sysadmin role 275ms
    [+] the MSSQLSERVER is running under the PowerLabUser account 63ms
Tests completed in 6.28s
Passed: 3 Failed: 0 Skipped: 0 Pending: 0 Inconclusive: 0
```

Everything checks out, so you're good to go!

Summary

In this chapter, you finally saw a more fleshed-out example of what you can do with PowerShell. Building on the work in previous chapters, you added that final layer of automation: installing software (SQL Server) on top of an operating system that was "layered" on top of a virtual machine. You did this in much the same way as in the past few chapters. You used a single example to figure out the code you needed; then you packaged that code in a reusable format and put it inside your PowerLab module. And now that that's done, you can build as many SQL servers as you want with nothing more than a few lines of code!

In the next chapter, you'll do something a little different: revisit code you've already written and refactor it. You'll learn about best coding practices and make sure your module is in the place you need it to be before adding the final piece in Chapter 20.

19

REFACTORING YOUR CODE

In the preceding chapter, you built a VM with a running SQL server using nothing besides an existing hypervisor, an operating system ISO file, and a little bit of code. Doing so meant linking together many of the functions you created in the previous chapters. Here, you'll do something different: instead of adding new functionality to your PowerLab module, you'll dig into your code and see if you can make your module a little more modular.

When I say *modular*, I'm talking about separating the functionality of the code into reusable functions that can handle many situations. The more modular the code, the more generally applicable it will be. And the more generally applicable your code, the more useful it will be. With modular code, you can reuse functions such as `New-PowerLabVM` or `Install-PowerLabOperatingSystem` to install many kinds of servers (which you'll see in the next chapter).

A Second Look at New-PowerLabSqlServer

You created two main functions in Chapter 18: `New-PowerLabSqlServer` and `Install-PowerLabSqlServer`. You did so with the goal of setting up an SQL server. But what if you want to make your functions more generally applicable? After all, different servers share a lot of components with SQL ones: virtual machine, virtual disk, Windows OS, and so forth. You could simply copy the function you have and swap out all the specific SQL references for references to the server type you want.

But I'm going to have to advise against this. There's no need for all that extra code. Instead, you'll simply refactor your existing code. *Refactoring* refers to the process of changing a code's insides without changing its functionality; in other words, refactoring is something for you, the programmer. It helps code be more readable, and it makes sure that you can keep growing your project without running into too many headache-inducing organizational issues.

Let's start by taking a look at that `New-PowerLabSqlServer` function you created, shown in Listing 19-1.

```
function New-PowerLabSqlServer {
    [CmdletBinding()]
 ❶ param
    (
        [Parameter(Mandatory)]
        [string]$Name,

        [Parameter(Mandatory)]
        [pscredential]$DomainCredential,

        [Parameter(Mandatory)]
        [pscredential]$VMCredential,

        [Parameter()]
        [string]$VMPath = 'C:\PowerLab\VMs',

        [Parameter()]
        [int64]$Memory = 4GB,

        [Parameter()]
        [string]$Switch = 'PowerLab',

        [Parameter()]
        [int]$Generation = 2,

        [Parameter()]
        [string]$DomainName = 'powerlab.local',

        [Parameter()]
      ❷ [string]$AnswerFilePath = "C:\Program Files\WindowsPowerShell\Modules
        \PowerLab\SqlServer.ini"
    )
```

```
❸ ## Build the VM
   $vmparams = @{
       Name       = $Name
       Path       = $VmPath
       Memory     = $Memory
       Switch     = $Switch
       Generation = $Generation
   }
   New-PowerLabVm @vmParams

   Install-PowerLabOperatingSystem -VmName $Name
   Start-VM -Name $Name

   Wait-Server -Name $Name -Status Online -Credential $VMCredential

  $addParams = @{
       DomainName = $DomainName
       Credential = $DomainCredential
       Restart    = $true
       Force      = $true
   }
   Invoke-Command -VMName $Name -ScriptBlock { Add-Computer
   @using:addParams } -Credential $VMCredential

   Wait-Server -Name $Name -Status Offline -Credential $VMCredential

❹ Wait-Server -Name $Name -Status Online -Credential $DomainCredential

   $tempFile = Copy-Item -Path $AnswerFilePath -Destination "C:\Program
   Files\WindowsPowerShell\Modules\PowerLab\temp.ini" -PassThru

   Install-PowerLabSqlServer -ComputerName $Name -AnswerFilePath $tempFile
   .FullName -DomainCredential $DomainCredential
}
```

Listing 19-1: `New-PowerLabSqlServer` *function*

How would you go about refactoring this code? Well for starters, you know that every server needs a virtual machine, a virtual disk, and an operating system; you handle these needs in the code block between ❸ and ❹.

If you look at this code, though, you'll see that you can't just pull it out and paste it into a new function. Parameters are defined in the `New-PowerLabSqlServer` function ❶ that you use in those lines. Notice that the only parameter that's specific to SQL here is `AnswerFilePath` ❷.

Now that you've identified the code that isn't SQL specific, let's pull it out and use it to create the new function `New-PowerLabServer` (Listing 19-2).

```
function New-PowerLabServer {
    [CmdletBinding()]
    param
    (
        [Parameter(Mandatory)]
        [string]$Name,
```

```
        [Parameter(Mandatory)]
        [pscredential]$DomainCredential,

        [Parameter(Mandatory)]
        [pscredential]$VMCredential,

        [Parameter()]
        [string]$VMPath = 'C:\PowerLab\VMs',

        [Parameter()]
        [int64]$Memory = 4GB,

        [Parameter()]
        [string]$Switch = 'PowerLab',

        [Parameter()]
        [int]$Generation = 2,

        [Parameter()]
        [string]$DomainName = 'powerlab.local'
    )

    ## Build the VM
    $vmparams = @{
        Name       = $Name
        Path       = $VmPath
        Memory     = $Memory
        Switch     = $Switch
        Generation = $Generation
    }
    New-PowerLabVm @vmParams

    Install-PowerLabOperatingSystem -VmName $Name
    Start-VM -Name $Name

    Wait-Server -Name $Name -Status Online -Credential $VMCredential

    $addParams = @{
        DomainName = $DomainName
        Credential = $DomainCredential
        Restart    = $true
        Force      = $true
    }
    Invoke-Command -VMName $Name
    -ScriptBlock { Add-Computer @using:addParams } -Credential $VMCredential

    Wait-Server -Name $Name -Status Offline -Credential $VMCredential

    Wait-Server -Name $Name -Status Online -Credential $DomainCredential
}
```

Listing 19-2: A more generic `New-PowerLabServer` function

At this point, you have a general server-provisioning function, but no way to indicate the kind of server you're creating. Let's fix that by using another parameter called `ServerType`:

```
[Parameter(Mandatory)]
[ValidateSet('SQL', 'Web', 'Generic')]
[string]$ServerType
```

Notice the new `ValidateSet` parameter. I'll give an in-depth explanation of what this does later in the chapter; for now, you just need to know that this ensures that the user can pass in only a server type contained within this set.

Now that you have this parameter, let's use it. Insert a `switch` statement at the end of the function to execute different code depending on which server type the user enters:

```
switch ($ServerType) {
    'Web' {
        Write-Host 'Web server deployments are not supported at this time'
        break
    }
    'SQL' {
        $tempFile = Copy-Item -Path $AnswerFilePath -Destination "C:\Program
        Files\WindowsPowerShell\Modules\PowerLab\temp.ini" -PassThru
        Install-PowerLabSqlServer -ComputerName $Name -AnswerFilePath
        $tempFile.FullName -DomainCredential $DomainCredential
        break
    }
    'Generic' {
        break
    }
  ❶ default {
        throw "Unrecognized server type: [$_]"
    }
}
```

As you can see, you handle the three types of server input (and use the `default` case to handle any exceptions ❶). But there's a problem. To fill out the SQL code, you copied and pasted code from the `New-PowerLabSqlServer` function, and now you're using something you don't have: the `AnswerFilePath` variable. Recall that when you moved your generic code to a new function, you left this variable behind, meaning that you can't use it here . . . or can you?

Using Parameter Sets

In situations like the preceding one, when you have one parameter that determines which other parameter you need, PowerShell has a handy feature called *parameter sets*. You can think of parameter sets as letting you use conditional logic to control which parameters a user inputs.

In this example, you'll use three parameter sets: a set for provisioning SQL servers, a set for provisioning web servers, and a default set.

You can define parameter sets by using the `ParameterSetName` attribute followed by a name. Here's an example:

```
[Parameter(Mandatory)]
[ValidateSet('SQL', 'Web', 'Generic')]
[string]$ServerType,

[Parameter(ParameterSetName = 'SQL')]
[string]$AnswerFilePath = "C:\Program Files\WindowsPowerShell\Modules\PowerLab\SqlServer.ini",

[Parameter(ParameterSetName = 'Web')]
[switch]$NoDefaultWebsite
```

Notice that you haven't assigned `ServerType` a parameter set. Parameters that are not part of a parameter set can be used with any set. Because of this, you can use `ServerType` with either `AnswerFilePath` or the newly created parameter you'll be using for web server provisioning: `CreateDefaultWebsite`.

You can see here that the majority of the parameters stay the same, but you add a final one based on what you pass in for `ServerType`:

```
PS> New-PowerLabServer -Name WEBSRV -DomainCredential CredentialHere -VMCredential CredentialHere
-ServerType 'Web' -NoDefaultWebsite
PS> New-PowerLabServer -Name SQLSRV -DomainCredential CredentialHere -VMCredential CredentialHere
-ServerType 'SQL' -AnswerFilePath 'C:\OverridingTheDefaultPath\SqlServer.ini'
```

If you try to mix and match, and use parameters from two different parameter sets at the same time, you'll fail:

```
PS> New-PowerLabServer -Name SQLSRV -DomainCredential CredentialHere -VMCredential CredentialHere
-ServerType 'SQL' -NoDefaultWebsite -AnswerFilePath 'C:\OverridingTheDefaultPath\SqlServer.ini'

New-PowerLabServer : Parameter set cannot be resolved using the specified named parameters.
At line:1 char:1
+ New-PowerLabServer -Name SQLSRV -ServerType 'SQL' -NoDefaultWebsite - ...
+ ~~~~~~~~~~~~~~~~~~~~~~~~~~~~~~~~~~~~~~~~~~~~~~~~~~~~~~~~~~~~~~~~~~~~~~~~~~~
    + CategoryInfo          : InvalidArgument: (:) [New-PowerLabServer], ParameterBindingException
    + FullyQualifiedErrorId : AmbiguousParameterSet,New-PowerLabServer
```

What would happen if you did the opposite and used neither the `NoDefaultWebsite` parameter nor the `AnswerFilePath` parameter?

```
PS> New-PowerLabServer -Name SQLSRV -DomainCredential CredentialHere -VMCredential CredentialHere
-ServerType 'SQL'
New-PowerLabServer : Parameter set cannot be resolved using the specified named parameters.
At line:1 char:1
+ New-PowerLabServer -Name SQLSRV -DomainCredential $credential...
+ ~~~~~~~~~~~~~~~~~~~~~~~~~~~~~~~~~~~~~~~~~~~~~~~~~~~~~~~~~~~~~~~~~~~~~~~~~~~
    + CategoryInfo          : InvalidArgument: (:) [New-PowerLabServer], ParameterBindingException
    + FullyQualifiedErrorId : AmbiguousParameterSet,New-PowerLabServer
```

```
PS> New-PowerLabServer -Name WEBSRV -DomainCredential CredentialHere -VMCredential CredentialHere
-ServerType 'Web'
New-PowerLabServer : Parameter set cannot be resolved using the specified named parameters.
At line:1 char:1
+ New-PowerLabServer -Name WEBSRV -DomainCredential $credential...
+ ~~~~~~~~~~~~~~~~~~~~~~~~~~~~~~~~~~~~~~~~~~~~~~~~~~~~~~~~~~~~~~~~~~~~~~~~~~~~~
    + CategoryInfo          : InvalidArgument: (:) [New-PowerLabServer], ParameterBindingException
    + FullyQualifiedErrorId : AmbiguousParameterSet,New-PowerLabServer
```

You get the same error about not being able to resolve the parameter set as before. Why? PowerShell doesn't know which parameter set to use! Earlier, I said you'd be using three sets, but you defined only two. You need to set a default parameter set. As you saw earlier, parameters that are not explicitly assigned to a parameter set can be used in conjunction with any in a set. However, if you do define a default parameter set, PowerShell will use those parameters if no parameters in any set are being used.

As for your default set, you could pick the defined SQL or web parameter set to be your default, or you could simply define a nonspecific parameter set like `blah blah`, which would create an inherent set for all parameters that do not have an explicit set defined:

```
[CmdletBinding(DefaultParameterSetName = 'blah blah')]
```

If you don't want to set a defined parameter set as default, you can set it to anything, and PowerShell will ignore both parameter sets *if no parameter in a parameter set is used.* This is what you need to do in this case; it's perfectly okay to not use a defined parameter set because you have the `ServerType` parameter to indicate whether or not you're going to deploy a web server or SQL server.

With your new parameter sets, the parameter portion of `New-PowerLabServer` looks like Listing 19-3.

```
function New-PowerLabServer {
    [CmdletBinding(DefaultParameterSetName = 'Generic')]
    param
    (
        [Parameter(Mandatory)]
        [string]$Name,

        [Parameter(Mandatory)]
        [pscredential]$DomainCredential,

        [Parameter(Mandatory)]
        [pscredential]$VMCredential,

        [Parameter()]
        [string]$VMPath = 'C:\PowerLab\VMs',

        [Parameter()]
        [int64]$Memory = 4GB,
```

```
        [Parameter()]
        [string]$Switch = 'PowerLab',
        [Parameter()]
        [int]$Generation = 2,

        [Parameter()]
        [string]$DomainName = 'powerlab.local',

        [Parameter()]
        [ValidateSet('SQL', 'Web')]
        [string]$ServerType,

        [Parameter(ParameterSetName = 'SQL')]
        [string]$AnswerFilePath = "C:\Program Files\WindowsPowerShell\Modules
        \PowerLab\SqlServer.ini",

        [Parameter(ParameterSetName = 'Web')]
        [switch]$NoDefaultWebsite
    )
```

Listing 19-3: The new `New-PowerLabServer` *function*

Notice that you have a reference to the function `Install-PowerLabSqlServer`. This looks similar to the function (`New-PowerLabSqlServer`) that got us into this mess. Instead of creating the virtual machine and installing the operating system, `Install-PowerLabSqlServer` takes over from `New-PowerLabServer`, installs the SQL server software, and performs basic configuration. You might be inclined to perform this same round of refactoring on this function. You could do this, but as soon as you look at the code that's inside `Install-PowerLabSqlServer`, you'll soon realize there are nearly no commonalities between the installation phase of SQL server and that of other types of servers. It's a unique process and would be hard to "genericize" for other server deployments.

Summary

Well, now that the code is nice and refactored, you're left with a function capable of . . . provisioning a SQL server. So back where you started, right? I hope not! Even though you haven't changed anything about the functionality of the code, you've built the foundation you need to easily insert the code for creating a web server (which you'll do in the next chapter).

As you saw in this chapter, refactoring PowerShell code isn't a cut-and-dried process. Knowing the ways you can refactor your code, and which of those ways is the best for your present situation, is a skill that comes with experience. But as long as you keep what programmers call *the DRY principle* (don't repeat yourself) in mind, you'll be on the right path. More than anything, abiding by DRY means avoiding duplicate code and redundant functionality. You saw this in this chapter when you chose to create a general function that created new servers, as opposed to another `New-PowerLab`*`InsertServerTypeHere`*`Server` function.

Your hard work wasn't for nothing. In the next chapter, you'll get back to automating, adding the code you need to create IIS web servers.

20

CREATING AND CONFIGURING AN IIS WEB SERVER

You're at the last step in your automation journey: the web server. In this chapter, you'll use *IIS*, a built-in Windows service that provides web services to clients. IIS is a server type you'll run into often enough when you're doing IT work—in other words, it's an area ripe for automation!

As in previous chapters, first you'll deploy an IIS web server from scratch; then you'll focus on getting the service installed and some basic configuration applied.

Prerequisites

By now, you should be familiar with how to get a fresh virtual machine created and set up, so we won't be covering those steps. I'm assuming that you already have a virtual machine up and running with Windows Server installed. If you don't, you could leverage our existing work in the PowerLab module by running this command:

```
PS> New-PowerLabServer -ServerType Generic
-DomainCredential (Import-Clixml -Path C:\PowerLab\DomainCredential.xml)
-VMCredential (Import-Clixml -Path C:\PowerLab\VMCredential.xml) -Name WEBSRV
```

Notice that you specify a `Generic` server type this time; this is because you haven't yet added full support for web servers (the task for this chapter!).

Installation and Setup

Once you've created a VM, it's time to set up IIS. IIS is a Windows feature, and fortunately, PowerShell has a built-in command to install Windows features called `Add-WindowsFeature`. If you were doing this as a one-off test, you *could* use a single line to install IIS, but since you're building this automation into a bigger project, you'll install IIS just as you did SQL: by creating a function. Let's call it `Install-PowerLabWebServer`.

You'll have this function adhere to the model you created earlier when you made the `Install-PowerLabSqlServer` function. As you begin to add further server support to this project, you'll see how creating a function for even just a single line of code will make using the module, and changing it, much, much easier!

The easiest way to mirror the `Install-PowerLabSqlServer` function as closely as possible is to take the "skeleton" of the function by removing any of the SQL Server–specific code. Normally, I'd recommend reusing an existing function instead of building another one, but in this case, you have a completely different "object:" a SQL Server versus an IIS server. It makes more sense to have a different function. In Listing 20-1, you simply copy the `Install-PowerLabSqlServer` function but remove the "guts" while keeping all of the common parameters (you exclude the `AnswerFilePath` and `IsoFilePath` parameters since IIS doesn't need them).

```
function Install-PowerLabWebServer {
    param
    (
        [Parameter(Mandatory)]
        [string]$ComputerName,

        [Parameter(Mandatory)]
        [pscredential]$DomainCredential
    )

    $session = New-PSSession -VMName $ComputerName -Credential $DomainCredential

    $session | Remove-PSSession
}
```

Listing 20-1: The "skeleton" `Install-PowerLabWebServer` function

As for actually setting up the IIS service, that's a piece of cake: you simply need to run one command that installs the `Web-Server` feature. Go ahead and add that line into your `Install-PowerLabWebServer` function (Listing 20-2).

```
function Install-PowerLabWebServer {
    param
    (
        [Parameter(Mandatory)]
        [string]$ComputerName,

        [Parameter(Mandatory)]
        [pscredential]$DomainCredential
    )

    $session = New-PSSession -VMName $ComputerName -Credential $DomainCredential

    $null = Invoke-Command -Session $session -ScriptBlock { Add-WindowsFeature -Name 'Web-Server' }

    $session | Remove-PSSession

}
```

Listing 20-2: The `Install-PowerLabWebServer` function

The start of your `Install-PowerLabWebServer` function is complete! Let's add more code to it.

Building Web Servers from Scratch

Now that you have an install function for IIS, it's time to update your `New-PowerLabServer` function. Recall in Chapter 19 that when you were refactoring your `New-PowerLabServer` function, you were forced to use placeholder code for the web server parts because you didn't have the functionality needed. You used the line `Write-Host 'Web server deployments are not supported at this time'` as filler code. Now's let's replace that text with a call to your newly created `Install-PowerLabWebServer` function:

```
PS> Install-PowerLabWebServer -ComputerName $Name -DomainCredential $DomainCredential
```

Once you do this, you can bring up web servers the same way you do SQL servers!

The WebAdministration Module

Once you have a web server up and running, you need to do something with it. When the `Web-Server` feature is enabled on a server, a PowerShell module called `WebAdministration` is installed. This module contains the many commands needed to handle IIS objects. The `Web-Server` feature also creates a PowerShell drive called IIS that allows you to manage common IIS objects (websites, application pools, and so forth).

A *PowerShell drive* allows you to navigate data sources just like a filesystem. You'll see next that you can manipulate websites, application pools, and many other IIS objects exactly as you would files and folders by using common cmdlets like `Get-Item`, `Set-Item`, and `Remove-Item`.

To make the IIS drive available, you first have to import the `WebAdministration` module. Let's remote into your newly created web server and play around with the module a bit to see what you can do.

First, you'll create a new PowerShell Direct session and enter it interactively. Previously, you were mostly using `Invoke-Command` to send commands to VMs. Now, since you're just investigating what's possible with IIS, you use `Enter-PSSession` to interactively work inside of the session:

```
PS> $session = New-PSSession -VMName WEBSRV
-Credential (Import-Clixml -Path C:\PowerLab\DomainCredential.xml)
PS> Enter-PSSession -Session $session
[WEBSRV]: PS> Import-Module WebAdministration
```

Notice the `[WEBSRV]` in front of the final prompt. This is a signal that you're now working on the WEBSRV host and can import the `WebAdministration` module. Once the module is imported into the session, you can verify that the IIS drive is created by running `Get-PSDrive`:

```
[WEBSRV]: PS> Get-PSDrive -Name IIS | Format-Table -AutoSize

Name Used (GB) Free (GB) Provider          Root     CurrentLocation
---- --------- --------- --------          ----     ---------------
IIS                      WebAdministration \\WEBSRV
```

You can peruse this drive as you can any other PowerShell drive: by treating it like a filesystem and using commands such as `Get-ChildItem` to list items in the drive, `New-Item` to create new items, and `Set-Item` to modify items. But doing all that work isn't automating; it's just managing IIS via the command line. And you're here to automate stuff! The only reason I'm mentioning the IIS drive now is that it will come in handy for automation tasks later, and it's always good to know how to do things manually, in case you need to troubleshoot automation when it goes awry.

Websites and Application Pools

The commands in the `WebAdministration` module manage and automate just about every facet of IIS. You'll begin by looking at how to handle websites and applications, as websites and application pools are two of the most common components that system administrators work with in the real world.

Websites

You'll start with a simple command: `Get-Website`, which lets you query IIS and returns all websites that currently exist on a web server:

```
[WEBSRV]: PS> Get-Website -Name 'Default Web Site'

Name             ID   State      Physical Path                  Bindings
----             --   -----      -------------                  --------
Default Web Site 1    Started    %SystemDrive%\inetpub\wwwroot  http *:80:
```

You'll notice that you already created a website. This is because IIS has a website called Default Web Site when it is installed. But let's say you don't want this default website and would rather create your own. You can remove it by piping the output of `Get-Website` to `Remove-Website`:

```
[WEBSRV]: PS> Get-Website -Name 'Default Web Site' | Remove-Website
[WEBSRV]: PS> Get-Website
[WEBSRV]: PS>
```

If you want to create a website, you can do so just as easily by using the `New-Website` command:

```
[WEBSRV]: PS> New-Website -Name PowerShellForSysAdmins
-PhysicalPath C:\inetpub\wwwroot\

Name             ID   State      Physical Path                  Bindings
----             --   -----      -------------                  --------
PowerShellForSys 1052 Stopped    C:\inetpub\wwwroot\            http *:80:
Admins           6591
```

If the website's bindings are off, and you want to change them (say you want to bind to a nonstandard port), you can use the `Set-WebBinding` command:

```
[WEBSRV]: PS> Set-WebBinding -Name 'PowerShellForSysAdmins'
-BindingInformation "*:80:" -PropertyName Port -Value 81
[WEBSRV]: PS> Get-Website -Name PowerShellForSysAdmins

Name             ID   State      Physical Path                  Bindings
----             --   -----      -------------                  --------
PowerShellForSys 1052 Started    C:\inetpub\wwwroot\            http *:81:
Admins           6591
                 05
```

You've seen a lot of what you can do with websites. Let's check out what's possible with application pools.

Application Pools

Application pools allow you to isolate your applications from one another, even if they are running on the same server. This way, if an error exists in one app, it won't take down other applications.

The commands for application pools are similar to those for websites, as you can see in the following code. Since I have only a single application pool, only the `DefaultAppPool` shows up for me. If you run this command on your own web server, you may see more:

```
[WEBSRV]: PS> Get-IISAppPool

Name             Status       CLR Ver  Pipeline Mode  Start Mode
----             ------       -------  -------------  ----------
DefaultAppPool   Started      v4.0     Integrated     OnDemand

[WEBSRV]: PS> Get-Command -Name *apppool*

CommandType     Name                                Version    Source
-----------     ----                                -------    ------
Cmdlet          Get-IISAppPool                      1.0.0.0    IISAdministration
Cmdlet          Get-WebAppPoolState                 1.0.0.0    WebAdministration
Cmdlet          New-WebAppPool                      1.0.0.0    WebAdministration
Cmdlet          Remove-WebAppPool                   1.0.0.0    WebAdministration
Cmdlet          Restart-WebAppPool                  1.0.0.0    WebAdministration
Cmdlet          Start-WebAppPool                    1.0.0.0    WebAdministration
Cmdlet          Stop-WebAppPool                     1.0.0.0    WebAdministration
```

Since you already created a website, let's see how to create an app pool and assign it to your website. To create an app pool, use the `New-WebAppPool` command, as shown in Listing 20-3.

```
[WEBSRV]: PS> New-WebAppPool -Name 'PowerShellForSysAdmins'

Name                     State        Applications
----                     -----        ------------
PowerShellForSysAdmins   Started
```

Listing 20-3: Creating an app pool

Unfortunately, not all IIS tasks have a built-in cmdlet. To assign the app pool to an existing website, you have to use `Set-ItemProperty` and change the website in the IIS drive ❶ (as shown next). To apply that update, you need to stop ❷ and restart ❸ the website.

```
❶ [WEBSRV]: PS> Set-ItemProperty -Path 'IIS:\Sites\PowerShellForSysAdmins'
  -Name 'ApplicationPool' -Value 'PowerShellForSysAdmins'
❷ [WEBSRV]: PS> Get-Website -Name PowerShellForSysAdmins | Stop-WebSite
❸ [WEBSRV]: PS> Get-Website -Name PowerShellForSysAdmins | Start-WebSite
  [WEBSRV]: PS> Get-Website -Name PowerShellForSysAdmins |
     Select-Object -Property applicationPool
```

```
applicationPool
---------------
PowerShellForSysAdmins
```

You can also see that you can confirm that the app pool was changing by looking at the applicationPool property returned from running Get-Website.

Configuring SSL on a Website

Now that you've seen the commands for working with IIS, let's go back to your PowerLab module and write a function that will install an IIS certificate and change the binding to port 443.

You can either get a "real" certificate from a valid certificate authority or create a self-signed certificate by using the New-SelfSignedCertificate function. Because I'm just demonstrating this concept, let's create a self-signed certificate for now and use that.

First, lay out the function and specify all the parameters you need (Listing 20-4).

```
function New-IISCertificate {
    param(
            [Parameter(Mandatory)]
            [string]$WebServerName,

            [Parameter(Mandatory)]
            [string]$PrivateKeyPassword,

            [Parameter()]
            [string]$CertificateSubject = 'PowerShellForSysAdmins',

            [Parameter()]
            [string]$PublicKeyLocalPath = 'C:\PublicKey.cer',

            [Parameter()]
            [string]$PrivateKeyLocalPath = 'C:\PrivateKey.pfx',

            [Parameter()]
            [string]$CertificateStore = 'Cert:\LocalMachine\My'
    )
    ## The code covered in the following text will go here
}
```

Listing 20-4: The start of New-IISCertificate

The first thing this function needs to do is create a self-signed certificate. You can do so with the New-SelfSignedCertificate command, which imports the certificate into the local computer's LocalMachine *certificate store*, where all the computer's certificates are housed. When you call New-SelfSignedCertificate, you can pass a Subject parameter to store a string that will give you information about what the certificate is. Generating the certificate will also import it into the local computer.

Listing 20-5 provides the line you'll use to generate the certificate using the passed-in subject (`$CertificateSubject`). Remember that you can use the `$null` variable to store the results of a command so that it doesn't output anything to the console.

```
$null = New-SelfSignedCertificate -Subject $CertificateSubject
```

Listing 20-5: Creating a self-signed certificate

Once the certificate is created, you need to do two things: get the thumbprint of the certificate, and export the private key from the certificate. A certificate *thumbprint* is a string that uniquely identifies the certificate; the certificate's *private key* is used to encrypt and decrypt the data sent to your server (I won't go into the details here).

You could have gotten the thumbprint from `New-SelfSignedCertificate`'s output, but we're assuming that this certificate is going to be used on a computer other than the one you created it on, as that's the more realistic scenario. To handle this, you first need to export the public key from your self-signed certificate, which you can do by using the `Export-Certificate` command:

```
$tempLocalCert = Get-ChildItem -Path $CertificateStore |
    Where-Object {$_.Subject -match $CertificateSubject }
$null = $tempLocalCert | Export-Certificate -FilePath $PublicKeyLocalPath
```

The preceding command will give you a *.cer* public key file, which you can use, along with some .NET magic, to temporarily import the certificate and retrieve the thumbprint:

```
$certPrint = New-Object System.Security.Cryptography.X509Certificates.X509Certificate2
$certPrint.Import($PublicKeyLocalPath)
$certThumbprint = $certprint.Thumbprint
```

Now that you have the certificate's thumbprint, you need to export the private key, which you'll use to attach to the SSL binding on the web server. Here are the commands for exporting the private key:

```
$privKeyPw = ConvertTo-SecureString -String $PrivateKeyPassword -AsPlainText -Force
$null = $tempLocalCert | Export-PfxCertificate -FilePath $PrivateKeyLocalPath -Password $privKeyPw
```

Once you have a private key, you can import your certificate into a certificate store on the web server by using the `Import-PfxCertificate` command. First, though, you need to check whether it was already imported. This is why you had to get the thumbprint earlier. You can use a certificate's unique thumbprints to verify whether it already exists on the web server.

To import your certificate, you need to use a few of the commands you saw earlier in the chapter: you'll create a PowerShell direct session, import the `WebAdministration` module, check whether the certificate exists, and then add it if it doesn't. You'll leave the last step out for now, and write up the code to do the rest in Listing 20-6.

```
$session = New-PSSession -VMName $WebServerName
-Credential (Import-CliXml -Path C:\PowerLab\DomainCredential.xml)

Invoke-Command -Session $session -ScriptBlock {Import-Module -Name
WebAdministration}

if (Invoke-Command -Session $session -ScriptBlock { $using:certThumbprint -in
(Get-ChildItem -Path Cert:\LocalMachine\My).Thumbprint}) {
      Write-Warning -Message 'The Certificate has already been imported.'
} else {
      # Code for importing the certificate
}
```

Listing 20-6: Checking whether the certificate already exists

The first two lines of code should be familiar from earlier in the chapter, but notice that you have to use `Invoke-Command` to import the module remotely. Likewise, since you're using a local variable inside the scriptblock in your `if` statement, you need to use the `$using:` prefix to expand the variable on the remote machine.

Let's fill in the code for the else statement in Listing 20-7. You need to do four things to finish setting up the IIS certificate. First, you need to copy the private key to the web server. Then you need to import the private key by using `Import-PfxCertificate`. Lastly, you need to set the SSL binding and then force it to use the private key:

```
Copy-Item -Path $PrivateKeyLocalPath -Destination 'C:\' -ToSession $session

Invoke-Command -Session $session -ScriptBlock { Import-PfxCertificate
-FilePath $using:PrivateKeyLocalPath -CertStoreLocation
$using:CertificateStore -Password $using:privKeyPw }

Invoke-Command -Session $session -ScriptBlock { Set-ItemProperty "IIS:\Sites\
PowerShellForSysAdmins" -Name bindings
-Value @{protocol='https';bindingInformation='*:443:*'} }

Invoke-Command -Session $session -ScriptBlock {
    $cert = Get-ChildItem -Path $CertificateStore |
        Where-Object { $_.Subject -eq "CN=$CertificateSubject" }
    $cert | New-Item 'IIS:\SSLBindings\0.0.0.0!443'
}
```

Listing 20-7: Binding an SSL certificate to an IIS

One thing to point out about this code is that you set the site binding on your website to use port 443 instead of port 80. You do this to ensure that the website adheres to the typical SSL port of 443, allowing web browsers to understand that you're using encrypting web traffic.

At this point, you're finished! You have successfully installed a self-signed certificate on the web server, created the SSL binding for your site, and forced the SSL binding to use your certificate! The only thing left to do is clean up the session you've been working in:

```
$session | Remove-PSSession
```

After your session is cleaned up, you can browse to *https://<webservername>* and you'll be prompted to trust the certificate. All browsers will do this because you issued a self-signed certificate, and not one issued by a public certificate authority. Once you trust the certificate, you'll be presented with the default IIS web page.

Be sure to check out the `New-IISCertificate` function inside the PowerLab module to see all these commands in one place.

Summary

This chapter covered yet another type of server, the web server. You learned how to create a web server from scratch, exactly the same way as you create SQL servers. You also learned some of the commands inside the `WebAdministration` module that comes with IIS. You learned how to use built-in commands to perform many basic tasks as well as looked at the IIS PowerShell drive that's created. To wrap up the chapter, you followed, in detail, a real-world scenario that required piecing together many of the commands and techniques covered earlier.

If you've made it through this entire book, congratulations! We covered a lot of ground and I'm glad you stuck around. The skills you've learned and the projects you built should give you a foundation to solve problems with PowerShell. Take what you've learned here, close the book, and get to scripting. Just start somewhere and automate it with PowerShell. The only way you'll truly master the concepts covered in this book is by practicing. There's no better than time than now!

INDEX

D

E

F

G

H

I

P

R

S

T

U

V

W

PowerShell for Sysadmins is set in New Baskerville, Futura, Dogma, and TheSansMono Condensed. This book was printed and bound at Sheridan Books, Inc. in Chelsea, Michigan. The paper is 60# Finch Offset, which is certified by the Forest Stewardship Council (FSC).

The book uses a layflat binding, in which the pages are bound together with a cold-set, flexible glue and the first and last pages of the resulting book block are attached to the cover. The cover is not actually glued to the book's spine, and when open, the book lies flat and the spine doesn't crack.